THE PRIESTLY KINGDOM

The Priestly Kingdom

Social Ethics as Gospel

JOHN HOWARD YODER

UNIVERSITY OF NOTRE DAME PRESS
NOTRE DAME, INDIANA 46556

"The Hermeneutics of Peoplehood" is reprinted with permission from the *Journal of Religious Ethics* 10/1 (Spring 1982), 40–67. "But We Do See Jesus" is reprinted with permission from *Foundations of Ethics,* edited by Leroy S. Rouner (Notre Dame, Ind.: University of Notre Dame Press, 1983), pp. 57–75. "Radical Reformation Ethics in Ecumenical Perspective" is reprinted with permission from the *Journal of Ecumenical Studies* 15/4 (Fall 1978), 647ff. "Anabaptism and History" is reprinted with permission from *Umstrittenes Täufertum,* edited by Hans-Jürgen Goertz (Göttingen: Vandenhoeck & Ruprecht, 1975). "The Constantinian Sources of Western Social Ethics" is reprinted with permission from *Missionalia* 4/3 (November 1976), 98–108. "The Christian Case for Democracy" is substantially rewritten, with permission, from the *Journal of Religious Ethics* 5/2 (Fall 1977), 209–223.

Library of Congress Cataloging in Publication Data

Yoder, John Howard.
 The priestly kingdom.

 Includes index.
 1. Christian ethics—Mennonite authors—Addresses,
essays, lectures. 2. Social ethics—Addresses, essays,
lectures. 3. Anabaptists—Addresses, essays, lectures.
I. Title.
BJ1251.Y6 1985   241   84-40358
ISBN 0-268-01627-5
ISBN 0-268-01628-3 (pbk.)

Contents

Introduction

Ever since *My Politics of Jesus*, and to a lesser extent in response as well to my even earlier booklets on Reinhold Niebuhr, on Karl Barth, and on *The Christian Witness to the State*, I have seen my views described, often by interpreters intending to be quite friendly, in ways that seemed to me to be beside the mark. The temptation is to take an occasion like this to clarify, explicate, and defend, or even explain myself from scratch in a complete and consistent way. Yet to do that with any thoroughness would replace or undercut the substance of the essays presented.

Then what is left to be provided in an introduction is a narrower, more biographical orientation, to locate the following texts within the wider horizon of the themes to which they relate.

These texts were commissioned separately, but they all are located near the intersection of the different fields where my responsibilities have lain. My first writing was done on the staff of a denominational service agency, under which my primary duties were with war sufferers' relief and social service administration. I was assigned to represent the denomination's convictions regarding Christian pacifism, in ecumenical conversations in Europe. As befits that context my articulation of the pacifist witness has been predominantly dialogical, addressing issues in the terms in which they are put by others rather than explicating my own views or those of the historic peace churches. The value of such a dialogical denominational format is that it educates one in respect for the thought systems of others. Its liability is that it exposes one to being misinterpreted by others as though one represented a "pure type" which they can use as a foil. Occasionally in what follows the reader will observe my discomfiture with being used as a foil rather than heard as an interlocutor.

A second set of assignments came to me as participant in the "conciliar" form of ecumenical relationships. World Council of Churches commissions and assemblies at Bossey, Montreal, Uppsala,

Nairobi, Melbourne, and Vancouver, and work with the Faith and Order Colloquium of the National Council of Churches demanded once again the exercise of accepting the way questions are put in the language which others use. Their focus was sometimes the missionary outreach of the Christian church, in which I was also serving in a denominational agency staff role. These conversations dealt as well with the more directly ecclesiastical dimensions of Christian witness and unity, mostly in ad hoc forms not productive of literature.

My doctoral research and one area of graduate teaching responsibility has been the history of the "radical reformation" vision of Christian renewal. Historical studies are worthy of investigation for their own sake; they also contribute their particular perspective to the contemporary discussion of Christian faithfulness. They are represented in this collection by three historical essays.

What historical studies investigate from a distance is also a continuing concern in the present. I was privileged to participate marginally in the coming into being of a number of intentional Christian communities, from both within and beyond the Anabaptist/Mennonite culture matrix. My contributions to the discussion of "practical theology" in the pages of *Concern, a Pamphlet Series for Christian Renewal* have subjected the learnings of history and the readings of Scripture to the test of empirical translatability.

The overlap of these several fields of concern locates the image of where I stand that was present in the minds of those program planners and editors who in different connections invited me to prepare, for occasional study events of divers kinds, the texts collected here. The interlocking dimensions of ecumenical, missionary, and ethical concern in these papers do not represent courses I have taught or ministries I have administered. They record what I was asked by others to contribute to their conversations, from an orientation whose horizon is formed by the fields named above.

That all identity is historical is a platitude, but not one that we can afford to leave unspoken. To be what one is always means both accepting and modifying a particular pattern drawn from the roots of one's society and language. This has not always been recognized. There have been cultures in which people were not obliged to be aware that change was involved in the movement between receiving from their parents and transmitting to their children what they thought to be the simple shape of truth. There have been cultures so provincial as not to be aware that their sense of who they were was particular. There have been social groups so powerful as to be able to assume that there was no other place to stand that could count but theirs.

The position represented here, on the other hand, is most openly and respectfully, repentantly and doxologically aware of particular historical identity. It is historically oriented as to *form*, in that what it holds to be the common Christian calling is a project: i.e., a goal-oriented movement through time. It is historical as well as to *substance:* for it recognizes that faithfulness is always to be realized in particular times and places, never assured and always subject to renewed testing and judgment.

There are visions of God's work in history whose claim is to be unambivalent and directional. One pretends to know for sure which way things are moving, and that that way is forward. The movement from the past is assumed to run toward greater truth and glory, thus limiting the authority of that past over us. One would not want to "retrogress" to an earlier "stage" if one could. There are divisions among the interpreters of that direction. Western and Eastern Catholic visions anathematized one another; Protestant and Catholic did it again in the West in the sixteenth century. Various forms of doubt calling themselves "enlightened," and various visions of dialectical certainty calling themselves "scientific" have since further contested the right of the historical magisterium to interpret, yet they all share the same trust in progress as the law of history. "Time will tell"; "a century from now historians will say . . . ." One's strongest certainties are clothed in the confidence that the future is moving farther in the good way our recent past has taken.

The stance represented here, while quite hopeful about some kinds of change and about God's ultimate project, is more skeptical than the views just mentioned of the directions "history" has been taking, more doubtful about the centralized authority of both its rulers and its interpreters. This approach is more careful than others with the epithet "apostate," which all of them used against one another in the past. It is more hopeful than others about the possibility of knowing and doing the divine will. To be both more hopeful and more critical means finding more clear lines within the (particular, historical) origins of the Christian movement and thereby being equipped to doubt (especially) those answers which have claimed a hearing because they were official. The more complex epistemology of such an appeal, within history, over the head of history, to history as canon is sketched formally below in chapter 3 and exemplified historically in chapters 5 and 6.

That sixteenth-century experiences can be cited in example does not mean that the position being described is a Mennonite view. Without disavowing my ethnic and denominational origins, I deny that this view is limited to people of that same culture or derived in its detail from that experience. It is a vision of unlimited catholicity because, in contrast to both sectarian and "established" views, it prescribes no particular institutional requisites for entering the movement whose shape it calls "restoration."

It is therefore an incorrect though natural reading of the position represented here to see it as first of all derived from denominational apologetics. To describe the position argued in the first three essays as "Mennonite" would be to demonstrate *par excellence* the genetic fallacy. Some very visible elements of the Mennonite denominational image are at best irrelevant to what is argued, and some are at worst misleading. Ethnic isolation, Germanic folkways, the simplicity of immigrant village culture, particular patterns of defensive discipline in garb, and the vocational selectivity that have marked Mennonite migration into North America are derived only very indirectly, if at all, from the distinctive theology spoken of above. Some aspects of Mennonite image are even farther from the target than that. The defensiveness and authoritarianism with which conservative mini-Constantinian establishments sometimes govern a rural colony or a church agency, the way in which immigrant farmers can without intending it be allied with authoritarian rulers against the interests of the previous, less technically advanced subjects of those same rulers, and the readiness to buy into some elements of the dominant culture while claiming to be clearly nonconformed on others, represent besetting temptations and at times direct moral failures in the Mennonite experience.

The first three papers demonstrate, from the present, that there is a stance whose claims are rooted intrinsically in the nature of the Christian faith, but which honest theologians from any tradition can affirm in the pursuit of their own vocation, as they are increasingly doing. The models of the historic "radical reformation" have for this enterprise a prototypical value, which does not depend on one's being a product of a denominational or ethnic subculture or on being oneself in a vise where the only options are radical revolt or apostasy.

I therefore describe the radical reformation model as a paradigm of value for all ages and communions, rather than as an apology for a denomination claiming the last—or the best—word. There is here no notion that all of the communities faithful to this vision relate genetically to one another, as a few of their teachers in the past argued. It is not assumed that everyone in these denominational traditions is faithful to the gospel. In fact, in contrast to other views of the church, this is one which holds more strongly than others to a positive doctrine of fallibility. Any existing church is not only fallible but in fact peccable. That is why there needs to be a constant potential for reformation and in the more dramatic situations a readiness for the reformation even to be "radical."

The posture of radical reformation, when understood as a recurrent paradigm, should then not be seen only through the lenses of one instantiation. The experiences of the sixteenth century produced an especially strong polar judgment upon the past establishment of Christianity. When taken alone, that example provides a too negative picture of the potential for constructive social change. The seventeenth-century British experience, within which the Society of Friends arose, was illuminated by a positive apocalypticism, whose hope for what good the Spirit of Christ might do was overly optimistic. The "restoration movement" of the American nineteenth century (the "Churches of Christ" of Alexander Campbell and Barton Stone; the "Churches of God" of Warner and Winebrenner), was especially concerned to reject sectarianism and to dismantle the structures of division. In our century similar movements have focused upon de-Westernizing the meaning of the faith (the Mukyokai of Japan, the Kimbanguists of Zaire). Any one of these leitmotifs taken alone pursues a too narrow agenda. Their commonality, not the specifics of one instantiation, is their witness. The historic "radical reformation" vision calls for both the acceptance of a particular agenda in particular cases and the insistence that the total agenda is far broader than that.

It is one of the widely remarked developments of our century that now one dimension, now another, of the ecclesiastical experience and the ecclesiological vision once called "sectarian" are now beginning to be espoused by some within majority communions. Karl Rahner sets about to prepare Catholics in the West for a "diaspora existence": one in which dominating a culture numerically or politically will no longer be presupposed. Juan-Luis Segundo projects how the church of the future needs to be a ministering, voluntary minority instead of the mass. Interpreters of the history of liturgy concede that the newly reworked Roman Catholic ritual for baptismal initiation of adults is nearer both to the practice of the first church and to the meaning of Christian commitment for our time than was the millennium-long routine christening of the newborn. Churches in Central and South America, whose national culture for centuries had been supported by the interweaving of the hierarchical church with the hierarchies of landownership and military government, now provoke willingly the travail in which a church of the poor is coming to birth, capable of talking back from below to the powers that be. In the North Atlantic world a growing capacity to speak with a mind of their own is being discovered by American Catholics, no longer preoccupied like their immigrant grandparents to prove their worthiness for citizenship, but rather speaking from their own more costly readiness for costly civic responsibility to challenge established public patterns that threaten life, whether it be in the womb, in the slum, or by the bomb.

The specimens just alluded to are most dramatically visible in the Roman Catholic experience of this decade, when we consider the rapidity with which a new ecclesiological vision has developed and the size of the communion exposed to that vision. Yet the components of the vision are far more widely shared. The new challenge to the moral propriety of war in the atomic age began in ecumenical Protestantism in the 1950s and is surging again in the early 1980s. Doubts about infant baptism were raised on theological grounds by Karl Barth in the 1930s and by East German Lutherans in the 1960s. That Christian presence in a society whose rulers are in principle not supportive to their witness can nevertheless be morally authentic was being explored in that same period by Christians in Eastern Europe, walking the narrow line between mindless conformity and reactionary resistance to the takeover of their countries by authoritarian regimes. In that search Josef Hromádka in Czechoslovakia and Johannes Hamel in the German Democratic Republic were among the first names to be noted with some prominence beyond their borders.

These few strands, drawn from what a sensitive history of renewal would need to untangle far more fully, suffice to indicate that the vision projected in this collection of essays about the foundations of Christian social ethics cannot be categorized as "sectarian," except in that very peculiar nonpejorative technical sense in which Ernst Troeltsch proposed to use that term to describe the social stance of the early Christians and of Jews since the second century.

Thus far this book's essays have been described as to their confessional setting; now to look to their substance. It would be wasteful duplication to seek in an introduction to summarize the content of the following essays. What may be helpful is to describe their interrelation.

Often a study of theological ethics seeks to ground the discipline in a description of the warrants which need to be found for dealing with it the way one does: i.e., what some call "meta-ethics." Such an argument discusses the nature of ethical language, what it means to be talking about ethics, and details the other presuppositions and subcomponents of the meaning of moral discourse within an intelligently self-critical community. The assumption is that such examination is in some sense prior to the teachers' or the communities' right or capacity to do ethics. One must first "lay a groundwork," in a realm that might be called "fundamental moral theology." It is thought that if that were not laid out first, then moral activity would be without foundation.

None of the present essays addresses that fundamental task, although in a sense the first few provide something of a substitute for it. While not at all disrespectful of the authentic self-critical ministry of conceptual analysis within any accountable community of discourse, I am skeptical about the possibility that such exercise could come first logically, chronologically, or developmentally. Establishing through theological analysis the conditions of meaningful discourse is an interpretive ministry at the interface between two cultures or two communities. It is not a place to start. There is no "scratch" to which one can go back to begin, anymore than there is any "onion per se" to be reached by peeling off one after another the layers of flesh. What must replace the prolegomenal search for "scratch" is the confession of rootedness in historical community. Then one directs one's critical acuity toward making clear the distance between that community's charter or covenant and its present faithfulness. The tension which is thus critically laid bare may help to discern the difference between wholesome evolution and falling away from the faith, as options within historical development (chapter 1). Thus to reformulate what much Western intellectualism has considered to be a necessary or promising search for "scratch" does not transcend particularity or relativity, as some other "constructive" approaches project the claim to do. It does however affirm the appropriateness of the concern for objectivity and can respond to the implicit but misdirected reproach which Western intellectuals have often addressed to the particularity of forms of faith.

If it be the case that Judaism and Christianity by the nature of things cannot be but particular historical communities, it will follow that the specific form of Christian commitment any given author espouses will be best understood by taking into account, rather than abstracting away, the particularity of the author's time and place. In that sense, this text is with no apology the exposition of a "radical reformation" confessional stance, and appropriately includes essays of a historical character. Yet, as already indicated, it would be a serious misunderstanding to cast upon this confessional quality the condescending light which a tolerant democratic pluralism casts on all "sects" and "marginal movements," which at the same time compliments itself for not persecuting them and determines not to listen to them. The folkloric distancing thanks to which the Amish of Lancaster, Pennsylvania, have been made a tourist attraction, or the Hutterian communities of the northern plains have become a favorite hunting ground for sociologists, should not be permitted to divert my claim that the vision of discipleship projected in this collection is founded in Scripture and catholic tradition, and is pertinent today as a call for all Christian believers. It is especially misinterpreted when it comes to be juxtaposed with a "mini-Constantinian" rural ghetto culture, or with a distinctive sectarian identity maintained not by effective evangelism but by migration and the cultivation of ethnic distinctiveness. These pages do not describe a Mennonite vision. They describe a biblically rooted call to faith, addressed to Mennonites or Zwinglians, to Lutherans or Catholics, to unbelievers or otherbelievers. The most that can be said about its relation to Mennonites or Disciples, Brethren or Friends is that, in the measure in which people of those communions claim faithfulness to their confessional traditions, we have less excuse for falling short of this vision.

As these essays should be understood as addressed to Christians in general, and not peculiarly "sectarian," so also they should be understood not as "radical" in any modern sense of that term, which places a premium on the far-out and unprecedented, but rather as classical or catholic.

I have already argued, with regard to the political pertinence of the humanity of Jesus, that to affirm the normativeness of discipleship is simply classical: the view of Jesus argued in my *Politics of Jesus* claimed to be "more radically Nicene and Chalcedonian than other views." I claimed not to "advocate an unheard-of modern understanding of Jesus." I asked rather "that the implications of what the church has always said about Jesus . . . be taken more seriously, as relevant to our social problems, than ever before" (pp. 100–105).

There my point was that that book's emphasis on the concrete historical-political humanity of the Jesus of the Gospel accounts was compatible with the classic confession of the true humanity of Christ (i.e., the core meaning of "incarnation"), whereas those who deny that humanity (or its normative exemplarity) in favor of some more "spiritual" message are implicitly Docetic. Secondly I argued that the New Testament's seeing Jesus as example is a necessary correlate of what later theology called his divine sonship (the other side of "incarnation"), in such a way that those who downgrade the weight of Jesus' example, on the grounds that his particular social location or example cannot be a norm, renew a counterpart of the old "Ebionitic" heresy. This is a small sample of a wider claim: the convictions argued here do not admit to being categorized as a sectarian oddity or a prophetic exception. Their appeal is to classical catholic Christian convictions properly understood.

It is not only the appeal to the authority of Jesus that is classical and catholic. The same is the case with regard to an understanding of morality in general which does not boil down to either the utilitarian management of consequences or the formal fulfilling of rules. The same is the case for reading the Bible as binding moral guide without subjecting it to fundamentalism or private whimsy. It is the case no less for my post-modern acceptance of the particularity of the Christian story without subjecting it either to the claimed objectivity of general consensus or to that of some specific "scientific method."

One of the marks of the "believers' church" heritage is that it sees movement within the canonical story, and therefore a difference between the testaments. Instead of a timeless collection of parabolic anecdotes for allegorical application, or of propositional communications ready for deductive exposition, the Bible is a story of promise and fulfillment which must be read directionally. The New Testament, by affirming the Hebrew Scriptures which Christians have come to call the Old Testament, also interprets them. Abraham and Moses are read through Jesus and Paul.

This directional array of former and later convenants, expectation and fulfillment, is easily misunderstood as a disjunctive dualism. Such dualism arises when the gospel is seen as characterized chiefly by its opposition to law, or when the Sermon on the Mount is opposed to the Torah. It may also happen when the free-church understanding of the mission of the church in the New Testament is seen as opposed to the nonmissionary ethnic theocracy of the Old.

Just as I have denied a polar tension with catholic identity, similarly a disjunction with the Hebrew history must be denied. There was evidently in ancient Israel an ethnic base, and (for a few centuries) there was a royal state structure (or two). Yet that "nation" was a very permeable unity. Provisions were made both formally and informally for the assimilation of the stranger and the sojourner. The function of both priest and prophet was to invite an uncoerced, voluntary response of the "heart" (a very personalistic and voluntaristic term, present already in the ancient texts) to the convenant initiative of Yahweh. The "free-church" dimension of Israel as a confessing community of moral identity is worth dwelling upon here.

The middle section of Psalm 24, like Psalm 15, is a priestly document in the form of a catechism. It says that only people characterized by a certain moral quality belong in the procession to lead the ark of Yahweh into the temple. It has always been clear that the "free-church" movement has a distinctive ethic. That is no novelty of modern renewal movements; it is already true of these psalms. There is no freedom and no history without Torah. There is no continuing authentic freedom without some way to put the question: who belongs in the procession (Psalms 15:1, 24:3)?

The place of the question, "who may ascend to the hill of Yahweh?" means that this procession into the temple is no fully voluntary parade, nor a mob. It is not a coalition group seeking maximum participation under minimum conditions of agreement. There are priestly marshals at the mustering point who ask, "who may enter?"

This procession is not a biological community nor a nation state. It is a disciplined community, a believers' church. The marks of the discipline in Psalm 24 are two: transparency (not swearing deceitfully), and freedom from idolatry (not lifting up one's soul to "emptiness"). Such marks have to do with the whole of one's quality or attitude. The rest of the moral catechism which could have been included (cf. 15:2–5) does not appear necessary.

It is appropriate that there be safeguards against legalism when affirming the authority of Torah. There is a point in the classical concern of Martin Luther to keep justification from being dependent on morality. There is a point in the recent concern of many to free ethical creativity from rigidity in order creatively to respond to one's "situation." In any Puritan context there is need to disconnect moral decisions from control by the magistrate or the parson. Yet these several legitimate antilegalistic points must not be permitted to issue in an antinomianism which would deny the communal quality of moral engagement.

Thus far my concern was to define an ethical style. Now its presuppositions can be discerned. The church precedes the world epistomologically. We know more fully from Jesus Christ and in the context of the confessed faith than we know in other ways. The meaning and validity and limits of concepts like "nature" or of "science" are best seen not when looked at alone but in light of the confession of the lordship of Christ. The church precedes the world as well axiologically, in that the lordship of Christ is the center which must guide critical value choices, so that we may be called to subordinate or even to reject those values which contradict Jesus.

Yet both in the order of knowing and in the order of valuing, the priority of the faith does not exclude or deny everything else. Insights which are not contradictory to the truth of the Word incarnate are not denied but affirmed and subsumed within the confession of Christ. Values which are not counter to his suffering servanthood are not rejected but are affirmed and subsumed in his lordship, becoming complementary and instrumental in the exercise of ministry to which he calls his disciples. This is the point at which H. Richard Niebuhr's notion of "Christ against culture" misinterprets the minority tradition as disjunctive rather than integrative.

It is therefore not a compromise or a dilution of the fidelity of the radical commitment when the obedient Christian community becomes at the same time an instrument for serving and saving the larger culture. The distinctive faithfulness of the church to her first calling does not undermine but purges and renews the authentic human interest and values of the whole society, well beyond the bounds of the explicitly known and confessed faith. In the present compilation this is exemplified especially by the analyses of democracy and of civil religion, and in "The Kingdom as Social Ethics." That discipleship means social withdrawal is a caricature projected by Troeltsch and the Niebuhrs, on grounds related to their own assumptions, not drawn from historical facts. By definition the disciple, like her/his Lord, is in the world although not of it. The style and the shape of the disciple's social pressure will be more critical, more flexible, less conformist and less patient, than the "responsible involvement" advocated by the majority traditions. That greater critical independence may include an occasional radical opposition. It may result in the disciples' being outvoted or excluded, which itself is a strong form of social participation. It will not withdraw *a priori*, as if obedience were thought to apply to some other world than this rebellious one.

The notion of the royal priesthood or kingdom of priests, echoing all the way from Moses to 1 Peter and the Revelation of John, capsules well that synthesis of apartness and representation, community and authority, whereby the people of God in present history live from and toward the promise of the whole world's salvation.

PART I

Foundations

1. The Hermeneutics of Peoplehood:
A Protestant Perspective

THE TASK OF THIS STUDY

It is not always necessary, and it is certainly not elegant, to begin an exposition with definitions of terms. Yet in this case it will be functional. Locating and justifying my subject is a major portion of this assignment.

"Protestant Ethics"

The territory of "Protestant ethics" is even less subject to being helpfully included in standard typological categories than the other major traditions. There are all kinds of diversities within Judaism or within Roman Catholicism; yet one can at least define an affirmative social and historic center around which those diversities cluster and can be clarified. No such simplicity for the "Protestant." Protestantism never was either a single social organization or a single intellectual system. Its common marks are negative, even when they are stated in affirmative form like the (historically not very well-founded) Tillichian notion of a "Protestant principle."

I therefore despair of coming up with any proper definition of what Protestant identity is supposed to be. That despair is not traumatic; nonetheless it separates me from some of the more easily constructed current typologies.

It would drive us even farther in the direction of a not immediately helpful cataloguing process if I attempted to define "Protestant" by way of the history of the term. My own ethnic and denominational orientation, by birth and by choice, represents a tradition which for most of the centuries since the Reformation has not been acknowledged by Protestants as belonging among them.[1] From this perspec-

15

tive, the camp which is usually called "Protestant" represents an unstable bridge position between, on the one hand, a fundamentally critical renewal of all Christian thought oriented by a renewed simplicity of understanding of the authority of Scripture and, on the other hand, the heritage of the medieval establishment in which the Bible, the established social order, and the sum of all human wisdom had flowed together in one great fusion.

Nonetheless, one trait which unites those called "Protestant," across the spectrum from "mainstream" to "radical," is the conviction that in the earlier history of Christianity something had gone wrong. For some, the corrective change that would be needed should be minimal, limited to those points "necessary for salvation," with no intention to call into question the inherited church order. For others, the change needs to be sweeping. But that there needs to be critical change at all means in any case that our moral reasoning cannot proceed unselfcritically. We can never simply stand on the shoulders of an unquestioned consensus from the past, claiming it to be "catholic" and assuming its acceptability simply by virtue of the claim that it has been believed always everywhere by everyone.

This does not mean that the classical Vincentian criterion always/everywhere/everyone becomes useless. Far from it: in Protestantism it became a critical tool to use in naming and rejecting what the Reformers believed to have been medieval or pagan accretions. (Especially was this done by John Oecolampad.) Its function was the "Protestant" or critical one of labeling aspects of medieval tradition which needed to be denounced because one can show when, or where, or by whom they had not been believed.

The implication of this one critical beginning move, once initiated, can then be projected minimally or maximally. For our present purposes, I suggest that there be no prior discussion of "how far" to carry the critical thrust, or "at what point" it needs to be buffered or diluted by "realistic" or "pastoral" or "ecumenical" considerations. This leaves me then to define the criterion of Protestant identity in the course of its use, in the perennially unfinished process of critiquing the developed tradition from the perspective of its own roots.[2] The critical process and the commitment to scriptural accountability which it incarnates are more important for definitional purposes than any particular denominational narratives (including my own) through which that critical concern has left its tracks.

If there is to be a fundamental skepticism about what everybody everywhere always thought, we shall expect it to include an element of challenge concerning who was doing the thinking before. That theology should only be taught by theologians, that catechesis and confession must be reserved to the duly ordained, and that decisions about the exercise of power need primarily to be made by the people who legitimately hold that power, are elements of the previously prevailing moral wisdom which it is not merely permissible but imperative to doubt. This doubt is expressed classically in the New Testament, which says that all of God's people should be kings, or priests, or prophets, or charismatics. Any reservation of the responsibility for moral discernment to a specialist must be challenged, especially if that specialist is understood to hold authority partly because he is one of a category of persons separated from the life-situations of people making moral choices.[3] Different "Protestant" criticisms have made this point with different degrees of radicality, but all have in some way or another sought to redefine or to relocate the prerogative of the priesthood in moral discernment.

To begin my definition modestly I should say that, for our purposes, all that is sure about "Protestant" identity is that it is not Roman Catholic: it does not have a pope or magisterium with theologically imperative, morally binding authority, nor a structure of confession and absolution wherewith to educate and to enforce. Yet that negation is not made on behalf of a counter-patriarch or an anti-magisterium, but rather by virtue of a critical principle of appeal to the sources, which can reach unpredictably farther than those who first called themselves "Protestant" dreamed.

"Practical Moral Reasoning"

By "practical moral reasoning" is meant (I take it) that people make particular choices which are illuminated by their general faith commitments, but which still need to be worked through by means of detailed here-and-now thought processes. Thus it is not possible in a strict sense to discuss "the place of" practical moral reasoning as if there could be ethics without it, i.e., as if one could choose to "use" or "not to use" it. Then the question is in what context it occurs, what weight it has.

It would be possible to construct a typology of the various ways Protestants talk about other things than practical moral reasoning, so that practical moral reasoning would take different places in the total context of their concerns. The other things they talk about have different relationships to ethics in general and to practical moral reasoning in particular. To orient ourselves on this extensive terrain, I shall allude to some obvious examples, but with no claim to fullness, nor even with much claim to fairness in detail.

1. One set of Protestants is concerned for the *authenticity* of religious self-understanding. They feel that morality, hard to separate from moralism, may easily become (or perhaps in fact always is) a barrier to authenticity, so that there is positive importance attached to *not* talking about practical moral reasoning. This approach has various pietistic and existentialistic variants.

For our present purposes Rudolf Bultmann, at least as he is received, may be taken as a prototype. Thomas Oden has written a very competent, sympathetic summary of the thought of Bultmann in this realm, under the heading *Radical Obedience* (1964). The agenda of ethics here becomes the occasion to work at the authenticity of religious self-understanding. The most important resource for such renewal is the lesson which must be learned, and learned again and again, that nothing that we can *do* makes us any better. So *Radical Obedience* is not about ethics. It is about authenticity, and about how authenticity is safeguarded, in Rudolf Bultmann's theology, by means of a preoccupation with openness to the present and the future, which forbids any material ethical content. It can only ever be known within a given situation what the needs of the neighbor in that situation are. The function of the statements of the law is not to tell us what to do, nor to provide substantial background to the interpretation of the "situation," but only to exemplify and dramatize our standing without any merits or righteousness of our own before God. So Oden's entire book makes no reference to any specific decisions, nor to any specific words of Torah which might illuminate moral decisions, nor even to any specimens to fill out the concept of "the concrete situation." All that we need to know about particular decisions is the drive of love and the grace of freedom with which we enter the situation, to discover then and there what it will mean, just then and there, to love the neighbor. Oden does not explain (and properly not, because Bultmann does not explain) how that process of "discovering" in the context what the neighbor needs will proceed. Neither the factual data explaining what the available choices are, nor those considerations which other people would call "value" data that explain why one choice is preferable to another, should be talked about ahead of time for fear of destroying the authenticity of the command of God in the moment. The reader is at a loss to know, on the one hand, whether this is because all values are assumed to be self-evident, so that there may be a very concrete process of practical moral reasoning going on. (Bultmann is not interested in talking about such a process, though, because it would be on a more mechanical level than he is interested in: one can hardly go wrong if one loves genuinely.) Or on the other hand is Bultmann actually claiming, as some existentialists and some pietists would like him to say, that knowing what is needed will come in a flash of intuition with no moral reasoning at all?

It goes without saying that there need be in such a subjectively concerned portrayal no reference to the social dimension of ethics: neither a word to the church as a community counseling me, nor any critique of or word to the "world" or the "principalities and powers" or multinational corporations or universities or races, as entities impinging upon me or upon the neighbor I am supposed to love *in this situation.*

Bultmann does not acknowledge the sociopolitical dimensions even by denying that they are important. There is nothing "radical" about the resulting behavior, in the ordinary social meaning of that adjective. Perhaps Bultmann's word "situation" *could* be expanded to include consideration of those matters; yet in the text itself the main function of the noun "situation" is not to draw our attention to a specifiable location of the person within structures beyond the self, but rather to draw our minds away from *any* temporal continuity, especially from any preparation before the "situation" in order to make an informed response to it.

It would be a mistake, in our brief sampling, to take this specimen as one of several possible ways to do moral reasoning. It is rather one of the few standard ways to do without it, or not to do it. Therefore it does not really show on the grid of our agenda. The detour was nonetheless important, precisely because it makes us recognize that there are particular protypically "Protestant" *pastoral* perspectives from which the possibility or the fruitfulness of practical moral reasoning are overshadowed or even set aside for the sake of other concerns, notably the salvation or the authenticity of the individual.

The radical discontinuity of Søren Kierkegaard's "suspension of the ethical" is one more failed way to drive home the same point. Ronald Green has shown that no one before Kierkegaard ever gave such a meaning to the story of Abraham's readiness to sacrifice Isaac,[4] but that is not why the point fails. Nor is it that Kierkegaard assumes a notion of a father's moral duties and the son's rights quite foreign to the age of Abraham.[5] It is that by writing about the text as he does, using it to make a point as he does, Kierkegaard after all makes the "suspension" of the (ordinary) "ethical" into a case to be explained "teleologically." "Whenever God himself tells you[6] to do something, even if it is something (otherwise) quite wrong, do it." Thus despite himself, Kierkegaard brings the *akedah* obedience of Abraham back into the realm of tragic necessity. It was after all the obedient thing, the right thing to do. (We need not blame Kierkegaard himself for the fact, but it is a fact that some have made his "teleological" suspension into a case for a utilitarian ethic, without being as clear as Abraham was about the voice of God. Instead of the suspension of "the ethical" by a higher order of faith imperative, we have the suspension of a norm in favor of a higher ethical value.)

2. Another set of mainstream Protestants would not go as far as Bultmann, but would retain, together with him, a strong concern for keeping ethics from distorting the framework of pastoral concern. The general Lutheran accent upon the discrimination between law and gospel does not set aside ethical deliberation, but is concerned to keep it in its place. This has a chastening impact upon the amount of time and attention which concrete ethical matters tend to be given, yet without rejecting practical moral reasoning. The great compendia of Thielecke or of Søe testify that one can still say a lot after the law/gospel preamble has been stated.

3. Protestant scholasticism, when in the seventeenth century it took its critical stance over against Roman Catholicism, claimed that the Bible was the only moral authority and announced a fundamental suspicion of moral discernment when (as in Catholic moral theology) such discernment claims rootage in reason, nature, and tradition. Yet when this official Protestantism turned to the problems of administering its own society, there resulted at the time no profound difference between it and Catholicism on any practical moral issues: divorce, usury, war, or truth-telling. Protestantism, by rebelling against Rome, had opened the gates for freer theological change from then on, but not intentionally: not because of fundamentally different ideas about the foundations of practical moral reasoning.

4. In that same seventeenth century Protestants could welcome the polemic of Pascal, in his *Provincial Letters,* over against the probabilism advocated by some of the Jesuits of his time. For the sake

of radical obedience Pascal took the position which Bultmann rejects, namely, that only a firm criterion not at all within our discretion can give roots to moral accountability.

It would be worthwhile in some other context to try to fill out and make fully fair this kind of inventory of types of reasoning. For present purposes, however, it suffices to show that the various concerns of a polemic or pastoral character do not in most cases correlate in any predictable or verifiable way with a different set of outcomes in particular decisions, e.g., about just war or justifiable divorce. The variations which we have observed do not create a balanced or rounded scheme or scale. They do not answer the same question differently. They rather attend to different questions. They do not correspond fully with classical denominational traditions or theological families. The argument with Pascal comes closest to making such a difference, but he represents the debate within one tradition of pastoral casuistry, rather than between different theological families.

Thus there is no reason, arising out of the comparison of major schools, to think that being "Protestant" is in itself a necessary and sufficient determinant of one distinctive style of practical moral reasoning. If we had hoped that some understanding of "Protestant identity" in the realm of moral reasoning would arise inductively out of the inventory of alternatives, as sometimes does happen for some questions, we should now be disappointed. But this is not the case. We have verified that the theme we are interpreting cannot be sorted out by means of some simple principles of classification. It is rather a variety of phenomena for which the phrase "practical moral reasoning" is too loose a grab bag. I take this conclusion not as a counsel of despair but rather as a step forward and as a reason to prefer my own definition to another that could (perhaps) be documented inductively out of the history of Protestant ethical thought. I therefore proceed to seek to define a coherent view without making the case that it synthesizes all the others.

This leaves me with a more modest and yet at the same time a more presumptuous definition of what perspective on practical moral reasoning ought fittingly to flow from what a Protestant identity is prototypically claimed to be. To the question, "which Protestantism?" I am now freer than I would have been before to give the simple answer: "my kind." The claim that it is prototypical as contrasted with other streams of Protestantism will have to remain implicit. An intra-Protestant debate would be worthwhile but not on this occasion. Some name the following account "free church" or "radical Protestant"; I would prefer to describe it as seeking to draw out consistent conclusions from the initial informal originality which marked the common Protestant origins in the early 1520s. But that it does that adequately, and in the only possible way, I do not now mean to argue.

AN OPEN PROCESS

> At all your meetings, let everyone be ready with a Psalm or a sermon or a revelation. . . . As for prophets, let two or three speak, and the others attend to them. . . . (1 Cor. 14:26, 29)[7]

Both Martin Luther and Huldrych Zwingli were challenged in 1523 to make the case for the canonical autonomy of the local congregation. In Zurich the occasion was the January "disputation" convened by the city fathers to hear testimony on the accusation that their preacher Huldrych Zwingli was heretical. The only representative of the hierarchy who bothered to show up was the episcopal Vicar of Constance, John Faber, who contested the right of that assembly of guildsmen to debate theology. Zwingli's response was based on 1 Corinthians 14, where the working of the spirit in the congregation is validated by the liberty with which the various gifts are exercised, especially by the due process with which every prophetic voice is heard and every witness evaluated. This dialogical liberty, which Zwingli once called "the rule of Paul," did not become a regular part of the life of the Swiss national church, but it retained its programmatic value in the congregationalism of the early Zwingli, as well as that of his followers, the Anabaptists and the British Puritans.

For Martin Luther the question was different: it was whether the congregation has the authority to name her ministers. But the argument was the same, and the appeal to 1 Corinthians 14 was the same.

For neither of these Reformers was this position an original one. It was, in fact, precisely a claim to catholicity that each of them was making. What earlier conciliarism had been saying on the scale of the world church, it had also always been saying (under its breath) with regard to local agenda. What Paul had said, no later council had doubted or revoked, so the Reformers could appeal to it with no fear of being heretical. God speaks where his people gather and are free to be led. The marks of the validity of the conclusions they reach are to be sought not alone in the principles applied but in the procedure of the meeting. Were all free to speak? Was every speech heard and weighed? Did the prophets grant their need to undergo interpretation?

That initial congregationalism was useful to Luther and to Zwingli as long as it justified the independence of what they were doing locally as over against the bishops or the Holy Roman Empire. It ceased to be attractive to them when their need for the support of the local civil authorities obliged them to choose between open congregational process and maintaining order. It is thus easy to see why by 1526 both Reformers had backed away from the announced autonomy of the gathered people and delegated the authority to be "church" to the city fathers (in Zwingli's case) or the territorial princes (in Luther's).

History demands at this point a brief excursus on the politicization of Protestantism. The slogan *ecclesia reformata, semper reformanda* expressed a conviction held by Luther no less than Calvin. Yet the institutionalization of church renewal in the hands of civil governments, whether directly through the consistory as an arm of the state of less directly through synods authorized and protected by the state, had the opposite effect from that implied in this slogan. It was the radical reformation which maintained the elbow room to keep on calling for change as new items arose on the agenda of reform.[8]

Most strikingly, with regard to our question of moral discernment, to assign matters of church order, and thereby also matters of teaching on morality, to the surveillance of civil government is practically to guarantee that some kinds of moral agenda will be much more difficult to manage. That such social advances as democracy and religious liberty in Western Europe had to come mostly at the urging of Enlightenment critics of Christian tradition, and therefore arose in often antichurchly and sometimes antireligious forms, is not a characteristic of the vision of democracy nor of the principle of religious liberty in themselves. This was rather the price paid for having entrusted reformation to governments, thereby preventing reformation on moral matters from being kept within the continuing control and responsibility of ecclesiastically committed Christians.

The divisiveness of sixteenth-century Protestantism was not the result of some people's seeking separation from other Christians in order to be free more easily to be faithful to their vision of some biblical imperative. The people who wished for such renewed faithfulness in the first generation of the Reformation wished it for the whole church. The divisions were the product of the fact that provincial and local governments became the instruments of reformation. This happened because in view of the failure to revitalize congregational process, the Reformers saw no other recourse in their conflict with the bishops and the empire than the help of local governments. Thus, they not only divided the Christendom which they had hoped to reform as a unit; they froze it into patterns of administration which were no longer reformable.

This early Protestant congregationalism is important for our purposes. First of all this is because it points to matters of due process in practical moral reasoning and to every individual's need for counsel. It is, though, still more fundamentally important as a perception of the corporate dimension in all of human nature. This needs to be said because a few generations later Protestantism was accused by Catholicism of being incorrigibly individualistic (because of the way in which the doctrine of the perspicuity of Scripture was interpreted), a reproach which the Enlightenment still later turned into a compliment. Western intellectual history ever since has been a pendulum swinging between the collective and the individual. This is clearly not what the Reformers intended when they argued the perspicuity of Scripture and the priesthood of all believers. Nonetheless, that openness to unaccountable individuality was potentially present in their logic, when the hierarchy as interpreter of Scripture was set aside, and when the universities, consistories, synods, and conventions which were expected to take its place became fragmented. The polemics of Bellarmine and Bossuet, understandably interpreting *in malem partem* this openness to individual arbitrariness, prepared the way for the flip over into the Enlightenment approbation of personal judgment. As long as the communal quality of belief is preempted by the sociology of establishment, the only social form that comes to mind with which to critique it is the lonely rebel. *Tertium non paret.*

It is the testimony of radical Protestantism that there does exist a third option, which is not merely a mixture of elements of the other two. Communities which are genuinely voluntary can affirm individual dignity (at the point of the uncoerced adherence of the member) without enshrining individualism. They can likewise realize community without authorizing lordship or establishment. The alternative to arbitrary individualism is not established authority but an authority in which the individual participates and to which he or she consents.

The alternative to authoritarianism is not anarchy but freedom of confession.

The model toward which the Protestant Reformation initially began to move, and which so-called "free churches" sought to incarnate more thoroughly than official Protestantism, is the voluntary community which has about it neither the coercive givenness of establishment nor the atomistic isolation of individualism. This has direct formal contributions to make to defining practical moral reasoning.

The moral validity of a choice one makes is connected to the freedom with which one has first of all made the choice to confess oneself a disciple of Jesus and to commit oneself to hearing the counsel of one's fellow disciples.

The long history of the struggle in the West between collectivism and individualism, with all of its themes and variations, is at least partially correlated with the fact that the mainstream Reformation did not call into question the principle of establishment, as this was expressed both in the baptism of infants and in the link between church and state, even though some questioning of both of those marks of establishment was implicit in the early years of the Reformation, and even though the challenge was carried to the point of implementation by a few radical Protestants in every century since the fifteenth. Voluntary commitment to a community distinct from the total society provides resources for practical moral reasoning of a kind which are by definition unthinkable where that option is not offered and where the only way to be an individual is to rebel.

We could run up and down the centuries, itemizing the ways in which it was thought by many that the only way to have authenticity was to foster individual rebellion, or that the only way to have common accountability was to deny the individual. From the perspective of individualism the communal quality of the radical Protestant moral witness seems to be tyrannical, if one fails to recognize that one's belonging to that community is free. From the perspective of establishment, the radical Protestant community is seen as anarchic, because one fails to see that the covenantal quality of its discipline makes it inwardly more coherent than that of establishment.

The importance of this alternative is difficult to appreciate in the present context, because my way of putting the point above converses with the alternatives of the sixteenth century more than with the present. In our time, on our continent, the direct equivalent of "establishment" is not immediately visible; so the shape of disestablishment or freedom of confession is not simple either. That does not mean, however, that pressures toward an inauthentic morality of conformity are absent in our culture. They simply take less overt forms. What in the sixteenth century was provided by the governmental sanction granted to the Reformers finds its analogues today in the conformity produced by the schools, the job market, and the media. Over against this kind of new establishment, sociologists of knowledge will continue to note the importance of voluntary associations, of which the free church remains a prototype.

A RECONCILING PROCESS

> Whatever you bind on earth shall be considered bound in heaven: whatever you loose on earth shall be considered loosed in heaven. . . . [I]f two of you agree on earth it will be granted by my Father in heaven. (Matt. 18:15, 18)

Twice in Matthew's Gospel Jesus is reported to have assigned to his disciples the authority to "bind and to loose." Those terms, although not widely used, were not neologisms. They had a meaning in the rabbinic thought of the time (or at least they have a documented meaning in rabbinic thought somewhat later, which permits us to presume that such a meaning was already present in the age of the Second Temple): namely, "binding and loosing" means what we have called "practical moral reasoning." When a rabbi was asked for moral advice, and he spoke to "bind" or to "loose," he made something obligatory or nonobligatory. The verbal sense of "binding" is still there in our word "obligatory." To explain a particular moral choice on grounds of its rootage in the tradition is to "bind" or to "loose."

The earliest Protestantism recognized this function to be assigned to the Christian community and used for it the precise technical term "rule of Christ." During the Reformation, we find this term in usage in the writings of Martin Bucer and of those radical Zwinglians who later came to be called Anabaptists. But the term is used as well by Martin Luther in 1526. Certainly Luther did not get it from the Zwinglians or vice versa; therefore it must have been a phrase that was current somewhat earlier in some other source accessible to both. It is one of the puzzles of early Reformation history that this usage has not yet been tracked down to its earlier common source. Like the ideal of congregational liberty, this vision was lost in the next generation.

What is said to the disciples by Jesus strikes one as presumptuous, if not preposterous or even blasphemous. "What you bind on earth shall be considered as bound in heaven." A transcendent moral ratification is claimed for the decisions made in the conversation of two or three or more, in a context of forgiveness and in the juridical form of listening to several witnesses.

Every fragment of the previous sentence matters. The context is conversation, not the jurist's simple deductive application of universally valid rules. The conversation takes place in a context of commitment to forgive (the theme of the entire chapter 18 of Matthew's Gospel). The deliberative process begins with only the two parties to the conflict being involved. The conflict is broadened only gradually, and only so far as is needed to achieve reconciliation. The tests of the validity of the process are procedural, having to do with the hearing of several witnesses, subject to correction and change over time. We have here then a kind of situation ethics, i.e., a procedure for doing practical moral reasoning, in a context of conflict, right in the situation where divergent views are being lived out in such a way as to cause offense. This rejects a rigid or automatic casuistic deduction on one hand and individualism or pluralism on the other. The obedience of the brother or sister is my business. There is no hesitancy in using the word "sin"; yet the intention of the procedure is reconciliation, not exclusion or even reprimand. Out of this utterly personal exchange comes the confirmation (or perchance the modification) of the rules of the community, which can therefore be spoken of, with the technical language of the rabbis, as having "bound" or "loosed."

Every element noted in the passage cited from Matthew 18 has something to say to the way we think today about decision-making in the context of faith. Most discussions of practical moral reasoning do not ask whether the intention of those doing the reasoning is to reconcile. Most treatments of this subject do not concretize the decision about issues in the form of a conversation between persons who differ on the issues. Most discussions of practical moral reasoning do not concretize that conversation by seeing it as surrounded by a church (i.e., a locally gathered body) which ultimately will ratify either the reconciliation or the impossibility of reconciliation. Most guides to practical moral reasoning do not have the nerve to claim that the discernment reached will stand ratified in heaven.

We have here an alternative both to individualistic intuitionism and to completely objective rigidity, in the form of a prescription for a valid, reconciling, decision-making process. That there will be rules, that these will sometimes collide and sometimes need to bend is neither affirmed nor denied, but rather located within a more important question: namely, "How are you going to go about it?" If you go about it in an open context, where both parties are free to speak, where additional witnesses provide objectivity and mediation, where reconciliation is the intention and the expected outcome is a judgment that God himself can stand behind, then the rest of the practical moral reasoning process will find its way.

For Luther, the actual functioning of a binding and loosing process was never more than an unreachable utopia. The passage where he uses the phrase, "Rule of Christ," is in fact part of the statement where he says he is abandoning that vision because he has no clientele for a "truly evangelical" form of community.[9] In the Upper Rhine, on the other hand, Zwingli's colleagues Martin Bucer, John Oecolampad, and then John Calvin, worked seriously at what Bucer called "genuine pastoral care." Yet there, too, the ambivalence of the interlock between this reconciling dialogical discipline and (standing behind the Reformers) the civil authorities, whose concerns were more punative the unitive, prevented the dynamics of dialogue from functioning in its own right.

Thus it was the "radicals" of the Reformed Reformation who, counter to their own intention, were driven into isolation. For them, the conversational structure of congregational reconciliation and intercongregational unity became their means of survival. Those who refused to delegate "being church" to the civil powers were thus placed before the new challenge of congregationalism's need to be civilly subversive and ecclesiastically schismatic, neither of which had been the original intent.

THE SHAPE OF CONVERSATION

To explain further how this communal hermeneutic operates in moral reasoning we need to ask not how ideas work but how the community works. We need a flow chart not of concepts leading into one another but of functions discharged by various organs within the community. Our task is aided by the way in which this community is described at several important points within the apostolic writings as a body needing to have each member do a different thing. The Apostle Paul says that *every* member of the body has a distinctive place in this process. I must limit myself to enumerating a few of those functions which have the most immediate and irreplacable contribution to make to practical moral reasoning. In describing them, I shall continue to interrelate elements of radical Protestant witness with their New Testament warrants, without claiming that the two outlines coincide completely, and without either one's being complete.

The community will have among it Agents of Direction.

> One who prophesies talks to others, to their improvement, encouragement and consolation. . . . Let two or three of them speak, and the other weigh what they say. . . . (1 Cor. 14:3, 29)

Prophecy is described as both a charisma distinctly borne by some individuals and a kind of discourse in which others may sometimes participate as well. Its primary focus is neither prediction nor moral guidance, yet it states and reenforces a vision of the place of the believing community in history, which vision locates moral reasoning. This understanding is clearly independent of any interest in satisfying our modern curiosity about explaining what people say without remainder in terms of their education and their complexes. There is no interest in claiming (like the modern "charismatic") that the phenomenon is "miraculous" nor (like the modern therapist) in "understanding" it. It is a matter of simple trust that God himself, as Spirit, is at work to motivate and to monitor his own in, with, and under this distinctive, recognizable, and specifically disciplined human discourse. It is because there is such a thing as prophecy and because there exist ways to evaluate its authenticity, that the process of weighing the words of prophets, which we saw to be the ground floor of early Protestant congregationalism, makes sense as a work of the Spirit and as more than a primitive, social contract democracy. This vision is thus as situational as is some modern existentialistic contextualism, yet without its arbitrariness. It is as institutionally verifiable as is established churchdom, yet without its rigidity.

Its verifiability is objective, formal. Anyone who prophesies is recognizable formally in that she or he will take turns talking and will wait for her or his discourse to be "weighed." Some prophets and prophetesses are furthermore recognized in the New Testament as regularly exercizing that "office." It is then a serious distortion, which does not arise only in "charismatic" circles, when the "prophetic" is associated with the erratic, impatient, unpredictable.

The community will be aided by the Agents of Memory.

> Every scribe who becomes a disciple of the kingdom of heaven is like a householder who brings out from his storeroom things both new and old. (Matt. 13:52)

This seems to be the only time a Gospel reports the use of the word "scribe" by Jesus himself, the only time it appears describing a function of social knowing rather than a member of a particular party in Palestinian society, and the only time the term is not at least lightly pejorative. Despite the opposition to Jesus reported as the regular stance of those who were "scribes outside the kingdom," we find here a striking affirmation of the place, within the moral life of the confessing community, of the function of memory and its renewed, flexible application. What is definitional for the scribe is that he does not speak on his own but as the servant of a community and of the communal memory. Whether the "treasures" which he brings to awareness be ancient or recent, they need to be brought out by someone who is acquainted with the storeroom, and who knows what to bring out when.

This is the necessary corrective to any purely occasionalistic ethic. The community's memory will never *make* a decision for the present. Because there is in the storeroom of memories a bewildering variety of "treasures," knowing which of them to bring out and how they fit is itself a charisma, different from the functions ordinarily ascribed to the people bearing the title of "scribe" in the Gospel story, yet calling for the same qualifications. The scribe as practical moral reasoner does not judge or decide anything, but he (or she) remembers expertly, charismatically the store of memorable, identity-confirming acts of faithfulness praised and of failure repented. As we in the age after Auschwitz reread the New Testament with concern to unlearn our anti-Judaic biases, we may take it less for granted that the pejorative Gospel references to "scribes" describe what most of the people in that leadership group in occupied Judaea were actually doing then. We may then be able to recover our respect for the needfulness of the positive scribal task.

This is the closest we come, in our amateur phenomenology of apostolic moral reasoning, to a place to locate the function of Scripture. Scripture is the collective scribal memory, the store *par excellence* of treasures old and new. The scribal skills and textual knowledge themselves are not identical with being "a disciple of the Kingdom," yet they represent access to Scripture as revered writing and to its story as our history. The "becoming a disciple of the Kingdom," the scribe's own integration into the Kingdom's Cause, must be added before the texts can live as the community's memory through the charismatic aptness of the scribe's selectivity. Scholastic Protestantism gave currency to the phrase "testimony of the Holy Spirit" to designate the mystery of the Bible's becoming a living Word, with one's receiving of that witness usually being thought of as quite individual and inward. Jesus' image of the householder's gift of resourceful selectivity is a more apt description.

American church life and scholarship have been concerned with deep debate about *just* how the reading of scriptural texts ought to proceed, with regard to patterns of literary and historical criticism, to theories of scriptural and magisterial authority, and (more recently) to sociopolitical analysis of the agencies of theological articulation. All of those considerations are worthy of attention. None of them must or can be resolved before making the affirmations of the above text. To make them logically prerequisite is itself an anti-people axiom. The utility of Scripture as common memory is not dependent on answering them first.

Jesus' image appears also to be as close as we can come, in New Testament vocabulary, to treating the function of "worship" as constituting a group ever anew around its common memory. We are reading and writing a lot these days about the interlock between worship and obedience or between liturgics and ethics.[10] That, too, should certainly be said here. We face one hindrance, however, in seeking to make much of the point, self-evident as it may be. Neither in the New Testament documents nor in radical Protestantism is there a discretely identifiable function called "priesthood" or a specific activity called "worship." The function which created the synagogue in central diaspora Judaism was the scribal one of reading the holy writings. What we call "worship" is hard to locate as the task of one officer. Breaking bread in the solemn memory of the Lord's suffering and the joyous acclamation of his presence and promised return was one of the things both the early Christians and the radical Protestants did regularly, but they needed no special officers for that. It was no more such action that constituted them as "church" than were the sending out of missionaries, the collection of famine relief moneys, or practical moral reasoning.

The community will be guided by
Agents of Linguistic Self-Consciousness.

On the lists of charismata in the Pauline corpus, and thinly scattered through Acts, we find reference to a particular function described as *didaskalos* or teacher.

It is said of this function that it is a dangerous one because the tongue is hard to govern. Not many people should be in this office, the Epistle of James says (James 3:18), because like the small bit turning a horse around or the small rudder turning a ship around, or the small flame setting a forest ablaze, language has a dangerously determining function. (Our understanding of this point is ill-served by our being the products of modern psychologizing individualism. We take "the tongue" to mean parabolically our individual capacity for impulsive, or unself-critical utterance: for hurting people by gossip, inappropriate humor, or intemperate anger. I do not intend to deny that many of us have that problem. But there is considerable room for doubt that that is what James meant. Modern psychologizing individualism is hardly the context for this admonition. In the Aramaic which James spoke and in the Greek which he wrote, as well as in many other mediterranean languages, "the tongue" means the language, or the phenomenon of language.)

It is a significant anthropological insight to say that language can steer the community with a power disproportionate to other kinds of leadership. The demagogue, the poet, also the journalist, the novelist, the grammarian, all are engaged in steering society with the rudder of language. This applies both to rhetoric as a skill and also to the place of any set of concepts in predisposing what kinds of thoughts the members of a given community are capable of having. Think for a moment about how much ink has been spilt over questions which were assumed to have been adequately stated in terms of reifications like "nature and grace" or "law and gospel." There is a fine balance when Timothy is invited at the same time to retain "the pattern of sound words" which he had received, and still "to avoid disputing about words" (2 Tim. 1:13, 2:16). There should not be many *didaska-*

loi, not many articulators in the church, because not many of those who use language are aware of its temptations.

The *didaskalos* as practical moral reasoner will watch for the sophomoric temptation of verbal distinctions without substantial necessity, and of purely verbal solutions to substantial problems. He will scrutinize open-mindedly, but skeptically, typologies that dichotomize the complementary and formulae that reconcile the incompatible. He will denounce the diversion of attention from what must be done to debate about how to say it, except when attention to language renews and clarifies the capacity for moral discourse. Metaethical analysis will be made accountable at the bar of common commitment, not the other way around. The prototype of the *didaskalos* is the apostolic theologian Priscilla, who when the rhetorically skilled Alexandrian Apollos arrived in Ephesus "gave him further instruction about the Way."

The community will be guided by
Agents of Order and Due Process.

A cross-referencing of the varied New Testament usages would seem to indicate that three sets of nouns and verbs covered roughly the same people and gathered roughly the same set of leadership functions. The functions to "oversee" or to "supervise" and the title "bishop" brought into the church the vocabulary of Hellenistic social life. "Elder" was a term evolved from synagogue usage. To "shepherd" describes the function parabolically. For our purposes they may be spoken of as constituting a "moderating team," whose function is to assure the wholesome process of the entire group, rather than some prerogatives of their own.

These people, far from being a monarchical authority, appear in the New Testament in the plural. Their ministry is not self-contained but consists in enabling the open conversational process with which our enumeration of skills began. The moderator or facilitator as practical moral reasoner is accountable for assuring that everyone else is heard, and that the conclusions reached are genuinely consensual. The nearest modern example is the Clerk of a Friends' Meeting. The apostolic prototype is the Lord's brother James, summing up (Acts 15:13) the mutually acceptable conclusion of a meeting in which minds had been changed because people had listened to one another. The attestation, "It has been decided by the Holy Spirit and by us" (Acts 15:28), was a testimony grounded in the formal validity of the conversational process, not in the status of James' throne.

ELUCIDATION BY CONTRAST

It would be important to explain how, within the multiplicity of factors already itemized and others not yet named, the priorities for moral discourse need to be set:

1) What the centrality of Jesus means and does not mean;
2) What valid meaning the "centrality of preaching" might have;
3) How "the world" properly should "set the agenda."

It would also be important to detail:

4) In what ways communal moral discernment risks normative choices where other traditions would tend to be more inclusive and pluralistic, yet without being misled by the caricatures so easily built upon the examples of ghettos, "sectarians," and come-outers:
5) By what logic most "free churches" are also "peace churches";
6) How it happens that most "free church" traditions are affirmative and creative about the values of family, neighborhood, and farm, whereas from the perspective of Troeltschian analysis "radicals" should be as suspicious of the "natural" as of the "cultural";
7) Why it is false, systematically and historically, to say with Tolstoy and Niebuhr that the free-church community "withdraws" from social responsibility, yet correct to say that it refuses to buy into the "given structures of responsibility" as the Constantinian churches do; how then its discriminating participation is guided.

But in the present overview it will be more fruitful to proceed by way of contrast with other current debates within the ethical guild.

When identifying my communal focus, I set aside the questions that are usually considered first in discussions of making particular decisions: the nature of the good, the place of the context, the validity of rules, and so on. I had to move those themes from the center; but that did not mean brushing them from the table. I now must suggest how they can be better dealt with in the context of communal process than in the more usual individual-casuistic frameworks. Having claimed that the churchly context of decision is important, that the contribution of the teacher is to be careful about the tyranny of language, and that the cultivation of spiritual memory through Scripture is a source of "treasures new and old," etc., it is fitting that I now specify the distinctiveness of that stance by commenting on some of those familiar questions in ethical analysis which I set aside as of less than central interest.

The Existence of a People Is Not Punctual.

By "punctualism" I mean to identify the predilection within ethics to consider primarily those decisions which are made at one time and place. Others call it "decisionism." Such singular decisions serve best to illustrate the dilemmas of casuistry and the inadequacy of tired old rules. They correspond to our sense of where the hardest problems lie. They distort reality, however, by filtering out the longitudinal dimensions of preparing for a decision before the crunch and confirming it (or repenting) afterward. Of course every choice is owned at some time by someone's choosing. Of course there are times when an individual must make a decision without community process, and still more painful ones where the individual must disagree with a disobedient or misinformed community. But these are the exception. They test but do not replace the rule.

To say that essentially and ideally practical moral reasoning is communal is not to disregard the intellectual processes of deduction, projection, analogy, or inspiration, but to attend more carefully to the agencies of a shared discerning process. This process is not reducible to a political-science model projecting who promotes what interests with how much power through which procedures, since the gathered community expects Spirit-given newness to suggest answers previously not perceived. The transcendent appeal to authority is moved away from the inspiredness of holy writ and from the centralization of an episcopal magisterium, as well as from any personal, unaccountable "fanaticism" (what Luther called *Schwaermertum*). The community pulls back as well from any claim to catholic generalizability and infallibility, yet it is believingly, modestly ready to say of consensus reached today, "it seemed good to the Holy Spirit and to us," and to commend this insight by encyclical to other churches.

From this perspective one will welcome the correctives currently being brought into the discussion of ethical method in the name of "virtue" and "character"; yet while not being punctualist these terms still tend to be used primordially of individuals and often to be conceived mentalistically. One will welcome the creative imagination of structuralists who protect narration from reduction to "truths" and "concepts"; yet an equal vigilance is needed to defend the particularity of Abraham and Samuel, Jeremiah and Jesus from reduction to mere specimens of a new kind of universals, namely narrative forms, lying deeper than the ordinary events and sufficient to explain them. In the order of being it is true enough that the crucified Lord is no stranger.[11] The way of discipleship is the way for which we are made; there is no other "nature" to which grace is a *superadditum*. Yet in the order of narration that account appears foolish to those who recognize wisdom and weak to those on the lookout for signs. Only from within the community of resurrection confession is the cruciformity of the cosmos a key rather than a scandal. Therefore the particular narrative is prior to the general idea of narrativeness.

Thus the hermeneutic community will share in the corrective concerns of each of these themes currently exercizing the ethicists' guild, yet in each case the corrective would be more naturally congenial and less faddish if rooted in the rest of the life of a body of people sharing the same moral commitment, rather than claiming validity "as such" or "for all."

Principle or Prudence?

One of the standard lessons any beginning student of religious or philosophical ethics learns is to tell the difference between an argument from duty and an argument from utility. While recognizing the difficulty of constructing a pure type of deontological or utilitarian reasoning, the academic ethicist still sees it as his contribution to call for relative purity of type in order to bring the debates more under control. In a more communal and less monolingual context of discernment, the task of the teacher will rather be the opposite: to contribute to the community's awareness that every decision includes elements of principle, elements of character and of due process, and elements of utility.

Without being able here to carry out the demonstration, I should expect that this same suspicion of methodological dichotomies will well be applied in many of the other cases where the analysts of logic have discerned structural differences: the debates over Scripture or tradition, Jesus as teacher or model or high priest, law versus gospel, nature versus grace. Each of these distinctions, important in the history of argumentative theology, contributes to ethical analysis by refining our awareness of certain pitfalls and potential lacunae in discernment. Yet any one of them raises the threat of an improper subservience to the helm or the bit or the incendiary torch of "words" if the dichotomy is allowed to become dominant in dictating how the church *must* think. It belongs to the "scribe" and the "teacher" (and in some degree to the scribelike dimension of every believer's mental maturity) to take note respectfully of those guides, and to genuflect to none of them. It belongs to the elder/moderator/bishop/shepherd to ask whether and how each proposed polarity or complementarity will "edify" (i.e., construct a place to be at home together).

When I suggest this kind of pluralism, with regard both to types of opposed ethical logics and to different formal principles and nodal points in theological debates, it may seem that I am delivering the discerning community into a markerless morass of inconclusive inclusiveness. By no means need that follow. For the radical Protestant there will always be a canon within the canon: namely, that recorded experience of practical moral reasoning in genuine human form that bears the name of Jesus. Far from being a fundamentalist view, this approach, which reads all the documents as ordinary human documents having come into being through ordinary human processes of remembering and retelling, reaching back to a real human career and the experiences of ordinary people with that extraordinary man, affirms the conviction that it is on the one hand more able than are the classical ethical traditions to be open with Scripture. On the other hand, persons holding this view are convinced that it makes them more able than some others to live with the recognition that to acknowledge that man Jesus as one's Lord, to confess him as risen and his Spirit as present, is an act of faith in which we follow the early biblical writers, for which there need not be claimed the coercion of evidence irrefutable by the historian's canons of uniformity or the scientist's axioms of repeatability. The insistence of the literary analysts that the Gospel accounts are biased in favor of faith is for this view no stumbling block.

I have been arguing against accepting traditional dichotomies. That concern led away from the specific dichotomy with which we began, namely utility versus duty. If Jesus Christ is Lord, obedience to his rule cannot be dysfunctional. Principled or virtuous behavior cannot be imprudent generally, though it may well appear so punctually. Torah is grace, not a burden. The covenant is liberation, not servitude.

Fiat justitia, ruat coelum is then a wrong way to make a valid short-range moral point. The heavens will not fall. If they were falling, my doing injustice would not hold them up. When it *seems* to me that my unjust deed is indispensable to prevent some much greater evil being done by another, I have narrowed my scope of time, or of space, or of global variety, or of history. I have ruled some people out of my Golden Rule, or have skewed the coefficients in my utility calculus.

Is "Intellectualism" the Error Needing Correction?

Daniel Maguire has argued that the enemy of practical moral reason is "the intellectual fallacy."[12] My perspective calls me to agree with his answer while doubting his question. Maguire presupposes at the outset, as if it needed no justification, that if we are to locate the root of moral obligation, both the knowledge of its material demands and its bindingness, we must do this for an ideal individual moral subject. When the issue is so put, then certainly the answer must include awe, emotivity, and affectivity as being deeper than "reason." But need Maguire have agreed to put the issue that way? Would Thomas have thus met post-Cartesian individualism halfway? Moral obligation is learned, after all, by growing up in historic communities. Our "knowing" it is prior, in the orders of both knowing and being, to the "reason" with which we question and clarify it, as well as to the awe and affectivity with which it grasps us.

The validity of Maguire's preference for the category of affectivity is not that it is a wider or softer way to describe *individual* moral experience, but that it better holds the door open for the more-than-individual or preindividual dimensions of how moral personality is formed.

Especially in an age of existentialistic intuitionism, the expectation of newness and bindingness needs to be disciplined; nonetheless it must be maintained in the face of every effort to reduce moral reasoning to any less local, less trusting, or more deductive model. Without any disrespect for the solidity of written and oral traditions, communal moral reasoning in the Holy Spirit will not be satisfied with logical conventions which proceed as if all that we were doing were the unfolding of what is already there.

When I accent the oneness of the hermeneutic community in process, being led to new light through new reformations, there is an obvious element of caricature in the juxtaposition with other tradi-

tions. Rabbinic moral counsel never really believed that the total tradition was solid and unchanging. It only spoke *as if* that were being
assumed. The rabbis were quite aware that the tradition was evolving
under their hands: only it was important not to *say* that. Similarly,
Roman Catholic confessional casuistry did not really believe that the
essence of morality was bearing its fruit in the confessional when a
man (who had to be ordained) listened to the recital of a person's im-
perfections, through the grid of a manual classifying offenses, with
both the manual and the status of the confessor being independent
of the sinner in their moral authority. But it seemed important to
think that that was the case. In actual lived experience, I suspect that
both ordinary Catholic believers and ordinary Jewish believers have
actually gone about living a life of shared practical moral reasoning
in a way not profoundly different from what I am talking about.

The debate about locating moral insights in the intellect or in the
will or the affections is not a debate that needs an either/or resolution.
I doubt that Thomas intended that either. His concern, in the passage with which Maguire began, was to explain how the contingency
of particular moral choices made utterly generalizable imperatives unattainable: property given one in trust is not *always* to be returned,
promises need not *always* be kept, life is not *always* sacred. Yet the
Maguire study concentrates on the *general* question of whether values
may be *known* in some nonintellectualistic way. Maguire does not
return to give us fresh guidance about how contingent decisions are
to come about, especially if (and this was Thomas's interest) they must
constitute exceptions to important obligations. When Maguire in his
own book *Moral Choice* deals with matters of this kind, the rootage
of such resources for decision to be found in community identity and
community process is not emphasized. Nor does he argue that affec-
tive or reverent knowledge is any more help in reaching contingent
concrete resolutions than a more intellectualist casuistry would be.
He has thus used Thomas's concern about *ratio practica* as a point
of departure rather than as a theme in its own right.

The reproach which Maguire addresses to what he calls "intellectualism" seems thus to me rather to belong somewhere else. It is an
offense committed as well by other kinds of people than intellectuals
and for other kinds of reasons than intellectualism. The punctualist
assumptions that moral decision is made by one person at a time,
and that the value of a given decision can adequately be interpreted
by abstracting out that person's community relationships, is one of

the reasons the intellectualistic reduction was possible. To say that intellectual knowledge must be rooted in religiously perceived values, as Maguire argues, is a necessary but not a sufficient correction for that abstraction.

PARTICULARITY: SCANDAL OR GOSPEL?

Is Our Ethics for Everyone?

Another classical checkpoint in academic ethics is the discussion of the public accountability of moral reasoning. Within one set of language conventions, we are told we should qualify as "ethical" only that level of discourse which we can claim applies to everyone, admitting that others of our commitments, because not widely applicable or generally verifiable, are only "private" or "particular" or "religious." Another set of conventions puts the divide at another place, considering ethics to be unverifiable because it makes "ought" judgments. Some would argue that one reason for a high view of natural law is a concern to sustain the possibility of moral discourse, if not verifiability criteria, which can be shared with the rest of mankind.

Some would argue that Protestantism, which proclaims a message which people who have not heard cannot yet know, and which even those who hear it are not coerced to believe, would care less than Catholicism about making sense to everyone.

The view I am seeking to interpret does not discount public comprehensibility nor the appeal to outside audiences. Yet it is suspicious of "natural" or "public" truth claims when it is proposed that they can stand alone, or come first.

The reason I do not trust claims to "natural insight" is that the dominant moral views of any *known* world are oppressive, provincial, or (to say it theologically) "fallen." This is true even if the terrain of the provincialism is large or if the majority holding those views is great. There is no "public" that is not just another particular province. We need a communal instrument of moral reasoning in the light of faith precisely to defend the decision-maker against the stream of conformity to his own world's self-evidence. Practical moral reasoning, if Christian, must always be expected to be at some point subversive. Any approach which trusts the common wisdom enough to make specifically subversive decisions unthinkable has thereby forfeited its claim to be adequate. (This is of course not a peculiarly Christian view. Socrates and Esther were subversive too.)

It is only from the point of view of established religion that the triune correlation seems logical between finding a vocabulary for public discourse, affirming the reliability of nonparticular sources of moral insight, and knowing that "reason" and "nature" or "creation" are the names for the same. It is not the case in logic or history that a thoroughly Protestant critique denies human wisdom, limits God's work to the confines of the Bible and the church, and rejects concern for civil righteousness or common discourse. It does doubt that the concepts and values accessible in the wider arenas are more clear or true for being less avowedly confessional. It doubts that it helps to call them "natural" or "created" or that one should assume that they should tend to coincide with custom. To say that *all* communities of moral insight are provincial, that there exists no nonprovincial general community with clear language, and that therefore we must converse at every border, is in actuality a more optimistic and more fruitful affirmation of the marketplace of ideas than to project a hypothetically general insight which we feel reassured to resort to, when our own particularity embarrasses us, but which is not substantial after all when we seek to define it. Certainly the current American debates about specifics like the governmental funding of abortions, or about limits on armament, or about transnational corporations are hardly helped by the fact that most parties in these debates claim to be using justice language that is naturally accessible to their adversaries as well.

Moreover, the discussion of how to speak of "values" of a public nature usually takes place in the post-Christian West. The examples of not specifically churchly moral insight represent post-Christian Enlightenment values. These values are, though, largely derived from the Hebraic and Christian world vision. They do not, therefore, constitute tests of the possibility of accepting, as complementary or compatible with distinctively Christian views, insights with a complete different rootage. It would be more fitting, if the point to be proven is that there are "values out there" which we need to affirm, that utterly non-Western samples be adduced, and that it be explained on what grounds Christians can affirm them. I am sure that this can sometimes be done, but not that the concept of a nonparticular "nature" or a nonfallen moral consensus will be of any help in that adjudication, nor that the concrete product of such encounter will bear much resemblance to the "natural" generalizations which Christians from within their embarrassed particularity *think* everyone else *ought* to understand.

The real test of the accessibility of a common moral language "out there," more general than confessional language, must then not be the times we find ourselves agreeing with "men of good will" (especially not if they be Western humanists); it must be the capacity of this line of argument to illuminate meaningful conversations with Idi Amin or Khomeini or Chairman Mao.

The preoccupation of some contemporary thinkers with what they think must be the difficulty of finding public moral language when beginning within a particular identity cannot be explained by any recorded experience of having succeeded in that search by means of appeals to "nature." Such appeals are as provincial in substance, as they work out concretely, as are appeals to revelation. The search for a public moral language is motivated rather by embarrassment about particularity, which is not willing to break through the embarrassment to confession by taking the risk of specific encounter, preferring to posit something argued to be more solid and less threatening than an open market place, even if that "something" be nonexistent or vacuous.

The function of the notion of "nature" in medieval Catholic thought was *not* the modern one of knowing how to talk with outsiders. The medieval concept of natural law was developed in a world where there were no non-Christians present in the neighborhood, and no non-theists in the known world needing to be convinced. If we were to look more pointedly at just that section of Thomas utilized by Maguire it would in fact seem that the purpose was the reverse of what he argues: it was to distinguish the things that everyone (including Christians) need to obey from those elements of divine moral guidance from Scripture which can be left to the Hebrews.[13] The appeal to "nature" was an instrument of *less* rather than *more* commonality with non-Christians. It was a way to protect Christians from the embarrassment of affirming scriptural authority and yet not holding to all of the Mosaic legislation. The concern with "nature" then bespoke not a growing readiness to converse with others in non-Christian language, but rather a growing conviction that the way Christians see reality is the way it really is. But the way to affirm our respect for others is to respect their particularity and learn their languages, not to project in their absence a claim that we see the truth of things with an authority unvitiated by our particularity. Our concern should then be not to limit truth to the sectarian but to suspect the common-sense epistemology which underlies at least some "natural revelation" claims.

It would also be wrong to claim, with a certain high Protestantism, that depravity is the most fundamental truth about human nature and moral insight; yet to put our trust in the generally accessible know-ability of the moral on the part of our secular humanist culture is certainly even farther from the truth. If moral discernment is not culture-critical, it has lost its connection with the gospel of grace and has fallen into the ratification of things as they are and choices as I want them.

The Unity of Worship and Morality

I referred briefly above to the "unity of worship and morality." It is at the point of the culture-critical or subversive dimension of the faith that we can see best why it was most fitting to affirm this. It appears at least to me as an observer-novice in liturgics, to be some-what of an innovation, or renovation, to pull up for analysis the kind of political commitment a particular cult form implies. Worship is the communal cultivation of an alternative construction of society and of history. That alternative construction of history is celebrated by telling the stories of Abraham (and Sarah and Isaac and Ishmael), of Mary and Joseph and Jesus and Mary, of Cross and Resurrection and Peter and Paul, of Peter of Cheltchitz and his Brothers, of George Fox and his Friends. How pointedly, and at what points, this cele-brated construction will set us at odds with our neighbors, will of course depend on the neighbors.

We need to doubt the focus upon the generalizability of ethical demands at the price of particular specifications, not only because all natural insight is fallen but because (to say it again in Christian terms) we confess as Lord and Christ the man Jesus. Then the par-ticular and the general cannot be alternatives. The general cannot be arrived at by subtracting the particular. Any embarrassment with par-ticularity which seeks to get at the general that way is a denial of faith.

Now, there is nothing wrong with denying the faith if that is what you want to do. Nobody *has* to believe. Nobody who claims to "be-lieve" has to believe that Jesus Christ is Lord. One of the reasons people deny the faith is, in fact (I suspect) that they think that every-one ought to have to believe; therefore they think that the meaning of belief must be adjusted so that it is acceptable or even irresistible to everyone. That is why the sharp edges of particularity must be honed off. One's own identity must be apologized for as the product of an irreducible, not culpable but not interesting, narrowness, so that what one commends to others is credible generally, untainted by the provincial. Now, I am embarrassed as anyone about the limits of my particularity. I too had a post-Enlightenment education. I can confess my culpability, personal and collective as male, as American, as Mennonite, as university employee, as property owner, as local church member, etc. Yet none of this embarrassment can be covered for by imagining a less particular Jesus than the one in the story, or a less particular path today than to be one specific community rather than another.

When I deny that the traditional appeals to "the nature of things" can serve to provide us an "unfallen" common language for public accountability, this does not indicate any disrespect for that need, but only realism about the impossibility of meeting the need that way.

A Missionary Ethic of Incarnation

If we cannot transcend the vulnerability of belief by positing as accessible a nonparticular "natural," might we then celebrate confessionally that light and truth have taken on the vulnerability of the particular? That would then call for and empower a *missionary ethic of incarnation.*

The challenge will still remain to find ways to translate and to work at a reciprocal adjudication of the varieties both of perception and of evaluation, where one provincial vision clashes and overlaps with another. But the way to do that is not to imagine or proclaim or seek or discover some "neutral" or "common" or "higher" ground, but rather to work realistically at every concrete experience of overlap and conflict. By "overlap" I mean that two provincial visions are dealing with the same subject matter of bringing people into common enterprises. By "conflict" I mean simply that people may have different commitments behind these common enterprises, and thus they need to wrestle with those differences in terms that take account of each other's distinct identity. Christians will never meet this challenge better by seeking to be less specifically Christian. They will meet it better if they take it on faith that Christ is Lord over the powers, that Creation is not independent of Redemption.

WE END WHERE WE NEED TO BEGIN

> It is to your advantage that I go away. . . . When the Spirit of
> Truth comes, he will guide you into all the truth. . . . He will
> take what is mine and declare it to you. . . . (John 16:7, 13–15)

This exposition necessarily has proceeded by negation and differentiation. That path intends to reopen the space for a style of practical moral reasoning genuinely free for this confessional, messianic, pneumatic empowerment.

A host of second-level questions remain unanswered, some even unasked. Can an isolated individual internalize something of this multiple-role conversational process when no such church is available? What differences will/would this approach make in specific social policy conclusions? Would that matter? The questions are proper; my inability to resolve them a priori is proper as well.

The stories can be told of how they have been answered before. The trust is not unreasonable that they can be answered again; yet this is not true a priori. It is true only in the actual encounter between a believing community and the next challenge. The only way to see how this will work will be to see how it will work.

2. "But We Do See Jesus":
The Particularity of Incarnation and the Universality of Truth

Let me begin with a landmark cliché, the words of Gotthold Ephraim Lessing which are so often taken as symbols of the threshold of modernity:

> Accidental truths of history can never become the proof of necessary truths of reason. . . . That . . . is the ugly, broad ditch which I cannot get across, however often and however earnestly I have tried to make the leap. If anyone can help me over it, let him do it, I beg him.[1]

It may be true for individuals that everything seems, only recently, to have come loose; but it is not true of the history of Christian thought. The new challenges which some take so seriously are not that new, except to them. It would be wrong to think that the issue of the credibility of particular claims is best represented only by some quite recent reformulation of historical skepticism, or religious pluralism, or the death-of-God language, or by the gap between contingent facts of history and the necessary truths of reason posited by Lessing, the dean of modern ditchdiggers. Each of those formulations is important. Yet none of them is at the bottom of our problem. None of them can find *beyond the ditch* a place to stand which would be less particular, more credible, less the product of one's own social location.

My task in this synthetic effort is not to respond to any one of those culture shifts alone in an adequate way, but rather to respond to the way in which they all address analogous challenges to a specifically Christian witness. Thereby several logically distinguishable critiques of particularity are telescoped. I shall not try to disentangle them:

1. There is the denunciation of the logical circularity of all claims to revelation.

46

2. There is the logical challenge of Lessing's dissatisfaction with particular proofs as not proving general truths.

3. There is the need for making sense to people of other backgrounds, who know ahead of time that our reasons are provincial.

4. Among the other backgrounds there is the special case of other faiths. Global cultural change no longer lets Christians assume the superiority of their belief system.

5. There is the need in public life (not only in politics) for a common denominator language in order to collaborate with relative strangers in running the world despite our abiding differences.

6. There is the need, in the interface of clashing or unrelated idea systems, for metalanguages to interpret why we misunderstand one another.

7. There is embarrassment about the provincialism of our predecessors, especially if they linked it with oppressive political and economic power.

8. There is doubt about the adequacy of an analysis using the dichotomies between grace and nature, the ideal and the real, the natural and the supernatural, with which we have tried to classify our problems, and by means of which the more private traditions had been defending themselves.

9. There is the fear that what we used to believe can all be explained reductionistically by some causation language (Freudian, Marxian, Skinnerian) which the wider culture knows.

For present purposes I propose an obvious simplification, lumping these variations under the code label pluralism/relativism, without claiming to define rigorously even those terms.[2] What is pertinent for our purposes is the point at which this stance is forearmed to box in the claims of Christian witness in the ready-made pigeonhole of the old absolute which it had destroyed.

For many, the great variety of convictions held in different cultural settings makes any absolute position unsustainable. The self-evidence of this claim is most convincing if it is not examined too closely, and it is in that form that I shall treat it.

This excludes my being fully fair to any *one* explanation for the skepticism which any breakthrough to a wider culture teaches anyone to direct toward the belief system he or she came from. Any living community is always moving from smaller worlds into wider ones, always challenged by the psychic dominance of each next wider world. Let the phrase "wider world" substitute for "universality" in my title, and let "pluralism/relativism" stand in for the varied ways in which truth claims from the smaller world find their credibility challenged.

SIX ADAPTIVE STRATEGIES

In the face of this challenge how many possible responses do we have among which to choose? Subject to the obvious limits of all reasoning with types, I suggest that there are at least six.

A first and obvious response is to stay by one's prior particular truth. But in the new context this fidelity will have a new meaning. What was before taken for granted as the way things are, simply "because my mother told me so," a natural identity, is now transformed by the threat into self-conscious narrow carefulness. Thereby the wider world has already exacted its tribute. Instead of being organic and natural as it had been "at home," the particularity will need to be defended against the wider spectrum of other particularities.

A second logical option is conversion. One grants that the wider world is not only larger and stronger but truer. Perhaps it is even thought to be truer just because it is larger and stronger.[3]

A third way will be that of the enlightened pedagogue. Since I was led—the convert says—from the smaller world to the larger one by an experience of rational growth and not by a simple irrational leap from one system to another, so I can with proper patience and intelligence lead along with me those who were born where I was and who should no less than I be helped by finding their way from there to here.

A fourth, more complex pattern is the apology. The *apologia* is a self-commendation or self-defense before a tribunal whose authority to judge one accepts. Yet instead of renouncing one's smaller identity, saying it had been wrong (the colloquial American meaning of "apology"), the apologete finds ways to commend his or her particular past by rephrasing it as another form of the mainstream value system, just as good as the other subforms.[4]

A fifth way, instead of looking for a common nature which is already there, would be to construct a new neutral metalanguage, an artificial instrument to talk about talking, to construct by conscious artifice a pedestal beyond all parties to the past conversations, thus being ourselves creators of the still wider world.

A sixth standard type of response is to retain one's stated loyalty to one's particular identity, but to accentuate the humility with which one recognizes the wider context. One does not, like the apologete, try to prove the smaller system right by appealing to the criteria of meaningfulness which rule the larger, nor to prove the larger right by explaining it in terms that make sense in the smaller world. One simply stands them side-by-side and talks about the interface in terms that accept particular identity for oneself and yet relativize the notion of truth.

What these six patterns have in common, behind a host of variations in secondary characteristics, is the acceptance of one way of putting the problem in the first place: namely, the priority in truth and value of the meaning system of the world claiming to be wider. That priority is not the product of a careful, debatable demonstration. Its own definition of what constitutes a wider or more public proof is precisely what we should be interested in debating. But that wider world, in any one person's experience of pilgrimage or in any interface between two groups, is still a small place. It still speaks only one language at a time, and that is still insider language. One adolescent's breath of fresh air is another's ghetto. Any given wider world is still just one more place, even if what its slightly wider or slightly more prestigious circle of interpreters talk about is a better access to "universality." Thus the first mistake which tends to be made by the apologetic person emerging from the smaller world is thinking that that wider society is itself the universe, or that its ways of testing validity beyond the provincial have succeeded, by dint of a harder and more thorough hauling away at one's own definitional bootstraps, in transcending particularity. How can particular truths be proclaimed publicly?

I shall draw a pattern inductively from a series of testimonies of cultural transition found in the literature of the early Christian missionary culture.

AN ANCIENT PARADIGM

In a very coarse-grained way we can say that the New Testament is the document of a transition made by a message-bearing community from one world to another. Born in Aramaic-speaking Palestinian Jewry, praying and socializing and theologizing only in that small society and its tongue, with its Scriptures, the messianic movement in two generations had reached the capital of the world and had produced a core body of literature in the trade-and-culture language of the Gentile world. Admittedly, the Hellenistic world was not one culture but a cosmopolitan melee; Jewry was already largely hellenized; and even Palestine had been infiltrated by Hellenistic cities and Hellenistic culture. Nonetheless, Jesus-believers with a relatively smaller, more homogeneous, poorer, less speculatively pretentious world view moved with their homegrown forms of faith into the encounter with peoples and meaning systems which have no place for their confident call to decision. The Jesus movement was utterly particular. The Hellenistic Roman world was classically pluralistic.

I propose to look schematically at five New Testament texts, chosen not arbitrarily but because of parallelisms within their differences. In very different language forms, they have in common the evident fact that in the process of organic expansion into the Hellenistic world, the particularity of the Jesus story, previously borne by predominantly Jewish communities into whose own world that story had first irrupted, must encounter the call of believers (and perhaps also of doubters) for a higher level of generality. In what sense can the Jesus story be reported as true for non-Palestinians? For non-Jews? As answering questions never put to Jesus?

We can readily project that the six prototypical strategies of submission to the wider world just described could be spelled out in as many ways to link Jewishness and Gentileness. They are analogous to the choices faced by any young person who discovers the jargon world of the peers on the street or the intellectual world of the teacher at school to be wider than the world one's parents had led one into at home; or to the choices faced by any immigrant, or any minority youth going to university.

Which of these choices does the New Testament support? Conversion to Gentile pluralism? Apology? Or is there another? Having sharpened the question, I turn to the texts. In what sense do New Testament writers already speak to this question?

The Prologue to John (John 1:1–14) seems to be addressed to people holding to a proto-Gnostic cosmology, in which a long ladder of mediating entities stretches from God to earth. The ladder's function is as much to hold its ends apart as to connect them, and it symbolizes the pluralism of Mediterranean culture. The pure ineffable Divinity at the top wards off particularity and contingency, so to speak, by interposing the Logos, a kind of cosmic provost, as the principle of order and rationality. Such a cosmology would have a natural, honorable place for Jesus and thereby for Christian proclamation. The cosmology, however, was bigger than and prior to Jesus, as Greco-Roman culture was prior to the church.

But the seer of the Prologue won't let them put Jesus in that slot. Encouraged by the analogy of Proverbs 8, where Wisdom seems to be a facet of deity, he does not hesitate to accept the language which this cosmology offers. He affirms the Logos as light enlightening every person, and before that as creator of the visible world. Yet instead of tailoring Jesus to fit the slots prepared for him, John breaks the cosmology's rules. At the bottom of the ladder, the Logos is said to have become flesh, to have lived among us as in a tent, symbol of mortality, and to have suffered rejection by us creatures. At the top of the ladder, the Logos is claimed to be coeval with God, not merely the first of many emanations. But then there is no more ladder: the cosmology has been smashed, or melted down for recasting. Its language has been seized and used for a different message. No longer does the concept of Logos solve a problem of religion, reconciling the eternal with the temporal; it carries a proclamation of identification, incarnation, drawing all who believe into the power of becoming God's children.

The addressees of the Epistle to the Hebrews also had a settled cosmology. Angels at the top have access to the divine presence from which they bear the word of the divine will to earth. Priests at the bottom are raised from among their fellows to mediate by bringing to the altar, on their own behalf and for all, the gifts and sacrifices which can cover sin.

Instead of claiming for the Son of Adam his place just *beneath* the angels, however, Messiah is declared to be *above* them at the Lord's right hand, appointed Son, reflecting the stamp of the divine nature, upholding the universe. Yet this cosmic honor was no exemption from human limits. His perfection is not a timeless divine status but was *attained* through weakness with prayers and supplications, loud cries and tears. Fully assuming the priestly system, as both priest and victim, once for all he ends the claim of the sacrificial system to order the community of faith, putting in its place a new covenant, a new universalized priestly order, an unshakable kingdom.

Yet this cosmic sovereignty is not a simple possession. Our contribution to proving or bringing about this sovereignty is our faithfulness to Jesus.

As it is, we do not yet *see* everything in subjection to him. *But we do see Jesus,* who for a little while was made lower than the angels, [now] crowned with glory and honor because of the suffering of death. (Heb. 2:8–9)

The Christians at Colossae also had their cosmology ready, with a modest slot for the Jewish Jesus. The world is held together by a network of principalities and powers, visible and invisible. Religious behavior (fasting, festivals) helps one to find one's way through the tangle. Visions and angelolatry help to manipulate the powers.

Once again Jesus is proclaimed, by the Paul of Colossians, not as part of the cosmos but as its Lord. The powers are not illuminated, appeased, manipulated by him, but subdued and broken. The believer risen with Christ has died to them and is no longer in their hold. That can be the case because the Son is the image of the invisible creator, holding all things together, reconciling all things, head of the body.

The first vision of the Apocalypse (Rev. 4:1–5:4) presents in classic visionary language the puzzle of history. No one is in sight able to break the seals on the scroll containing the meaning of it all. John weeps. There is no one worthy among the elders, the angels, or the seraphim. But then the Lamb appears, next to the throne, perfect in the sevenfoldness of his horns and eyes, able because he was slain to take history in his hands, unstick the seals, and unroll the world's judgment and salvation.

The fifth analogous text is one which we cannot locate in an initial communication context. It must have been in use in some churches as a hymn before Paul wove part of it into the letter to the Philippians (chapter 2). The imagery behind the hymn would seem to be that of a Prometheus/Adam/primeval king, who as representative of the human race grasped at equality with God, thereby representing the picture the poet projected of the human predicament. The contrast with that is not a more successful Prometheus or an unfallen Adam, but the willing self-emptying of the one who really had divine sonship in his grasp, to identify himself with humanity and in fact to die the death of a criminal. "Wherefore," the hymn goes on in a dramatic reversal of the *kenosis,* "he has been divinely exalted and given the name of Lord" (Phil. 2:9), which fact all of the cosmos shall one day acknowledge. The ground for this exaltation is the free willingness of his humiliation. The low point of the humiliation is not entering humanity but dying on the cross.

Five times, in utterly independent ways, an apostolic writer has responded to the challenge of a previously formed cosmic vision. Each time, in completely different vocabulary, and with no commonality of structure to indicate that one might have learned from one of the others, the writer makes the same moves. We could call it a syndrome or a deep structure. What are those moves? We have seen, each time:

1. That the writer becomes quite at home in the new linguistic world, using its language and facing its questions;
2. That instead of fitting the Jesus message into the slots the cosmic vision has ready for it, the writer places Jesus above the cosmos, in charge of it;
3. That there is in each case a powerful concentration upon being rejected and suffering in human form, beneath the cosmic hierarchy, as that which accredits Christ for this lordship;
4. That instead of salvation constituting our integration into a salvation system which the cosmos holds ready for us to enter into through ritual or initiation, what we are called to enter into is the self-emptying and the death – and only by that path, and by grace, the resurrection – of the Son;
5. That behind the cosmic victory, enabling it, there is affirmed (without parallel in the synoptic Gospels) what later confession called preexistence, co-essentiality with the Father, possession of the image of God, and the participation of the Son in creation and providence;
6. That the writer and the readers of these messages share by faith in all that that victory means.

> Brother and sister saints, who share in the heavenly call, contemplate Jesus, Apostle and High Priest of our confession. He was faithful in God's house. . . . Now Moses was faithful in all God's house as a servant, to testify to the things that were to be spoken later, but Christ was faithful over God's house as a Son. *We are his household,* as we hold fast our confidence and pride in our hope. (Heb. 3:1–2, 5–6)

To be fair to this event in the first century we must protect it against anachronistic tendencies which our twentieth-century agenda would impose upon it. One thing we cannot say about the impact of these texts upon their readers, or upon their readers' unbelieving neighbors, was that it was alien or meaningless. They addressed a profound challenge to the contemporary pagan mind, and they did it in terms familiar to that mind, from within its linguistic community.

The other thing we cannot say about this new communication move is that it leaves Judaism behind. That would be anachronism again; the writers of these texts and the singers of the hymn in Philippians were all Jews. They were proclaiming the pertinence and the priority of the meaning-frame of messianic Judaism, with all its concentration upon empirical community, particular history, synagogue worship, and particular lifestyle, over against the speculative and skeptical defenses of its cultured despisers. Instead of requesting free speech and room for one more stand in the Athenian marketplace of ideas for a new variant of already widely respected diaspora Judaism, their claim was that now the Hebrew story had widened out to include everyone; that, with the inbreaking of the messianic era, the Jewish hope in process of fulfillment was wide enough to receive all the nations and their riches.

So we must step back a moment from our own concern with the usability of ancient language in our time if we would follow how it was usable then. A handful of messianic Jews, moving beyond the defenses of their somewhat separate society to attack the intellectual bastions of majority culture, refused to contextualize their message by clothing it in the categories the world held ready. Instead, they seized the categories, hammered them into other shapes, and turned the cosmology on its head, with Jesus both at the bottom, crucified as a common criminal, and at the top, preexistent Son and creator, and the church his instrument in today's battle.

It is not the world, culture, civilization, which is the definitional category, which the church comes along to join up with, approve, and embellish with some correctives and complements. The Rule of God is the basic category. The rebellious but already (in principle) defeated cosmos is being brought to its knees by the Lamb. The development of a high Christology is the natural cultural ricochet of a missionary ecclesiology when it collides as it must with whatever cosmology explains and governs the world it invades.

PARTICULARITY AS GOOD AND AS NEWS

As I try to identify how the apostolic sample differs from the other ways of relating the wider and the smaller worlds with which I began, the best adjective I can find is "evangelical."

I take the term in its root meaning. One is functionally evangelical if one confesses oneself to have been commissioned by the grace of God with a message which others who have not heard it should hear. It is *angellion* ("news") because they will not know it unless they are told it by a message-bearer. It is *good* news because hearing it will be for them not alienation or compulsion, oppression or brainwashing, but liberation. Because this news is only such when *received* as good, it can never be communicated coercively; nor can the message-bearer ever positively be assured that it will be received.

What distinguishes this view from the apologete and from the convert is the challenge it addresses to the truth claims or salvation claims of the wider world. This challenge does not prove that people at home in that other wider world view are bad. It simply brings them news.

Its reason for not remaining in the ghetto is not merely some kind of psychic drive, nor a sense of deprivation, nor a lack of esteem projected upon ghetto dwellers by outsiders. The message cannot remain in the ghetto because the good news by its very nature is for and about the world. The good news is not information which will remain true even if people in a ghetto celebrate it only for themselves; it is about a community-building story for which the world beyond the ghetto is half of the reconciling event. It moves on from the verifiable fact that the world of the God of Abraham is higher and wider than the world of the mystery religions or the Athenian Sophists. This is simply true of the story of the Abrahamic people, which has already run through its contacts with Babylonia, with Egypt, with Persia, as well as it is true of the Hebrew cosmology, which makes sense of the world as the meaningful product of the purposive activity of a single, coherent, invisible creator. Abrahamic particularity is not bad but good news, not embarrassing but worth sharing, not arcane but illuminating.

That the world of Abraham and Moses and Jeremiah was (and still is) larger than the world of the Sophists and the Gnostics is not an apologetic argument needing to be waged in the midst of ambivalent claims and counterclaims about what constitutes an argument for wider validity; it is a simple cultural experience. While messianic Jews in the first century are a sliver of a minority population, the story they tell has been around farther and longer than the Athenian story. That does not make it true. Age, like size, is not in itself verification. But the memory of centuries does support its credibility, and perhaps it explains why for those Jewish witnesses their particularity was less embarrassing than ours sometimes is for us.

How Not to Say It

It would have been the wrong question had the early Christians asked, "Shall messianic Jews enter the Hellenistic world and adjust to its concepts?" Should Paul use Greek? The question was not whether to enter but how to *be* there: how in the transition to render anew the genuine pertinence of the proclamation of Christ's Lordship, even in a context (*particularly* in a context) where even the notion of such sovereignty is questionable.

Then must we not say the same for other times and places, for here and now? Pluralism/relativism as a pervasive meaning system is not, like Kantianism or Thomism, a total seamless unity; it is more, like Greek or Fortran, a language. We are now called to renew in the language world of pluralism/relativism an analogue to what those first transcultural reconceptualizers did; not to translate their results but to emulate their exercise.

The last thing we should ask, then, would be whether we can translate into our time from theirs the notion of preexistence or of the participation of the Son in creation. That would be to contrast the rules of two language worlds instead of finding a message to express within both. That would be like asking whether with the bases loaded you should try for a field goal or use a number three iron. What we need to find is the interworld transformational grammar to help us to discern what will need to happen if the collision of the message of Jesus with our pluralist/relativist world is to lead to a reconception of the shape of the world, instead of to rendering Jesus optional or innocuous. To ask, "Shall we talk in pluralist/relativist terms?" would be as silly as to ask in Greece, "Shall we talk Greek?" The question is what we shall say. We shall say, "Jesus is Messiah and Lord"; but how do you say that in pluralist/relativist language? If that language forbids us to say that, do we respect the prohibition? Or do we find a way to say it anyway?

We won't play with the utopia of getting out of our own pluralist/relativist skins by going either backward or forward. It is within these skins that we need to restate whatever our claims are. Since for some even the phrase "truth claim" evokes echoes of theocratic compulsion or of pretensions to infallibility, let us use the more biblical phrases "witness" and "proclamation" as naming forms of communication which do not coerce the hearer.

We shall not ask whether Christianity, or Jesus, or anything, is absolute or unique or universal in some way that could be supported, kept dry above the waves of relativity. A claim to absoluteness can be adjudicated meaningfully only in the frame in which it is pronounced, and then only if the way that that frame is self-understood provides some kind of fulcrum and a place to stand to make such a judgment.

What we need to try to do now may be further clarified by contrast with the six strategies of adaptation with which we began. Those strategies granted in different ways the priority, in the orders of both knowing and being, of the wider world. They then defended or diluted or translated the particular identity in subordination thereto. Now we are asking, in the same kind of intersystem encounter, what would be the shape of an evangelical alternative—one which would agree with the above strategies in the practical affirmation that the present world, the wider and the widest worlds of our day, is the arena within which it speaks; but one which would claim to have something more to say than to concede the sovereignty or the adequacy of the ideas currently dominating that wider arena.

What then can we do to transpose faithfully into a self-contained immanent frame the equivalence of the "Christ is Lord" claim, in some continuity with what it meant in the first-century context, where all parties to the conversation lived in cosmologies with the top open for transcendent validation?

There is no need to assume that that question can have only one answer. Maybe it has to have several, each fragmentary, but which might severally add up asymptotically to a functional equivalent of a proclamation of lordship. One partial answer might be that in an encounter between two different—not fully compatible but not fully alien—meaning frames, reference to Jesus might make it easier to converse about things which in both frames are important. Modern meaning systems being independent, might they still overlap? Might Jesus be located on common turf?

Jesus participates in localizable, datable history, as many religious hero figures do not. Jesus intervenes in the liberation from violence and he identifies with the poor as many savior figures do not. He contributes to the nuts-and-bolts reconstruction of forgiving community, as many people planning to change the world do not. His memories have created, despite much betrayal by his disciples, a nearly worldwide communion, as some of the great culture religions have not yet done. His message interpenetrates with the realms of politics and culture, as some forms of devotion do not. Let these specimens stand for the longer list of traits of "relative" fruitfulness of Jesus as mediator in culture clashes and changes.

But, you will say, these samples of transsystem meaningfulness are only relatively true; none is fully unique. Of course! It would have been contradictory to expect that Christian commitment—even less Christians' performance—should be at the top of every scale. What we are looking for, I repeat, is not a way to keep dry above the waves of relativity, but a way to stay within our bark, barely afloat and sometimes awash amidst those waves, yet neither dissolving into them nor being carried only where they want to push it.

Some meaning frames, such as the early modern natural science vision of the closed causative system, claim or assume no historical variability and therefore cannot handle historical particularity. They can neither verify nor falsify it. They cannot deny that Jesus is Lord because they have no definition of what affirming it would mean.

Sometimes the internal claim of a meaning system applies only criteria of inward consistency: wholeness, coherence, happiness, or self-fulfillment. Of course these will work as criteria only if we assume in a circular way that it is better to be whole or happy or coherent, however we measure those virtues, and that whatever meets those standards is true.

There are those whose skepticism is more thorough, and who will make a point of setting aside any hypothesis which they don't need. Yet that response does not remove them from the conversation, since the first-century witness never understood itself as a hypothesis needing to verify itself by someone else's standards. No communication in any meaning framework needs to accept being tested by people who have decided ahead of time not to listen. Then an evangelical vision will seek no validation and fear no falsification.

A second usable choice would be to look again for other extant meaning frames in which larger questions can still function. Is there some still wider world? There is, for instance, the wider world of past history which, although interpretations of it will keep changing *somewhat*, is not completely a wax nose. Historical memory of the Hebraic and Christian contributions to Western culture may then contribute to reordering any debates between later meaning systems, all of which claim to take account of the past.

A third line of advocacy would be to make more of the family of epistemological paradoxes which gather around the truth claim of relativism/pluralism itself, whose proponents constantly tend to disregard its own warnings and to claim the authority to accredit other value systems with more substance than their own. The pluralist/relativist view differs from (some) other value systems in that it is our own world, the air we breathe. It is also a second-order system, which lives from interpreting other views. It leaves much of morality and more of worship to other communities. It does not baptize babies (or adults). It does not fight just wars (or love its enemies). It does name heretics, but when it does so firmly it tends to refute itself.

Another path we noted could be projected to reach past the varieties of peoples to a knowledge of nature which is common to all, as we could know it either by finding it everywhere or by constructing it out of necessary truths of reason. Instead of being a renunciation of particular claims, can it be made usable as an evangelical instrument? Perhaps, but a fair test of that alternative would take us too far.

To glance back for a moment at our starting point: we shall no longer try to help Gotthold Ephraim Lessing to leap across his ditch, nor to build him a bridge. The solidity of the necessary truths of reason concerning fundamental ideas of the nature of the Godhead, which Lessing's doubt posited on the other side of the ditch, is not there, should not be, need not be. The solid ground beyond the ditch is not there. The less narrow truth over there is still also provincial. Reality always was pluralistic and relativistic, that is, historical. The idea that it could be otherwise was itself an illusion laid on us by Greek ontology language, Roman sovereignty language, and other borrowings from the Germans, the Moors, and the other rulers of Europe. Yet within this relativity and in the style of noncoerciveness, we can and must still proclaim a Lord and invite to repentance. We report an event that occurred in our listeners' own world and ask them to respond to it. What could be more universal than that?

This debate about the context in which it again makes sense to talk of Jesus has been the bulk of my assignment. What then remains to be resaid cannot be new, but only the context for restating it.

THIS LAND IS OUR LAND

To begin that restatement I would take my first cue from the early proclaimers' confidence that they were not on foreign ground when they laid claim to the Hellenist cosmologies as one more place to make peace. They believed they were mopping up after an invasion in which their general had already established his lordship. Similarly, pluralism/relativism is a confusing world, but it is not an alien one. It is the child of the Hebrew and Christian intervention in cultural history. It is the spinoff from missionary mobility, from the love of the enemy, from the relativizing of political sovereignty, from a dialogical vision of the church, from a charismatic vision of the many members of the body, from the disavowal of empire and of theocracy. It lays before us the challenge of convincing interlocutors who are not our dependents, of affirming a particular witness to be good news without being interested in showing that other people are bad. Its corrosive critical power seems at first to be alien to the claim of the witness to bear good news, when that critical perspective is first encountered as a threat to the self-evidence of the smaller world in which one grew up. Yet it still is the case that pluralism/relativism is itself a part of the ripple effect of the gospel's impact upon Western culture.

What the challenges of relativism do threaten, and threaten profoundly, are two other kinds of epistemology. One of those, the epistemology of the establishment, was validated by placing the power of political authority and social consensus behind a particular belief system. In the primitive tribe, in an ancient Near-Eastern metropolis, or in Caesaro-Papism from Constantine to recent times, the vision of a local monocultural unity could remove all subjective choice from the belief question. This still is the normative vision in most of the world. Not until Vatican II did the Church of Rome reject it formally. But the knowledge of geography and the interpenetration of cultures make that option logically inaccessible for us even if we had found it psychologically attractive.

The other option to reject is one we have not finished dallying with, which we described at the outset as a subset of the apologetic approach: the search for some operation—be it linguistic, statistical, or logical—to define a kind of solid ground no longer subject to the reproach of others or to self-doubt as being vitiated by any kind of particularity. This is to renew the vain effort to find assurance beyond the flux of unendingly meeting new worlds, or to create a metalanguage above the clash, in order to renew for tomorrow the trustworthiness and irresistibility of the answers of the past.

By confessing that Messiah has been placed by God above and not within the cosmology and culture of the world they invade, the messianic Jewish witnesses also affirmed that under his lordship that cosmos will find its true coherence and meaning. To use the example of Colossians, the powers are not merely defeated in their claim to sovereignty, and humbled; they are also reenlisted in the original creative purpose of the service of humanity and the praise of God. Or in John, the *logos/sophia* vision of the rationality of the universe and of history is not only dethroned but is also put to work illuminating everyone who comes into the world, and empowering sons and daughters. To know that the Lamb who was slain was worthy to receive power not only enables his disciples to face martyrdom when they must; it also encourages them to go about their daily crafts and trades, to do their duties as parents and neighbors, without being driven to despair by cosmic doubt. Even before the broken world can be made whole by the Second Coming, the witnesses to the first coming — through the very fact that they proclaim Christ above the powers, the Son above the angels — are enabled to go on proleptically in the redemption of creation. Only this evangelical Christology can found a truly transformationist approach to culture.

We still do not *see* that the world has been set straight. We still have no *proof* that right is right. We still have not found a bridge or a way to leap from historical uncertainty to some other more solid base that would oblige people to believe or make our own believing sure.

As it is, we do not see everything in subjection to him. *But we do see Jesus,* revealing the grace of God by tasting death for everyone. (Heb. 2:8–9)

That should be enough for us to begin reconstructing God-language on this side of the ditch. We shall often be tactical allies of some apologetic thrust, when it rejects the results of a previous too-close identification of church and dominion. We may be tactical allies of the pluralist/relativist deconstruction of deceptive orthodox claims to logically coercive certainty, without making of relativism itself a new monism. We will share tactical use of liberation language to dismantle the alliance of church with privilege, without letting the promises made by some in the name of revolution become a new opiate. For the reconstruction we shall find other tactical allies. In the realm of ethics we shall not grant, with Tolstoy and Reinhold Niebuhr, that to renounce violence is to renounce power. We may then find tactical alliances with the Enlightenment, as did Quakers and Baptists in the century after their expulsion from the Puritan colonies, or with the Gandhian vision, as did Martin Luther King, Jr.

For our world it will be in his ordinariness as villager, as rabbi, as king on a donkey, and as liberator on a cross that we shall be able to express the claims which the apostolic proclaimers to Hellenism expressed in the language of preexistence and condescension. This is not to lower our sights or to retract our proclamation. It is to renew the description of Christ crucified as the wisdom and the power of God. This is the low road to general validity. It frees us from needing to be apologetic in either the popular or the technical sense. It thereby frees us to use any language, to enter any world in which people eat bread and pursue debtors, hope for power and execute subversives. The ordinariness of the humanness of Jesus is the warrant for the generalizability of his reconciliation. The nonterritorial particularity of his Jewishness defends us against selling out to *any* wider world's claim to be really wider, or to be self-validating.

Paul Ricoeur speaks of a second naïveté in which – after having taken all the critical distance we must, both from a text as literary product and from its ideas as artifacts of a not fully recoverable cultural matrix, we after all read a text as it stands. It is such a second level of ordinariness for which our tactical alliance with pluralism/relativism/historicism has freed us, by suspecting all the remaining claims of any wider worlds, however accredited, to have the authority to pass judgment on the Lord. The particularity of incarnation *is* the universality of the good. There is no road but the low road. The truth has come to our side of the ditch.

But then my assigned problem was not the real problem, but a screen. The real issue is not whether Jesus can make sense in a world far from Galilee, but whether – when he meets us in our world, as he does in fact – we want to follow him. We don't have to, as they didn't then. That we don't have to is the profoundest proof of his condescension, and thereby of his glory.

3. The Authority of Tradition

> "Why do you transgress the commandment of God for the sake of your tradition? Isaiah rightly prophesied of you: 'This people serves me with their lips, but their heart is far from me; the worship they offer me is in vain, for they teach as doctrine nothing but human regulations.'"
>
> Matt. 15:3, 8f.

How tradition exercises authority is one of those questions which put to us the prior challenge of choosing which league we want to play in. In the classical debate between scholastic Protestantism and scholastic Roman Catholicism after Trent[1] the term "tradition" not only pointed to the general observation that the substance of faith and the framework of its interpretation are passed on from one generation to the next: "tradition" also meant the specific set of units of information which have been passed down and cherished in such a way that they can claim a kind of revelatory authority, complementary to and not completely dependent on that of the canonical Scriptures.[2]

For the Protestants in that debate, it was profoundly important to say that *all* necessary information bearing revelatory authority is contained in the Holy Scriptures as they stand, sufficiently clear and self-interpreting as to need no more hermeneutic aids than every believer has available in the Holy Spirit and his or her human reason. Thus it was important for the Catholics to say the opposite: namely, that there are specific items of information (not merely additional perspectives useful for interpretation) which have been handed down without being written (or at least without being written in sacred Scriptures) "as if from hand to hand." It lies within the authority of the teaching hierarchy to clarify and promulgate this knowledge as they may see fit, subject to the internal accountability structures of the hierarchy, but independent of what other believers may hold the Bible text itself to say.

Reconception or Evasion?

As this debate was framed after Trent and administered from both sides until a generation ago, it by definition cannot move to a resolution. It could however be bypassed, if one could step back from the issue of locating in the papal office the authority to declare *which* units of information have the status of revelatory tradition. Thus it is no surprise that it was first in the Faith and Order movement (that division of the World Council of Churches which devotes its attention to classical issues of dogma and polity, and which for all practical purposes was long mostly a bilateral conversation between mainstream Western Protestants and the Eastern Orthodox) that the post-Tridentine formulation of the problem could be bypassed. In the documents of the Faith and Order Assembly in 1963 at Montreal, the issue was raised to a higher level of sophistication, and thereby practically laid to rest. The absence of formal Roman Catholic representation in the WCC at that time, and the practical silence within the Faith and Order conversations of the radical free-church traditions, made this major progress easier. The Montreal formulation used "Tradition" with a capital *T* to refer globally to all that each Christian community and all the Christian communities together think and speak. It is a stream of handing-down processes which is prior to and wider than the tradition of any one denominational communion. Secondly, the "traditions" (small *t*) are the several sets of sectarian understandings. They may properly be cultivated in separate places, but by their nature do not justify dividing the church. Thirdly, "tradition" (singular with a lower case *t*) means the event or process of handing down the substance of a community's faith. Everyone affirms all three. Since it is fitting that local "traditions" (lower case, plural) should differ, we can recognize one another without demanding uniformity or centralization.

But then what has become of the problem, the classical problem of Bellarmine and Canisius? Has it been resolved? or has it been simply declared nonexistent by definition or repressed? Is this like a military retreat from a battle line, where the trenches had been dug at the wrong point, without its being clear that we know now where we will meet an enemy? Has something been learned by backing away from that wrong battle? Albert Outler, one of the participants in the Montreal process (whose own brief book *The Christian Tradition and the Unity We Seek*[3] had contributed to that development), does think we have learned something. Of most disagreements between Christians that went to the point of schism, Outler argues that the break was not necessary. Even at the point of schism, the common beliefs remaining were more fundamental than the crucial differences. Outler holds that the wider stream of common experience and confession, binding all Christians together even though they have never met, is weightier than the issues about which we do battle with one another. Tradition and Scripture are not separate forces or substances but two different expressions of the same function of "handing on" what has been "given over" to us all in Christ.

That handing-on process includes organic evolution such as produced the later definitions of Nicea and Chalcedon. Simply facing that fact will, according to Outler, be a strong step forward toward "the unity we seek."

I grant that this sense of progress and learning is appropriate on the level of etiquette. Christians of all kinds have learned to be more polite and pluralistic in dealing with difference. If we had not been taught this by the gospel, we should have had to learn it from the culture of disestablishment.

The reading Outler gives is appropriate as a description of the mutual recognition for which mainstream Western Protestant churches are ready. Openness of previously separated denominational bodies to mutual recognition has been purchased partly by serious theological labor like Outler's and partly by the extent to which these Protestant denominations have bought into the pluralistic mood of their surrounding cultures.

Yet I must record doubt as to whether this more appeased mood has taken care of the root of the problem. This kind of irenic restatement was achieved in a context where the parties with the strongest convictions were absent, namely the Roman Catholics and the "free-church" Protestants. The old agenda was also left in the shadow, in favor of this more formal analysis. The specific issues that had been fought about before were not resolved but left to withdraw into a penumbra of polite pluralism. That is no reproach. Ecumenical movements do not have to discuss all the issues all the time. Some issues to which a new generation turns may well be of more immediate importance, without claiming that the older ones have been resolved.

My task here is not so much to add to the discipline of ethics[4] some new resource which might be discovered in the name of "tradition," but rather to ask with reference to ethics whether the issue of tradition, as irenically reorganized at Montreal, is rightly put and readily resolved.

I mentioned before the absence at Montreal not only of Roman Catholics, but also of radical evangelicals and conservative Protestants. The absence of conservative Protestants made it easier to reach a relatively moderate consensus. Yet their critique of inclusive pluralism is valid in one way that I must mention.

THE ABIDING CHALLENGE

The critical claim of evangelical biblicism is not answered by the "you-too" of the Catholics from Bellarmine to Patrick Murray. To retort to the "biblicists" (a label I propose to use descriptively, not pejoratively), who claim to grant authority to "the Scriptures alone," "you too have a context of interpretation, you too make assumptions, you too choose arbitrarily a canon within a canon" is true but is not to meet the issue worthily. This kind of put-down speaks to the cultural naiveté of some precritical evangelicals, but it does not speak to their theological tradition, which in its original age (that of Wyclif and Hus or of Luther and Calvin) was by no means naive nor disrespectful of tradition as a hermeneutical matrix. To recognize that there is no reading of Scripture without an interpreting frame does not set aside the canonical witness as a baseline and a critical instance, or make it only one of "two sources." One's "hermeneutical matrix" is like the microscope in microbiology. You cannot see the tiny organisms without the microscope, but the microscope never becomes the microbe. The use of the microscope might impose upon the microbe certain very severe conditions before it can be seen. The microbe will need to be put on a slide. It may need to be killed or dyed, but still it remains distinct from the microscope. If the microscope is immensely more powerful we approach the frontier where the interference of the instrument with the object becomes uncontrollable: but even here the electron which the microscope uses to see with is not the molecule. It is, in other words, thoroughly possible to distinguish in principle between the object of knowledge and the way of knowing it, and to affirm the priority of the former. In a similar sense, Protestant biblicists do not deny that they use language and logic, but they need not grant that that makes their reading hopelessly subjective.

They can grant that the Scripture was produced by churches out of traditions that were not "Scripture" until long after they were edited and recorded, and that contemporary interpretation is moved by contemporary priorities and challenges, without thereby conceding as desirable or even as possible that all of that process be controlled by a particular agent in the teaching church.

The old notion of tradition, as challenged by the Protestants, is inadequately represented by such concepts as unfolding, clarification, or reformulation. There can very properly be forms of change to which the "biblicist" would not object, if they have about them the organic quality of growth from seed, faithful translation, or fecundation. In fact, most of the theology of the conservative Protestant was reformulated after 1500 and much of it has evolved since 1600 (though not much since 1900). What is at stake is not whether there can be change but whether there is such a thing as unfaithfulness. Is there a difference between compatible extrapolation and incompatible deviation?

The linguistic line between treason and tradition is very fine. Both terms come from the same root. Yet in substance there is a chasm between the two, a chasm which the modern debate about tradition has not helped to survey. The semantic puzzles are enormous when we try to distinguish between faithful organic development on one hand and a sell-out on the other. Both are formed in historical continuity. Both are explainable within historicist axioms of causality and analogy. Both use the same words. Yet if the notion of fidelity is not to fade into a fog where nothing is verifiable, the notion of infidelity as a real possibility must continue to be operational.

New Forms of the Issue

Current examples will demonstrate that the problem is still with us. In the World Council of Churches the label "syncretism" has long functioned as an identity marker. William Visser 't Hooft, the Council's first General Secretary, wrote the book *No Other Name,* which denied any path to saving knowledge of God other than Jesus Christ. He denounced mixed forms of religious expression as intrinsically idolatrous.[5] The fact that the World Council arose in close association with the Protestant World Missionary Movement and the World Student Christian Movement forged a linkage with missionary Protestantism at large. The centrality of Christ was for a time more important in the Council than any search for ways to dialogue with outsiders. Since the New Delhi Assembly (1961) and still more since Nairobi (1975), this easy rejection by Westerners of "syncretism" as a peculiar temptation of Africans or Asians is no longer credible to Christians at home in the "third world." Though they affirm the need for vigilance to avoid diluting or confusing the gospel by the admixture of genuinely incompatible alien elements, they remind Europeans that such mixing has gone on for centuries in Europe, whereas the task of authentic communication in the forms of any non-Western culture has only recently been tackled. Until we know how faithfully to speak of Christ in some non-Western language, we can hardly know what identifies culpable syncretism.

Another variation on the faithfulness theme is the current conservative evangelical discussion of what is called "contextualization." Making use of the tools of cultural anthropology and comparative linguistics, evangelical missionaries are newly open to far-reaching reformulations of the gospel message. The founders of their missions would have considered illegitimate such adaptation to local pre-Christian patterns. The movement is impressive in its anthropological competence and creativity. It has not been at work long enough for us to determine whether it will develop criteria for defining heresy.

Still another variation is the cultural criticism being formulated by the "theologies of liberation." The way in which Christians have come to be at home with the powers of the wealthy world and the alliance of the older churches with colonialism and capitalism are denounced as a failure faithfully to represent the gospel's liberating impact.

Obviously a fourth variant is the broad current Roman Catholic review of the possible religious value of other faiths.[6]

In each of these cases someone claims that someone else has permitted the faith to evolve in a way that denies something of its essence. They claim that such evolution can be evaluated so as to be found acceptable (as in contextualization) or heretical (as in syncretism or oppression). Thus in order to make the fundamental Protestant point, we need not claim that all developments are wrong, or that any one specified development is all wrong. It suffices to have illustrated how it is possible in principle for an important error, when not promptly corrected, to jeopardize the claim of the church to be speaking credibly for her Lord.

PERPETUAL REFORM

The problem with which we must wrestle is one that Albert Outler and Montreal were not trying to solve. We are not plagued merely by a hard-to-manage diversity, by a wealth of complementary variations on the same theme. We are faced with error, into which believers are seduced by evil powers seeking to corrupt the church and to disqualify her witness. To denounce those errors we must appeal to the common traditions from which those who fall into error are falling away, which they previously had confessed together with us. As the Apostle Paul was already doing in 1 Corinthians 15 and Galatians 1, we appeal to a prior commonality against an innovation. Such an innovation, already having been handed down for more than one generation, but recognizable as not valid from the root, is what Jesus in Matthew 15:3ff. (followed by Zwingli and the Puritans) called "human traditions." The need is not that *those* traditions be integrated in a richer pluralism. They must be uprooted (v. 13). There are no grounds for claiming that they had been handed down in unwritten form "as if from hand to hand" ever since the apostles. Against these new-fangled "traditions of man" we appeal to the original traditions which enshrine the commandments of God. The clash is not tradition versus Scripture but faithful tradition versus irresponsible tradition. Only if we can with Jesus and Paul (and Francis, Savonarola, Milton, and the others) denounce *wrong* traditioning, can we validly affirm the rest. Scripture comes on the scene not as a receptacle of all possible inspired truths, but rather as witness to the historical baseline of the communities' origins and thereby as link to the historicity of their Lord's past presence.

Far from being an ongoing growth like a tree (or a family tree), the wholesome growth of a tradition is like a vine: a story of constant interruption of organic growth in favor of pruning and a new chance for the roots. This renewed appeal to origins is not primitivism, nor an effort to recapture some pristine purity. It is rather a "looping back," a glance over the shoulder to enable a midcourse correction, a rediscovery of something from the past whose pertinence was not seen before, because only a new question or challenge enables us to see it speaking to us. To stay with the vinedresser's image, the effect of pruning is not to harm the vine, but to provoke new growth out of the old wood nearer to the ground, to decrease the loss of food and time along the sap's path from roots to fruit, and to make the grapes easier to pick. *Ecclesia reformata semper reformanda* is not really a statement about the church. It is a statement about the earlier tradition's permanent accessibility, as witnessed to and normed by Scripture at its nucleus, but always including more dimensions than the Bible itself contains, functioning as an instance of appeal as we call for renewed faithfulness and denounce renewed apostasy. The most important operational meaning of the Bible for ethics is not that we do just what it says in some way that we can derive deductively. It is rather that we are able, thanks to the combined gifts of teachers and prophets, to become aware that we do not do what it says, and that the dissonance we thereby create enables our renewal.[7]

There is no reproach involved when we affirm this need for correction. *Sometimes* a need for correction is the result of culpable failure or disobedience. Sometimes it is the result of not having listened or waited. Yet often the need for continuing historical correction is blameless, intrinsic to the quality of historically rooted community. We should feel guilty not when we need to be corrected but when we claim to bypass that need, as if our link to our origins were already in our own hands.

What we then find at the heart of our tradition is not some proposition, scriptural or promulgated otherwise, which we hold to be authoritative and to be exempted from the relativity of hermeneutical debate by virtue of its inspiredness. What we find at the origin is already a process of reaching back again to the origins, to the earliest memories of the event itself, confident that that testimony, however intimately integrated with the belief of the witnesses, is not a wax nose, and will serve to illuminate and sometimes adjudicate our present path.

New Receptivity

One way the same old data yields new information is that we bring to it another set of questions, just as the natural sciences find more facts in the same plant or animal than before their present instruments were developed. A new question permits the old event to respond in ways that earlier patterns of questioning had not made self-evident or perhaps had hidden.

Within the last century, and for many of us within the generation, there has been a fundamental paradigm shift in the readiness to see the Gospel story in particular, and the biblical revelatory story in general, as social and political. Earlier generations had intentionally filtered out that part of the light, considering it as the particular conditioned dimension that should not be permitted to get in the way of the more authentically religious data. It is now possible to talk about the Eucharist as relating to world hunger, or about Jesus as a liberator. We are finding in the old sources help which was always there, but which previously was not drawn from them because we did not expect them to speak to those issues. Nor did we think that we needed much help in that area anyway. In other words, we have just lived a new episode of the "reaching back" phenomenon. Having learned that our models for understanding social structures and their moral weight in the light of the faith were not adequate, we were free for a new approach to the same old canonical texts. Some of our questions are now reformulated in such a way that the texts are ready to speak to them.

There have always been radio waves bringing messages to us from distant stars. Only the development of radio technology has empowered us to receive those signals. The Bible was always a liberation storybook: now we are ready to read it that way. Tomorrow some other question will provoke another "reaching back" for yet another level of meaning that was always there. In this study, our interest is that what the "reaching back" has brought forward recently has to do with ethics. It corrects a model of Christian social ethics that thought it did not need that specific story, because it got its guidance from "nature" or "conscience" or later history.

The commercials invite us to "reach out and touch someone." They tell us we can do it by phone. The healing communication we need for ethical reforming is also to reach and to touch someone. Here, though, the touching must be done through documents, and through our modest capacity for understanding what documents originally meant. More than when the reformation debate arose, we are aware that these documents point to events beyond themselves, namely to the utterly human, vulnerable, dubitable, rejectable presence of Jesus among us, and that the quality of historical testimony which they offer is that of believing witness. Nonetheless this process of "reaching back" once again, to participate in the process of the believing witnesses' "reaching back" at their time, must be the shape of our discipline if our claim to be his disciples is not to be evacuated of moral substance.

The radio analogy stated in lay cultural terms what a free-church alternative to the Tridentine debate would have said biblically. There is continuing revelation. Jesus promised that there would be (John 14:12–26; 16:7–15). The Lucan and Pauline pictures of prophecy assume that there will be. 1 John 4:1ff, and 1 Corinthians 12:1ff. assume that there will be and provide criteria for it. At Trent the defense against Protestant biblicism made the wrong move. Instead of granting to the Protestants that all revelation must be apostolic and then claiming to have some leftover unwritten apostolic information, Trent might have granted that later developments had gone beyond Scripture, but agreed to face the challenges of dialogue about justifying at the bar of Scripture the movement beyond Scripture. Then it would have surfaced that the real debate was not about apostolic memories but about which kind of church can have an open dialogue.

So the term "tradition" has exploded beyond the point where it could have functioned as a "second source." It now represents a river in which we all float, or swim, seeking our bearings as we move. It is not like Scripture in the high scholastic Protestant view, uniquely inspired literature, whose credibility has been undermined by the perspectives of historical criticism. The acids of historicism that have weakened it are not challenges to the precise historicity of particular Gospel accounts, or to naive traditions about authorship and redaction, but rather the broader awareness of the plurality and the conditioned quality of all meanings and institutions.

Most of the above applies intentionally to the wider questions of how tradition functions in all social groups claiming to be faithful to some formative or founding event. It may apply more specifically just now to ethics because it is a realm where the reality check is met soon. In ritual or in dogma it is not surprising or alienating for language to be a little old or other-worldly. There the past, at least the moderately recent past, has a hold on us against which we do not rebel. Social behavior has by its nature a present meaning.

MODELS OF UNFAITHFULNESS

It is in the realm of ethics that the strongest appeals have been made to kinds of information that do not need scriptural warrant, since they are held to be common to all mankind: the famous "natural" sources of moral insight. People would be less likely to suggest there are natural sources of ritual knowledge or of creedal information.

The realm of the social is accordingly the one where the dynamics of accommodation and the tendencies to sell out are the strongest, as the church lives at the interface with the world of unbelief, its powers and pressures. Thus if we want to know how we need to proceed in a debate about tradition going astray and being called to order by tradition, we should find such a mistake to analyze.

If I knew more, I should like to begin with the betrayal of the Jewishness of the early church, as the Christian apologetes of the second and third centuries moved into Hellenistic culture, or with the betrayal of the feminist thrust that had begun with the Gospels. I would, if I could, study when the veneration of the saints became a new paganism, or when Easter became a fertility ritual. If I were a Marxist, or a historian of the eleventh century in Milan, we could talk about wealth as apostasy.

Instead of focusing on a debatable negative case of ethical evolution that needs to be called into question, it might have been desirable first to use some positive ones, which we would all agree to be good, and others that we would all agree to be bad. As an example of good change we could have taken the acceptance by most Christians in our time of religious liberty, or of democracy. I doubt, however, that that would really have produced more clarity. The grounds on which these affirmations, ancient in some Christian communities and recent in others, have been integrated in recent Christian thought are not agreed upon. It seems to have been a part of the price of the acceptance of religious liberty, by Vatican II, as desirable from now on in the modern world that there needed to be no express disavowal of its rejection by Catholics in past centuries. There is not full agreement about whether the particular lines of argument which led to the acceptance of religious liberty in Vatican II, thanks to the leadership of John Courtney Murray, were the best way to move in that case. It would seem then that the acceptance of religious liberty is not a better test case for evaluating our differences about how tradition functions to criticize tradition.

The other approach would be to broaden our conspectus with something that we would all agree was a bad evolution, properly rejected by "all Christians everywhere always," on the grounds of an appeal to the older tradition. We might ethically agree to condemn support given to Adolf Hitler by the *Deutsche Christen,* but that case would not really count, because it was not sanctioned by a hierarchy. We could critique the Crusades, but that would involve us in a complicated conceptual debate among specialists about the sense in which the Crusades were and were not expressions of the just war logic.

We could discuss the Iberian conquest of South America and the first four and a half centuries of bad colonial manners, but that would point us to an unfinished debate still going on within in the dominant Catholic communion rather than to real agreement. Even many theologians of "liberation," while very clear in their present criticism of the colonial heritage, do not want to use ethical concepts which would reject the colonial pattern in principle, nor the pattern of Constantinian establishment from which it was derived. Some would seem to say that Constantine was all right for his time, and Charlemagne for his, and Charles V for his: then it is only in our age that we must replace the imperial vision of civil righteousness with a revolutionary one.

This would leave us with the Inquisition as one possible case where we might all agree today that that pattern, once solidly accepted by the entire hierarchy, has come to be rejected on the grounds of a fundamental appeal to what the earlier Christian tradition was about. Yet even here, we would have some more history to study before we could be sure that what undercut the Inquision for those whose direct predecessors had believed in it, was really a renewed appeal to the New Testament, or to Christology, or to the fundamental nature of religion or of the human being as a religious person, rather than acquiescence to the power of modernity, which tore such instruments from the hands of the hierarchy on quite other grounds.[8]

The Legitimation of War

Yet the demonstration will be simpler if I stay with the classical agenda of the divergent Christian views about the morality of the violence of the state, not to be argued for its own sake but as a well-known specimen of what we are trying to isolate.

From Tertullian and Origen at the end of the second century to Bernard a millennium later, the view of Christians on the morality of violence in the public realm was reversed. The development came in phases. The first was a rather modest borrowing from the Roman legal tradition by Ambrose and Augustine, to speak to questions the New Testament did not help them with. The legitimate violence which they approved was the function of the police in domestic peacekeeping or at most the defense of the empire against the Vandals. The category of "vengeance" was present in their thought, to account for the wars in the Old Testament, but they did not see the contemporary international undertakings of the Roman Empire as being vengeance commanded by God. The Crusades were quite another phase, which went far beyond the old Roman just war categories to make the Middle East adventures a specifically religious cause.

The end product of these and other shifts is a fundamentally new political ethic, not organically evolved from the social stance of the early Christians, as that stance had been evolving up to and through Tertullian and Origen. The new stance rejects the privileged place of the enemy as the test of whether one loves one's neighbor. It rejects the norm of the cross and the life of Jesus Christ as the way of dealing with conflict. It assigns to civil government, not only to Caesar as an ecumenical savior figure but even, later, to fragmented local regimes, a role in carrying out God's will that is quite incompatible with the fruit of the progressive relativization of kingship from Samuel to Jeremiah to Jesus and Jochanan ben Zakkai.

This "just war tradition" is now dominant.[9] It has crowded the earlier pacifist tradition to the Franciscan and Waldensian fringes of Christendom. Yet it has never been promulgated as an official teaching by a council or a pope, never studied with great intensity, never formulated in a classical outline, and never applied with much consistency. It is dominant without being clear. It has taken over without being tested.

Having a real case of change in view, there is no difficulty in observing that the Tridentine notion of a second source is ludicrously inept. There was not a "just war" undercurrent in the first centuries, waiting unused yet faithfully passed on orally until the Constantinian opportunity let it come out of the catacombs. Rather, there were new challenges to which the separatist ethic of the apocalypse or of the pacifist fathers did not seem to speak sufficiently. It would have been good at that time to have had a new prophetic voice to save the church of the third and fourth centuries from the no-win choice between separatism and sell-out. Tragically, there was no such prophet. Ambrose and Augustine did the best they could. They did not mean to sell out, but they did buy into a system whose inherent dynamism they could no longer control. The one explanation that can *not* be claimed is that they got their new ideas about the just war from a not yet recorded oral treasury of apostolic memories. They themselves would not have said that. They knew they were borrowing from Cicero. What needs to be debated is not the "two sources" notion but the criteria for the church's necessary appropriation of non-Christian moral ideas.

Our concern here is not to debate the ethics of violence as an issue for its own sake. The observation is purely formal. A change has taken place which must be described as a reversal rather than as an organic development. This case shows that when the issue is whether change has been faithful or unfaithful, *then* the reason the reformers challenge some usage or idea is not that it is not in the Scriptures, but that it is counter to the Scriptures; not that it is an ancient idea insufficiently validated by ancient texts, but that it is a later introduction invalidated by its contradicting the ancient message. So the issue —if there be a genuine issue—is not tradition versus Scripture, nor Scripture versus some one fragment of the rest of tradition, nor (as Montreal said) the scriptural fraction of tradition versus some other one of many traditions. The issue is (as Jesus said it) the traditions of men versus the commandment of God. That rough word of Jesus introduces seriousness that ecumenical politeness had hidden. Not all varieties of vision—or of ethics—can fit together within a tolerant pluralism. What we need is tools to identify and denounce error, while welcoming variety and celebrating complimentarity.

The problem with which the truce of Montreal cannot help is not that we talk different languages, or that each of us is so integrated in his own culture that our several patterns are very different. The problem is that within the same culture we take positions so fundamentally contradictory that we cannot both be faithfully serving the same Lord. To adjudicate that question, the thrust of Trent and Bellarmine is no help. However prestigious be the center which claims to rule over the universal community, it will always be in some sense provincial. Its claim to possess a side channel of revelation reaching all the way back to the apostles by an unbroken oral chain is even less credible, in the face of the perspectives of scientific historicism, than are the claims for the univocal meaning of Scripture texts. Nor has it ever been seriously claimed in the field of social ethics that there exist particular data preserved within the unbroken hierarchy by oral transmission. If we treat as more or less equivalent (a) the claim that there is valid nonscriptural tradition received from the apostles and (b) the practice of Roman councils and popes of promulgating specific claims, if necessary *ex cathedra*, then it is significant that it is not in the field of social ethics that this authority has been exercised. Such a fundamental innovation as the just war attitude was never given that kind of ratification. A stronger claim in fact would have been to exploit the promises in the New Testament of further leading beyond the teachings of Jesus, and to claim continuing specific concrete guidance in line with Matthew 10:19f., yet for other reasons Trent could not have taken that path, and the just war doctrine would not have fit the context of Matthew 10.

The scholastic Protestant view has been no less undermined by the age of historical awareness. With regard to the Bible itself, we know, without being threatened by the fact, that a process of traditioning had been going on for a generation before the texts took on their present form, that those texts were always interpreted within a wider context of meanings and logic, and that the plurality of the texts testifies to an even greater variety in those early communities. In a similar way, historical relativity makes us aware that the way we read a text is also the product of our education, language, and logic.

Thus both sides of the scholastic debate have been undermined. The three definitions from Montreal, while not harmful, are of no help here. It was not the intention of the Montreal redefinition to adjudicate apostasy or heresy. Its purpose was to insist that not all divergence is heresy and that no one is without tradition. That approach is especially fitting when the divergences we talk about are matters of ritual, where the variations in the language of the doxology need not be measured in dogmatic terms, because they do not exclude the appropriateness of quite different language in other places. This same quality of pluralism will not work in the same way, and has not been advocated aggressively by any convinced theologian, in the field of social ethics.

We are not talking about "the authority of tradition" as if tradition were a settled reality and we were then to figure out how it works. We are asking how, within the maelstrom of traditioning processes, we can keep our bearings and distinguish between the way the stream should be going and side channels which eddy but lead nowhere. Can we do this by some criterion beyond ourselves? The peculiarity of the term "tradition" is that it points to that criterion beyond itself, to which it claims to be a witness. We are therefore doing no violence to the claim of tradition when we test it by its fidelity to that origin. A witness is not being dishonored when we test his fidelity as an interpreter of the events to which he testifies. That is his dignity as witness; he wants to be tested for that.

Returning to the particular sample case: how would we proceed if we desired to let reforming and renewing through memory apply to the tradition of the just war? It would not suffice to say that these new ideas came into Christian thought in the fourth century and are therefore wrong. Neither can we say that they were brought into Christian thought in the fourth century by bishops who were later sainted and that therefore they are all right. Nor can we bring justification like that of Reinhold Niebuhr, to the effect that any growing community will have to dilute its morality a little in order to take charge of a society for the good of that society.

We must therefore ask much more careful questions about the vision of history as a whole that led to this change in ethics. What kind of formulation of the Christian hope was at work when this ethical change seemed to make sense? What was the quality of Christian spirituality and character that made the shift seem "natural?"

If this questioning is careful and is not simply polemic, we shall come to the awareness that the early just war thinkers, more than our contemporaries who use the same words, were still thinking in terms of a minority ethic. They were attempting to "drag their feet" as the mass of Christianity rapidly moved into a new relationship of church and world. Unwilling to admit that their ethical commitment to the sacredness of life and the dignity of the enemy was irrelevant, or to accept that their morality was only for the monastery, they transposed their Christian defense of the sacred life of the enemy into a doctrine of the right of the enemy not to be harmed except for cause, which should have made sense to the Caesars and their heirs. They were not saying that war is "just" in the sense of moral righteousness. They were saying that, to the extent to which this exceptional degree of violence, which obviously is *prima facie* opposed to the gospel, can be justified at all, it must be subject to the vigilant application of the solid criteria of just cause, right intention, legitimate authority, necessary and proportionate means, etc. They were not describing a good society or a Christian moral order but continuing to drag their feet as they saw Christians drawn into administering a bad one.

Seeing the pastoral and culture-critical intent of early just war thought provides us the criteria by which we can evaluate it after a trial run of fifteen centuries. It has very seldom functioned as an efficacious restraint, as it was supposed to. It has more often been transmuted, in the hands of people less critical than Augustine or Aquinas or Vitoria, into a simple affirmation that war is acceptable if it meets certain requirements. Augustine himself would reject that use made of his language. He was adapting the *prima facie* original Christian pacifism, which he still thought he was faithfully supporting, in his continuity with the early Christians, against abuse by people improperly claiming that their responsibilities for the civil order authorized them to be free of restraint. He said it in the language of human rights (the right of the enemy not to be jeopardized without due cause) rather than in the simple language of the Gospel, because he was willing to grant that this simple language would be written off as irrelevant. He had given up on the claim that the Jesus of the Gospel account was relevant and was accepting the apologetes' demand that ethical insight be transmuted into Hellenistic and Roman juridical forms.

A fundamental critique must then address not merely the space that was made for justifiable violence, but the prior acceptance of the irrelevance of Jesus to the political existence of his disciples, or the prior commitment to the imperative of using the world's language if we want to challenge the world's imperatives. That is the point at which the sell-out can now be seen to have occurred. The debate is not about whether the Christian prohibition of violence might have loopholes. The question is whether the pertinence of the Jesus story for our present agenda has to be filtered through some other language and its frame of reference.

I have in the past said it affirmatively: Jesus is presented by the Gospel writers as a model when he renounces the justifiable insurrection of the Zealots. Now I say it as critique. A millennium and a half of efforts to use the more "natural," and therefore supposedly more "applicable" categories of the just war tradition have not successfully translated Christian concern for the enemy's dignity into real politics. We are more able than the medievals to see that justifiable insurrection, as a form of the "just war," *is* a theme to which Jesus does speak: a perception for which neither Saint Francis or Tolstoy was yet ready. The newer urgency of the arms race and of liberation rhetoric frees a deeper stratum of the Gospel. We reconstruct by critiquing and by remembering.

4. The Kingdom As Social Ethic

The years have confirmed the aptness of observing how a distinctive stance in social ethics both follows from and contributes to a distinctive social location. There are still corners of the ethical field where that awareness has not penetrated; but in its essence the point was established by Ernst Troeltsch. One might unfold with more examples the reasonableness of the connection between the social status in which radical reformation communities have usually found themselves in the post-Renaissance West and the specific social style which they have developed: migration, pacifism, vocational specialization, and so on. But this too has been done repeatedly and some might think repetitively.

It would be a mistake to trivialize our topic with ecumenical good manners. In an age when every confessional family is willing to recognize that others have something to say, it is natural that some of the churches of the majority Western traditions should take notice of the distinctive "peace church" presence as one of those families whose witness has not been heard and which it would be appropriate to give attention to. Since it is assumed that every denominational family must possess some charisma which the others should hear of, and since the phrase "peace church" has become current,[1] the suggestion normally arises that maybe something these churches could help the rest with would be the questions of war and peace with which others recognize that their own traditions have not adequately prepared them to grapple.

Such intentions to seek to learn from the peace churches have recently been expressed by such agencies the World Council of Churches and the Lutheran World Federation. Another kind of recognition is the suggestion that other denominations might declare themselves to be "peace churches" by adopting some kind of antimilitary statement.

We see here at work the ordinary ethos of liberal Western ecumenism. One assumes that it is proper for each denominational communion to have "their thing," perhaps thought of as their "gift" in analogy to the language of 1 Corinthians 12, or as their "talent." One assumes that each denomination's particularity is somehow "true," in that others should listen to it respectfully rather than calling it heretical as they used to. At the same time, one assumes that the kind of "truths" which the others hold is not overpowering, since that "respectful listening" does not obligate one to agree with them, or even to weigh seriously the reasons *they* give for their views. One listens to the others when and because one has one's own timely reasons to think that what they say might be interesting; one listens to them on one's own terms and at one's own convenience. Thus the price of this good-mannered ecumenical openness to hear one another at our points of distinctiveness is a pluralism that may replace the truth question with a kind of uncritical celebration of diversity. Our recognition of how it is that those other people, from their other place in history, can hold to those other views does not necessarily mean expecting those views to have any hold on us because they can claim to be true or biblical or prophetic. After all, ecumenical etiquette must be reciprocal. If I grant that what makes you distinctive is worth listening to, it is appropriate that you should return the compliment and accept that my having been led in another direction is equally authentic.

My task here is to exposit, noncoercively and dialogically, the case for claiming that that stance which has here been variously labeled as "peace church," "minority," "non-established," "radical reformation," is closer to the gospel and more properly to be recognized as the imperative under which Christians stand than are the major alternatives.

Instead of asking what ethical positions come naturally to a church which finds itself in a minority, or which ethical positions, if taken consistently, would probably leave any church in minority status, I should be trying to state that particular set of convictions about what should be the stance of the *whole* Christian community. Such a stance is most appropriately understood from within the social context of being outvoted, but whose truth claims are not dependent on that social situation. I should not ask what complementary corrective is needed from a minority perspective after granting that the majority establishment does most of the work of being the church. I should ask rather what the whole church is called to be in the world where she is (really) in a minority position. I shall use the memory and perspective of minority experience only to clarify the credibility of such positions, and to spark creativity about the possibility of a counter-establishment stance for the whole church, but without granting either that Christians if they took these positions would *always* be voted down or excluded, or that it only makes sense to hold such positions when the believing community is numerically insignificant.

THE DIFFERENCE STATUS MAKES

Even though it is being done in this book, it is not obvious to all modern readers why it should be significant to take account of the minority status of a faith community in understanding its ethical perspectives. To understand the perspective of the book of the Apocalypse, or of the prophecies of Jeremiah and Ezekiel, or for that matter of the records of the message of Jesus, many of our contemporaries do not stop to take account of what it contributes to the shape of the writer's ethical guidance that he is not assuming that his listeners dominate the society where they live. The reader of such literature knows that to be a fact, but often does not take account of that fact as helping to explain why the ethical orientation projected in such literature takes the shape it does.

The way we put this question in modern times is therefore itself the product of our times. It is only possible to think seriously about what difference it makes that a moral community is a minority if one has come to grips with the difference that dominant status may make. Thus an indispensable detour toward our theme must be a sketchy inventory of the difference it makes, specifically for Christians, when the ethical guidance which they derive from their faith is adjusted to their having become the dominant element of their society.[2]

1. The ethical orientation may need to change in the minds of most when the ruler has become a member of the church. During the Christian Middle Ages Constantine became the symbol of this.[3] The assumption tends to be that in order to continue being a sovereign, he needs to continue to act the way a (non-Christian) sovereign "naturally" acts, thereby creating some tension with what the later prophets and Jesus taught about domination, wealth, and violence. A strongly conversionist ethic might have held forth the possibility that a converted ruler could also transform his office and might resolve differently the challenges of dominion, wealth, and killing (much later there will be some conversionists with visions like that); but in the fourth century there was no recorded strong advocacy of the possibility that

the conversion of Constantine might change his behavior or that of his heirs. We have thereby discovered what later Protestant social ethics will call "the ethic of vocation," whereby what it means to do the proper thing in one's given social setting is determined by the inherent quasi-autonomous law of that setting,[4] whose demands can be both known and fulfilled independently of any particular relation to the rootage of Christian faith.

2. The influx into the membership of the Christian church of larger numbers of persons for whom that new affiliation is not the expression of a strong personal faith experience or commitment means that there will be a need to adjust the expectations of ethical teachers with regard to how insightful and how unselfish we can ask people to be. The conversionist ethic of a minority under pressure can expect of its members a "heroic" level of devotion: a church of the multitudes must on the other hand be satisfied with a run-of-the-mill level of understanding and devotion. Here we discern the point of entry of two notions which the earlier Christians or the Jews of the same epoch would not have taken for granted:

a) the notion of a distinction between the minimal morality of the "precepts" and the higher "volunteer" level of the "evangelical counsels," and

b) the independent but congenial notion that the kind of life compatible with the call of the gospel is manageable only by virtue of some degree of special motivation, usually expressed in a vocational withdrawal from ordinary life.

3. Once we dominate society, the way we want things to go is the way they might very well be able to go. Therefore one can think of social behavior in terms of controlling social process or of goal-oriented causation. The rightness or wrongness of behavior can now be translated or interpreted in terms of good and bad outcomes. If we want something not to happen we can declare it a crime, we can punish it when it does happen, and it will happen less or not at all. If we want something to happen, we can make it an obligation or reward it, and it will tend to happen. Thus there enters into ethical thought

a) that entire set of styles of discourse which later analysis will speak of as teleological or utilitarian, i.e., as orienting evaluation around intended or actually achieved outcomes, as well as

b) the distinguishable but compatible notions of "compromise" and
the "lesser evil," whereby it is a part of moral decision to play against
one another a variety of competitive values that are at stake, and
to take responsibility for the particular value mix and cost/benefit
trade-off that will come out to be the most desirable "for the good
of the whole."

4. Behind these adjustments, where the logic flows from the
changed social setting to a changed pattern of ethics, it will then be
natural to develop as well a changed set of express philosophical or
semantic assumptions. It will now be appropriate to speak about nature and grace in such a way as to affirm the knowability through
"nature" of kinds of moral insight which correspond to the new ethic.
It will be assumed that the moral insights of Gentile antiquity and
the teachings of the Old Testament are for some reason closer to "nature" than are the teachings and example of Jesus. The general tone
of the argument will be formal: i.e., a discussion of why one should
believe in general that those other sources of moral guidance may have
some validity. Yet the stake in the argument is material, i.e., the fact
that those other moralities are more affirmative than is the New Testament about the uses of coercion, violence, wealth, status, tradition,
and the justification of means by ends. Later versions of the same kind
of reasoning for modern times will take account of non-Christian contemporaries and of other cultures, or of post-Christian skeptics in the
West, as representative of the access that people may have to moral
insight independently of the channels of the community of faith.

It is not my present concern to project an argument about whether
these changed approaches are biblically or logically or realistically acceptable, but only to report it as a matter of the history of Western
moral thought that their coming to dominance in Christian and post-
Christian thought is correlated with Christianity's becoming the faith
of the dominant segment of society. They would not be thinkable in
this same simplicity from the perspective of a persecuted or isolated
minority.

The way this evolution has been described retraces the path of the
dominant thought of Christendom. The ethicist will recognize it as
touching the main traits of the form of social thought which Ernst
Troeltsch called "churchly."

By charting the natural changes in social thought which derive
logically and historically from the churches' acceptance of a position

of social dominance, we have traced backhandedly the major traits which we shall expect obviously to characterize a church which (whether naively or self-consciously) seeks to live and to keep thinking in a setting parallel to that of the early Christians. But before we advance to the affirmative statement of what we have already projected obversely, let it be recalled that (contrary to a common misinterpretation) the initial intention of the "sectarian" communities which in the course of Western history have renewed a minority ethic has not been to be sects. Division was not their purpose. They have called upon all Christians to return to the ethic to which they themselves were called. They did not agree (with paragraph b above) that their position was only for heroes, or that it was only possible for those who would withdraw from the wider society. They did not agree to separate themselves as more righteous from the church at large. They rather called upon the church at large to accept as binding for all Christians the quality of commitment which would in effect lead them all to be separated from the world once again in order to be appropriately in mission to the world.

THE NOTION OF RADICAL HISTORICAL CRITIQUE

What it takes to explain one group of people to another group will depend upon who the others are. There is no such thing as just one central definitional trait which defines the radical reformation view, except as we specify what is the other position from which a given "radical" group differs. Since, however, most of the other positions are those which are the products of some experience of "establishment," let us name as definitional for beginning our characterization of the radical Protestant reformation the very notion of challenging establishment: i.e., of rejecting, or at least doubting fundamentally, the appropriateness of letting the Christian faith be the official ideology of a society, especially of the elite within a society.

Why then should there be anything wrong with Christianity's becoming an official ideology? It must be because that change itself calls into question something definitional about the faith. Perhaps this would not need to be absolutely true. It nonetheless tends to be the case, in the experience of the Christian community, that the only way in which the faith can become the official ideology of a power elite in a given society is if Jesus Christ ceases to be concretely Lord. Some other value: power, mammon, fame, efficacy, tends to become (the radical would say must become) the new functional equivalent of deity. The radicals' condemnation is then not addressed to popularity or visibility or social responsibility, not to growth in numbers or being tolerated as such, but to purchasing such value at the expense of fidelity to the jealousy of Christ as Lord. It makes no difference for the present analysis whether the claims of some other Lord than Jesus be made effective because a believer follows them out of the conscious conviction that he should be serving an unbelieving community, or whether the rejection of Jesus be more tacit or even unwitting. Nor does it matter whether we think of specific "crunch" decisions where someone chooses to do evil with a good intent or whether deeper matters of character and commitment be thought of as more basic.

Obviously it will never happen, at least not in the first generation, that anyone will say explicitly that another deity has been elevated beside Jesus Christ. They will rather say that these other values, which they call by less judgmental names like responsibility, nature, efficiency, wisdom, are also affirmed as a part of the meaning of "Christ," standing in some complementary relationship to the Lordship which is still ascribed to Jesus. This supplementary or complementary insight deals with some realm to which Jesus had not spoken, or fills in a gap which the radicality of the gospel had not taken time to deal with. It takes its cues from other positive values which Jesus can hardly be against, like reason and created nature, like the orders which it takes to keep a society operating, even though at certain crucial points this means specifically not doing what Jesus said or did or asked of his disciples.[5] This peaceable complementarity seems self-evidently acceptable as a way to widen the relevance of the faith to more people and more questions. Only the distance of later generations or unbelieving criticism will name the contradiction more bluntly.

If it is the case that this kind of adjustment to other loyalties is a step on the way to unfaithfulness and should be condemned, then it would seem at first that the necessary corrective would be to reject all change, restoring things as they had been before, For the early centuries the concept of "renewal" was this "simple"; it asked for the restitution of the way things had already been. Only in recent centuries has historical consciousness made it impossible to think that way. Any effort to restore what one thought had been there before changes that ideal by the very fact that it is now being sought, whether successfully or not, as the goal of retroactive change. For over a thousand years this is what both "catholics" and "radicals" thought the debate was. The party of accommodation identified the movement they had made with movement forward. Accordingly the critics could conceive of no other alternative but artificial movement backward.

The genuine alternatives arise when one faces the fact that neither of those pure options is real. No one can say that the movement up to the present has all been simply forward. In fact it has not been all in one direction and has not brought us all to one place. But to criticize the way things have developed is not to propose that history must be reversed. The call is not for a "return to go" but for a mid-course correction enabled by the insight that the path things have taken has not all been good, or not only good. This midcourse correction is illuminated by the better picture of where they should have gone. The reference of the "radicals" to the early centuries is not made with a view to undoing the passage of time but with a view to properly reorienting our present movement forward in light of what we now know was wrong with the way we had been going before.[6] The truth claims being made by critics of the unfaithfulness into which Christians have fallen through the centuries are therefore not posited upon a vision of some pristine clarity that could be regained by going back to the first century. That is a frequent misconception of what the Protestant Reformation in general and the radical reformation in particular were about. The point is rather that they deny absolute authority to any later epoch, especially to the present, and especially to arrangements which came about in the medieval period through a tacit or explicit relativizing of the normativeness of the incarnation. It is those who believe their own present truths to be the culmination of univocal progress who are unaware of historical relativity and whose truth claims are circular (and usually elitist). The critic whose historical criticism is rooted in the Bible, far from denying the risks of particularity, identifies them by putting the question of faithfulness in historical terms.

This appeal to Scripture as judge over our unfaithfulness came into the classical denominational documents of Protestants out of the dramatic situation of historic schism. That context should not be permitted to make us think that schism is in its normal form. Its normal form is the regular exercise of the office of teacher in the Christian community. It is regularly, and in regular circumstances peaceably the function of the *didaskalos*[7] to serve as the instrument of tense interaction between the community's memory and its contemporary articulation. We must express our faith in terms which make sense to our neighbors in their own language and which face the challenges with which they live. At the same time we must defend that sense-making function against selling out, against cheap conformity, by finding new and newly relevant ways to remind ourselves that it is always the God of Abraham and the Father of Jesus that we are talking about. Ordinarily, when the gift of *didaskalos* is being properly exercised by its bearer and properly received by those it serves, this procedure of reminding and remembering operates in a permanent reciprocity of exchange between the concern for contemporary relevance and the concern for historic community unity.

The appeal to canonical warrant for one's critique provokes division only when some other power in the community has withdrawn itself from the purview of the appeal to Jesus, or when the *didaskalos* has fallen into inflexible modes of articulation. The act of looking back to the origins, which in cases of radical reformation provokes the crystallization of new and independent forms, should normally not take the shape of schism. The proper exercise of the moderating vocation of *episkopos* will normally find ways to let the renewing reminder of our rootage in Jesus be effective without division.[8]

It is thus not a part of the definition of the "radical reformation" position that it should go beyond some other reformation. What is definitional is the ultimate normative claim of the appeal to Jesus. In extreme circumstances, in the face of entrenched apostasy, it is true that the readiness to take the shape of a radical reformation – i.e., the readiness to let the price of faithfulness be expulsion from the established mainstream – may be the test of faithfulness. Yet what matters to the radical reformation position is not its radicality but its Lord. In situations where that appeal to the normativeness of Jesus does not trigger defensive expulsions, the free church has no commitment to schism or to extremism.

Minority Language: Mainstream Voices

I must therefore not label the orientation which I here describe as an updating of something modeled by Peter Chelčický or Pilgram Marpeck or George Fox. Those "radical" positions were worked out by people who had been expelled from the regnant Christian community without a serious hearing. They therefore represented responses to exile as much as they did projections of the shape of the faithful community. I am more interested in finding *within* majority Christianity people who at least begin to ask fundamental questions, even though their being in majority position may keep them from following those questions to their natural conclusions.

Two generations of college students have come to know the heritage of H. Richard Niebuhr mostly through reading his *Christ and Culture.* The book is a most impressive synthetic vision of how the variety of different positions which Christians take all make sense, each in its own place, and how they all need each other, culminating in the best case to be made for the most complex and pluralistic of the five typical orientations. Some whose picture of Richard Niebuhr is the product of that book would be surprised to encounter his 1935 work, *The Church Against the World.*[9]

> The world has always been against the church, but there have been times when the world has been partially converted and when the churches lived with it in some measure of peace; there have been other times when the world was openly hostile, seeking to convert the church. We live, it is evident, in a time of hostility, when the church is imperiled not only by an external worldliness but by one that has established itself within the Christian camp. Our position is inside a church which has been on the retreat and which has made compromises with the enemy in thought, in organization, and in discipline. (p. 1)

> Only a new withdrawal followed by a new aggression can save the church and restore to it the salt with which to savor society. (123ff.)

Niebuhr spoke of the church as being in bondage to idolatry, to capitalism and nationalism and the spirit of class, but also to optimistic humanism, to a too easy identification of the church with worthwhile social causes and valuable human experiences. Companion essays by Wilhelm Pauck and Francis Miller elaborated further the critique of the liberal identification of the church with worthy causes and human self-fulfillment.

This call to the church to rediscover an identity of her own, independent of the support of the world, as the prerequisite of a renewed validity in contributing to the world, did not mean a call to reach back to some earlier phase of Protestant integrity. These writers were neither "evangelical" nor "neo-orthodox." Niebuhr, Pauck, and Miller wrote from within the mainstream of institutionally coopera-tive, intellectually and socially liberal Protestants. It is perhaps partly for that reason that their witness has been forgotten. The academic and ecclesiastical perspective of responsibility from which these men wrote is nonetheless noteworthy: Niebuhr had been president of a de-nominational college and was now teaching ethics at a divinity school; Pauck was an immigrant Reformation historian interpreting the con-temporary crisis in European Protestantism in order to throw light on the American experience; Miller wrote from twenty years' experi-ence in the World Student Christian Movement. They could together say that the church must begin by affirming an identity not derived from or tailored for a contribution to society, but by getting ready to speak to and for the world from a stance independent of the estab-lished institutions into which churches had previously been drawn.

A decade later John C. Bennett provided a pluralistic synthesis somewhat like *Christ and Culture*. Bennett's book[10] describes five dif-ferent social strategies, among which the fifth is the most adequate, the most flexible, and the least clearly defined. Yet somewhat inde-pendently of that discussion of ethical orientations toward society as a whole, Bennett also restates a distinctive vision for the church as community. The church, he says, should be

> a base for operation in a world that is still alien . . . an ethical
> laboratory . . . to push further in the realization of Christian goals
> for human life than can be done in society at large . . . a school
> to train for dual citizenship . . . and a voice of criticism that con-
> tinues to sound when most other voices have been silenced. (90f.)

Richard Niebuhr never wrote his next book about the church against the world. One can even argue that his pluralistic typology later in *Christ and Culture* was his apology for backing away from so decisive a judgmental stance, or for not having found a church to fit that vision.

Similarly the later published work of John C. Bennett was not de-voted to working out more fully his vision of the church as commu-nity over against the world. It cannot be said that he retreated from that affirmation, but it was most of the time not his calling to be sharpening it.[11]

The following summary can best be understood as an effort to for-mulate what Bennett and Niebuhr might have said if they had gone further in the direction projected in the texts here cited. Niebuhr,

Pauck, and Miller say on the grounds of theological integrity that if the church testifies to a God who is other than or more than our best common sense, then she must stand over against the world and the world's wisdom. Bennett says that if the things the church wants to help Christians to do in the wider society, and to help the wider society to do for itself, are to have direction and integrity, there must be an empirical body of people who help one another define and fulfill the concrete social meaning of their loyalty to Jesus Christ. That logic is intrinsically authentic, whether or not the people testifying to it have been led by it into ecclesiastical separation. How would they have fleshed out such beginnings?

We know that it is congruent with the radical ecclesiology to be nonviolent in a violent world, and not to take its signals from consensus. What more can be said of its style?

THE WEIGHT OF WEAKNESS

The believing community as an empirical social entity is a power for change. To band together in common dissidence provides a kind of social leverage which is not provided by any other social form. The subordinate community with its own internal covenants is able to provide economic and social as well as moral support to individuals standing with it against the stream who could not stand alone.

1. There is the psychic or moral support of knowing that others see it my way.
2. There is the psychic support of others who are up when I am down, to protect the activist from indispensability.
3. There is the far more concrete support of social security and survivor's aid. The early Hutterian and Quaker missionaries were courageous in risking their lives overseas because they knew that if they did not return their loved ones would be taken care of.[12]
4. A special form of psychic support is helping us to live up to our stated goals. If I have secretly told myself, in the face of some challenge, that I will go this far and no farther, and then the challenge pushes me a little farther, I may, if I am standing alone, give in a little more. If, however, I have covenanted with you to go no farther than that, our solidarity will augment my power to resist. This is the psychic power of Alcoholics Anonymous; why should it not also guard against other intoxications?
5. People who because of their dissent are driven from home or live-

lihood or land can find a refuge if there is a wider supporting community.

6. Dissenters support one another in opposition in such a way that their combined power of resistance is far more than the sum of the resistance potential of each member taken separately. When one leader is "burned out" the others are rested. When one is shot down another can step into her place. No one of them needs to carry the whole burden of responsibility alone. What modern analysis calls the division of labor and the New Testament calls the diversity of gifts makes the organism as a whole more efficient in each function than if each individual were seeking alone to do all it takes to stand against the stream. Thus the plurality of members of the body provides not simply more strength quantitatively but more skills and special contributions qualitatively.

7. When the powers of evil are for a time so successful that all resistance seems to be crushed, it is from the ranks of that community, just now bludgeoned into quiescence, that will come another generation's prophets, in their time.

First Fruits

The alternative community discharges a modeling mission. The church is called to be now what the world is called to be ultimately. To describe their own community Jews and Christians have classically used terms like those claimed by the structures of the wider world: "people," "nation," "kingdom," even "army." These are not simply poetic figures of speech. They imply the calling to see oneself as doing already on behalf of the wider world what the world is destined for in God's creative purpose. The church is thus not chaplain or priest to the powers running the world: she is called to be a microcosm of the wider society, not only as an idea, but also in her function. Let us look at some examples:

1. The church undertakes pilot programs to meet previously unmet needs or to restore ministries which have collapsed. The church is more able to experiment because not all ministries need to pay off. She can take the risk of losing or failing, more than can those who are in charge of the state. Popular education, institutionalized medicine, and the very concept of dialogical democracy in the Anglo-Saxon world generalize patterns which were first of all experimented with and made sense of in free-church Christianity.

2. The church represents a pedestal or a subculture in which some truths are more evidently meaningful and some lines of logic can be more clearly spelled out than in society as a whole. The credibility and the comprehensibility of an alternative vision which does not always convince on the part of an individual original or "prophetic" person, is enormously more credible and comprehensible if it is tested, confirmed, and practiced by a community. This theme will be treated under another heading later.

3. The church exemplifies what has come to be called "sacramentality," which means that meanings which make sense on an ordinary level make more of the same kind of sense when they are embedded in the particular history of the witness of faith. Catholics now talk about the existence of the church as itself a "sacrament," in the sense that the church represents the kind of society that all of society ought to be. The church is able to be that because of the presence in her midst of witness and empowerment which are not in the same way accessible to the wider society. Sometimes this sacramental quality is read in the direction of saying about the church what one says about the rest of society. For instance, if in society we believe in the rights of employees, then the church should be the first employer to deal with workers fairly. If in the wider society we call for the overcoming of racism or sexism or materialism, then the church should be the place where that possibility first becomes real.

More striking and more concrete cases of "sacramentality" can be developed if we look at those specific activities which the church has more traditionally called "sacraments." Here the logic flows the other way; from what the sacrament means to what the world should be.

a. The Eucharist originally was and could again become an expression not only of the death of Christ for our sins but also of the sharing of bread between those who have and those who have not.
b. Baptism could again come to be, as it was in the New Testament, the basis of Christian egalitarianism, in the face of which male and female, barbarian and cultured, slave and free, etc., are all ascribed the same dignity.
c. The process of binding and loosing – i.e., deliberative morally accountable dialogue, dealing with offense and forgiveness (and thereby dealing with moral discernment) – may recover the connection with forgiveness and with decision-making which "church discipline" lost when it came to be tied with formal excommunication and the sanctions of hierarchical authority.

4. The church can be a foretaste of the peace for which the world was made. It is the function of minority communities to remember and to create utopian visions. There is no hope for society without an awareness of transcendence. Transcendence it kept alive not on the grounds of logical proof to the effect that there is a cosmos with a hereafter, but by the vitality of communities in which a different way of being keeps breaking in here and now. That we can really be led on a different way is the real proof of the transcendent power which offers hope of peace to the world as well. Nonconformity is the warrant for the promise of another world. Although immersed in this world, the church by her way of being represents the promise of another world, which is not somewhere else but which is to come here. That promissory quality of the church's present distinctiveness is the making of peace, as the refusal to make war is her indispensible negative transcendence.

If One Is in Christ, the World Is New

The church cultivates an alternative consciousness. Another view of what the world is like is kept alive by narration and celebration which fly in the face of some of the "apparent" lessons of "realism."

1. The experience of isolation/oppression/suffering/powerlessness, when it is experienced together, in a situation where acquiring the power of establishment is not possible, or not desirable morally, renews the community in its awareness that it is nonetheless worthwhile to go on living. One experiences the spirituality of *The Desert is Fertile*[13] and the long history of spiritual and material poverty as a respectable way to be human. One learns empathy for others who are also victims; one learns to understand the power game from below and to see how different it looks from there.

2. A sign or a fruit of the creativity of the spirit is genuine innovation, surprise and paradox in the ways one learns to see reality, as over against the monolinear "realism" of the established power system.

a. One learns to trust in the power of weakness. There are some kinds of strength involved in being weak, or in accepting weakness, or in facing the facts which make one weak.

b. One learns to see through the weakness of power. The ability to achieve one's goals may constitute bondage, or an obstacle to the genuine freedom to achieve what one thought oneself able to do. With too large a weapon one cannot even reach one's enemies.

3. There is an alternative narrative. It is not merely that minority peoples tell stories and majority people don't tell stories, although that is in fact often the case. The believing community has a longer sense of history past and future than do their oppressors, or than majorities unaware of alternatives to their own world. They also see the same facts differently. They do not assume that the only way to read national and political history is from the perspective of the winners. To remember that in every battle there was another side, and sometimes that there were more people on the other side and sometimes more worthy causes, sustains a different understanding of how we want to help history move.

The creative potential of alternative narrative does not only throw a new light on the majority story. Also on "our side," things could have gone differently: we may discern in the minority experience absences of creativity or shortness of will, impatience or evil will, so that the story as it is told is a subject for repentance and not merely remembering, for making amends as well as for giving thanks. A repentant view of history is more creative than a eulogistic one.

4. There is reason for hoping when there is no reason to hope. In Christendom, both optimism and despair are correlated with the direct reading of how it is going for us in the rising and falling of power structures. The minority community reads these events otherwise, if not simply contrariwise. When things seem to be going well, they refuse to trust the rosiest promises, knowing how deeply embedded in human optimism are the seeds of pride and how easily when welcoming what we think to be good news we miss part of the picture and plan wrongly. That all seems to be going badly is not grounds to abandon hope, not only because we have heard promises "from beyond the system," but also because we have learned that sometimes our pessimistic readings of the present are shadowed too much by taking some setback too seriously.

It is then not merely a matter of there existing a perspective from which occasionally to see things differently: it is that the minority community provides a training ground for cultivating the concrete expectation that things will usually be seen inadequately by those who read events from a posture of control or of seeking to control. Thus we educate ourselves in the reasonable expectation that when we see things differently from others, we will often be seeing them more truly.

What is called "consciousness" is far more than a different set of ideas or of assumptions; it is also style and skills. The minority community, through its ordinary social process and its rituals of reconciliation, through its dialogue and disputations, is an arena for training in conflict resolution and in the search for truth.

SERVANT STRENGTH

There are other ways to do Christian ethics than to ask, "How can we help to move the total social system?" When Christians count among their number a monarch, or the majority in a democratic system, or a sizable and significant minority in a pluralistic democratic system, it can be practically taken for granted that one way, perhaps the only right way to do moral deliberation is to work out a consequentialist calculation of the direction one wants the whole social system to take. For a small minority such calculation would be an irrelevant or at best utopian way of looking at things.

This is the particle of truth in the idea, given considerable currency since Max Weber, that an ethic of rules will be unconcerned for the results to be expected from a given line of action. In that perspective it might even be taken as a sign of unfaithfulness that one should give as much attention as this study does to how the minority ethic "really works." Concern for effectiveness, we are told, is only fitting for those who can live up to that concern by actually managing the world. True obedience to suffering love must therefore presuppose that one disavows concern for results.

Seldom would the advocate of this Weberian patter of division recognize that it is itself based upon the establishment perspective. Only the person who believes that the "responsible use of power" from a position of domination is necessary in order to be useful will then presuppose that the alternative is moral purity at the price of ineffectiveness.

Then there may well be dimensions of effectiveness to a minority position even though its logic works on other levels:

1. A minority group with no immediate chance of contributing to the way things go may still by its dissent maintain the wider community's awareness of some issues in such a way that ideas which are unrealistic for the present come to be credible later. This is the American record for such matters as Social Security, which was quite un-

thinkable when first of all commended by the American Socialist Norman Thomas and then became a possibility for a majority party to implement.

Minority groups can also exercise pioneering creativity in places where no one is threatened. They can do jobs nobody else is interested in doing, and thereby gradually draw attention to some realm of social need for which it would have been impossible to find an imposed solution. An example of this is the variety of recent exploratory visions developed by minority agencies in the realm of ministries to victims and offenders. The presence on the stage of a very different position, even if not a possible model to be imposed as official policy by a majority, or even to be negotiated by a sizable minority in a coalition situation, still does change the total spectrum of positions, and thereby moves the balance point of the system.

2. Integrity and consistency are good policy in the long run, despite the fact that in the short run exceptions often seem to be justified. Quaker merchants in the eighteenth century progressed in merchandizing because of fair prices and good products, even though their prices were sometimes higher than those of others. Quakers as employers developed better relationships with employees, including forerunners of modern visions of worker involvement in management and profit sharing, so that the work quality was greater than that of other employees, even though these better wages and employee rights represented an initial competitive disadvantage to the Quaker employer. The Protestant work ethic, although more demanding than other styles of productive organization, turns out to be more efficient in productivity for all parties involved. The conviction that one's morality and social style are expressive of a transcendent commitment and not just of consequential calculation (i.e., what some call an ethic of "principle"), contributes to the holding power of individuals in the face of short-range conflict and opposition and protects against giving up the battle or "burning out," standard temptations to those whose reason for doing good is too closely correlated to manageable projections of effect. The support of a group reinforces social reliability, enabling people to stand against the stream in the face of short-range ineffectiveness until longer-range factors have time to work.

3. In yet one other way a morality based on principle has a special moral power. In most cultures there is some such thing as a public conscience or public opinion. Moral rhetoric has a kind of sacramental effect before the public at large, in both democratic and totalitarian

cultures. The hard-nosed political realist can always say that moral rhetoric is not binding or convincing, yet it still tends to have some power of conviction to ordinary people. In the context of Anglo-Saxon democracy it has far more power than that, reaching in fact to the point where a Gandhi, a King, or a Chavez can call forth a special new kind of social power by appealing symbolically to the idealism of the majority culture's moral language.

4. If we have learned to step back from the preoccupation with the kind of measurement of effectiveness that expects results tomorrow by virtue of seizing control today, we can discern other kinds of "utility" which previously were either taken for granted without attention being given to them, or depreciated or ignored.

One thing that minorities learn to do is to survive: i.e., to provide for the presence a decade or a generation later of the alternative options for which there was no hearing this year or last. They can do this because their grounds for holding to what they believe have been conceived of in a way needing no ratification by present acclamation or success.

5. Whereas both democracy and demagoguery would have us believe that the course of events is determined by "the people" as a majority, social and political realists know that most societies are divided in such a way that the reality of the decision process under the surface, whether in totalitarian or "free" countries, is a matter of bargaining and brokering among fractions. A minority faith community is more able to maintain a strong bargaining posture in such a mix than all those fractions whose identity is determined only by ideology or by group interest. The advantage of American life is that such fraction politics, especially in our major metropolitan centers, is out in the open, so that we can see that some groups do that negotiating shrewdly and others clumsily. The faith community has both the cultural and normative wherewithal to make that fractional bargaining constructive and honest, and the internal cohesion to keep its leaders accountable and its bargaining goals realistic. A faith community differs as well from other pressure groups in that, without denying an element of self-centered bias and interest, it is able to claim that its social goals are in the interest of others. This is dramatically visible for the Quaker involvement in corrections and abolition in early America, or for the Jewish involvement in civil liberties in our time.

6. I have already noted how a minority community can appeal to the conscience of society at large and call it to outdo itself occasion-

ally in moral commitment. Another way in which a minority can be the conscience of a society is to continue to voice the claims of unrepresented peoples and causes, when they do not yet have the ear or the heart of the majority. A minority may do for a society what the conscience does for an individual. A current example is visible in the field of "corrections." Insightful minorities are telling our society that what we are doing with offenders is counterproductive, even when no one has ready the outlines of a better solution. If truth were left·to a market philosophy, there would be no point in continuing to make an argument for which there are no takers, or to ask a question for which there are no answers. The minority community has other grounds to sustain a wholesome discomfort and thereby keeps the door open for solutions not yet found.

In these ways, and in others which could be spelled out at greater length by more sophisticated interpreters, a position which is not justified on the grounds of calculating effectiveness will turn out in the long run to be more effective than one which at every step along the way is the object of a cost/benefit calculation. This only seems paradoxical.

It is therefore a misperception when radicals, responding to the way issues have been put by Tolstoy and by Niebuhr, tend to concede that this ethic of "obedience" sacrifices "effectiveness." It does reject some ways of deriving ethics from effectiveness calculation, but it represents a commitment to and not against long and broad usefulness. It is ready in extreme either/or cases to place clear moral obligation above calculable short-range utility, but so is any other serious ethical system. This is not to grant that apparent calculable short-range utility is sufficiently knowable and even such a "crunch choice" is a clear case of duty versus ends.[14]

LET IT BE

It is difficult to find a label for the next category of description which must be condensed here. One might call it "acquiescence." Minority perspective makes more nuanced the vocabulary of moral evaluation. This is one of the points of most profound difficulty in dialogue between majority and minority people.

In a majority situation the normal expression of "responsibility," by those who hold power, and who believe they have been given it by God, is to work to approximate a coincidence between what is right and what really happens. Right behavior is sanctioned positively, wrong behavior is sanctioned negatively, with the degree of rigor depending on the size of the offense and the degree of need to prevent it or compensate for it. The only elements left unregulated are those concerning which there is either honest ignorance or acceptable difference of opinion, or concerning which no means of enforcement can be found proportionate to the weight of the principle at stake. In this situation, then, any morally aware person associated with the majority that has power is seen as being in more than an accessory sense "responsible" (i.e., accountable) for everything that happens. To let something happen by inaction is *practically* as grave as to do it oneself, since it is presumed that one could have stopped it. To let something happen is therefore also *morally* the same as doing it oneself. Not stopping Hitler is the same as helping him.

The entire landscape looks different from a position of weakness. If you could not have stopped something, then you are not to blame when it happens. A set of both logical and psychological differences arises from that. No longer have we simply the two categories of "right" which we must foster or even enforce, and "wrong" which we must prohibit and punish. Between the clean categories a host of other gradations arise. These are not the same as the moral gradations in the Niebuhrian scheme, where the persons who are responsible find their unselfishness mixed with self-interest and their servanthood to others diluted with pragmatic realism: that is still a modulation within doing the morally right thing.

In a situation of majority control, if something happens it is because you let it happen and you are to blame for it, even for results which are partly evil. Reinhold Niebuhr was more frank than his predecessors had been about the fact that some of the things you believe you have to take responsibility for are harmful or hurtful to others and are to some degree selfish. Yet he was still able to claim that on balance a particular expression of hurtfulness and selfishness was the best available choice, everything considered, for the sake of the whole community. Thus it would be a positive expression of moral responsibility to use whatever violence and self-interest is necessary to bring about the least evil outcome.

There are evils which minority agents cannot prevent which are not thereby condoned as "right." There are sins which is it not possible or desirable to treat as crimes, even if one had the kind of majority status that would permit making the laws. One major American experience in this respect was with prohibition. There are also voices today suggesting that drug abuse, like adult homosexuality and heterosexual adultery, like most of the other deadly sins (gluttony, sloth, avarice, pride . . .) could not properly be dealt with in the courts even if there were a majority to declare them worthy of civil punishment.

There are things which we cannot control, which nonetheless are going to happen, which are going to impinge upon the situation where we ourselves are trying to do something else. This means that it will be an expression of wisdom, and not of self-righteousness or unconcern or isolation, if we accept the fact that those deeds are going to be done and that we cannot stop them, and concentrate for ourselves on doing other things which no one will do. This looks to our friends of a majoritarian cast of mind like acquiescence in evil. It is; one of the differences between being powerful and powerless is that one has thought more about the fact that there are evils one cannot prevent.

The entire calculation of responsibilities is different in a situation where one disposes of no capacity to impose one's preference. One will not claim that the result of one's not intervening effectively is the least evil possible but only that, since the situation is decisively controlled by other powers, one does the best one can to serve as can be served and save what can be saved in a bad situation. In that context most pacifists accept the fact that nonpacifists will be running the world violently. They interlock their own rejection of violence with the knowledge that others will keep on killing and coercing. The reckoning of what it takes to bring about desired results is disconnected from realistic short-term measurements of feasibility. Instead of asking about one's action, "if I do this how will it tip the scale . . . ?", one rather asks, "in a situation where I cannot tip the scales, on what other grounds might I decide what to do?"

BACK TO TRUE NORTH

The imperatives of dialogue with majority mentalities have skewed this description toward the problematics of weakness and effectiveness. An authentic portrayal of "the peace church vision" from the inside would have spoken more of worship and servanthood, reconciliation and creativity, *Gelassenheit* and the Power of the Light, "heartfelt religion" and transforming hope, and the person of Jesus Christ. But if this paper had been thus affirmative then the reader would have wondered why any of that should be "sectarian."

PART II

History

5. Radical Reformation Ethics in Ecumenical Perspective[1]

In the broadest sense a "free church" is any ecclesiastical body which does not enjoy the institutional support of, or control by, the organs of civil government. This is the ordinary British usage. However, when disestablishment is the definition, the utility of this definition to determine the character of the church or of the ethics derived therefrom is not very precise. The Presbyterians are a free church in England and the Anglicans in Scotland.

It is thus more functional to ask for a stronger definition, one which will make of disestablishment not simply an acceptable accidental trait but an affirmative definition. A *doctrine* of the church, according to which it would be wrong for it to be supported and governed by civil government, begins to take on additional substance as defining what it means for a church to be free. Even this position can be adopted in our age by communions which would not have accepted it in their classical periods. Catholicism adopts this position with conviction in America, but not in Alsace. Most Lutherans and Presbyterians would hold to this view with conviction today in North America, but the opposite was the conviction of Luther and Calvin.

Thus we have not made the definition an instrument of meaningful discrimination until we push one degree further and say that a free church is one in which membership is voluntary. This is the functional meaning presupposed and advocated by Franklin H. Littell, prolific pioneer author in the field twenty years ago.[2] This insistence on meaningful membership based upon voluntary adult decision can be expressed in either of two natural forms. One natural expression is to make baptism contingent on an informed, articulate confession of faith by the one baptized, which means the rejection of infant baptism. Another alternative is that effective membership is contingent upon a further experience or ceremony of instruction and commitment, whether considered sacramentally as confirmation or not. This may occur in Methodist or Reformed or Lutheran churches, especially when confirmation is linked with a notion of personal decision or conversion, as has been the case in some of those traditions since the age of Pietism, or with substantial catechesis.[3]

Instead of continuing progressively to narrow the definition of what I am supposed to be talking about by extending the enumeration of distinctives and thereby decreasing the radius of the circle enclosing the remaining relevant sample, I propose now to leap across the remaining scale of differentiae and to begin to state the heart of the definition toward which the shrinking circles were leading us.

Setting aside the assigned identity label "free church" as too broad and flexible, I shall rather resort, despite some of its shortcomings, to the label "radical reformation," as representative of a genuinely distinctive vision of what the church is about in the world. This view is most thoroughly worked out in the thought and experience of the Swiss Brethren among the Anabaptists of the sixteenth century and among the Quakers and Baptists arising out of seventeenth-century Puritanism. Before that, only slightly less clear formulations can be encountered in the Waldenses and the Czech Brethren. Later there are radical pietists, several kinds of groups called "Brethren," and the Disciples. The label "radical reformation" has been given currency by Professor George H. Williams of Harvard Divinity School.[4]

When these groups are talked about as one form of "reformation," it means that they deny that the faithfulness of Christian community can be defined adequately and without remainder in terms of organic institutional continuity.

There needs to be (or once needed to be) a reformation. This means that historic Christianity has fallen short of faithfulness, and that there is some other criterion (most centrally Scripture) whereby the shape of the Christian life should be reformed. This is something of course which all Protestants and many Catholics believe in some way or other. But the mainstream of the Protestant Reformation concentrated its call for reform on selected matters of faith and order, which were deemed to be of predominant importance for the salvation of souls and the validity of churchly practice while retaining many of the marks, especially ethical, of what established Christianity had become. The Lutheran, Reformed, and Anglican reformations retained infant baptism, which identified an entire population with the church. They retained (or rather established more strongly than before) the control of the church by civil authority. They retained the compulsory membership in the church of all but Jews, and retained as well the approbation of the violence of civil government within the doctrine of the just war.

The groups called "radical reformers" carried the initial reformation vision through to reject as well these indices of the post-Constantinian synthesis. Thereby they changed not simply the definition of certain ministries or churchly practices, but also the entire understanding of what it means to be Christian, and consequently also of how the body of believers relates to the powers of this world. Obviously this must have profound implications for the structure and content of ethics.

Our focus upon ethics dispenses us from fuller analysis of the other ways in which radical reformation ecclesiology is incommensurate with the other streams. Majority ecumenism is accustomed to using contrasts and convergences among traditions as "handles" for negotiation toward greater unity, but that is to make assumptions about the unity we seek and how to seek it which are themselves part of the debate.[5]

I begin with a matter of ethical content so as to work back from there to distinctive logical criteria. The fallenness by virtue of which it is held that the church is in need of radical reformation is not merely an accumulation of a series of unrelated mistakes but a fundamental flaw of structure and strategy. The church of the Middle Ages had come to be marked by the alliance of the clergy with the sword, with wealth, and with hierarchy. Some would group these three marks of violence, money, and social stratification under the broader heading of "power," but such shorthand would cause us trouble if we took it too seriously.

The issue of power as a spiritual temptation had already been discerned by ancient Israel. In the New Testament "mammon" and "the sword" were clearly identified and renounced by the teachings and example of Jesus and the apostles. The church after Constantine reversed the New Testament attitude toward these matters and thereby changed the very nature of what it means to be church.[6] The official Reformation of Luther and Zwingli made significant changes, but did not fundamentally reverse the structural decisions of the age of Constantine. The radical reformers restored the New Testament standards as their goal.[7] Wealth, they held, is to be dealt with by sharing and simplicity of life. The sword is to be avoided by believers and left, as in the New Testament times, in the hands of pagan Caesars. Believers are to be equal within the body. The ethical issues are at the heart of what we differ about. They need not be derived from some deep insight into metaphysical method or from a general doctrine of nature and grace: ethical dissent is itself the subject matter, the agenda of reformation.

Obviously, the ethical analyst can demonstrate after the fact that these distinctive ethical commitments do have presuppositional correlates which may be clearly identified and stated theologically. A different ethic obviously involves the possibility of a different doctrine of humanity, of Christology, or of nature, of sin or grace or law. I am therefore not saying that there was not always a theological dimension to free-church origins, or even that the integrity of theology and ethics was any less coherent with the radical reformers than with others (one might discuss whether the criteria of "coherence" would be the same in all traditions). I am making the descriptive, formal observation that ethical agenda have a different place in the debate. The difference between Lutheran and Calvinist confessions or between Anglican and Roman confessions in the sixteenth century does not focus on any significant ethical differences. The debates between the Anabaptists and all those others did include ethical differences at the surface. Those ethical differences were debated for their own sakes, not simply derived deductively from intellectual struggles with the implications of prior systematic commitments formulated by intellectuals.

A Different Mood and Method

From the perspective I represent there should not have to be one particular answer to the classic method questions about the status of the law, the status of institutions, the nature of information about obligation, valid catholicity, valid secularity, or a doctrine of creation or of human nature. For more academically oriented ethical traditions those concerns came to matter very much, but in free-church tradition they were of little interest.

What I say here about self-conscious attention to formal matters of ethical method is parallel to what I suggested above about doctrinal issues. Obviously, if we were to analyze the reasoning processes of free-church preachers and teachers, we could not avoid identifying specific types of arguments that could be so classified as to constitute answers to the classical questions that ethicists always discuss. It is still significant that, as distinguishable from the ethical thinkers in the majority traditions just referred to, free-church preachers and teachers tend not to be self-conscious in the first generation about how they make those intellectual moves, and the people who do offer ethical instruction are not regularly the experts in those techniques.

What is of interest is far less the question of how ethical obligation is to be formulated and far more the question of whether or not one is going to obey the Lord who commands. The radical reformers differed with their mainstream contemporaries not so much about what Jesus said but about whether it was to be taken simply and seriously as moral guidance. A "catholic" perspective, out of concern for patience with the immature and the weak, has often tended to distinguish between minimal "precepts" to be expected of everyone and "evangelical counsels" for the spiritually heroic, with the more striking teachings of Jesus falling in the latter category. A certain kind of popular Lutheranism (not exactly what the early Luther had called for) was so preoccupied with the need to recognize that we are always and remain always sinners, that any attention to decision-making in a mood of responsibility to do what we were told seemed presumptuous, and it had to be rejected on the grounds that it would jeopardize the gratuitousness of justification.

A certain Calvinist vision would limit the realm of applicability of Jesus' commands by placing them within a larger framework, consisting (historically) of the abiding binding force of theocratic social models from the age of Israel's kings and (conceptually) of the "vocational" guidance derived from the relatively autonomous "orders of Creation."

Thus, in each of the best known classic cases, the debate was not about the right thing Jesus or the apostles say we should do, nor about the meaningfulness of ethical discourse. It was about whether to do what we are told or how serious it would be if we did not, and how one's status in the Christian community was correlated with obeying or failing to obey.[8] It will thus be part of the nature of things, and not a result of clumsiness or a surprise, that my giving account of my community tradition will fail to mesh with the analogous services of my colleagues. We shall not find ourselves agreeing about what the questions are to which we have divergent answers.

Instead of getting lost in an attempt to sketch a broad outline of many ethical issues, the historian can easily identify two simple controversies which are the most representative of the challenge addressed by the radical reformation tradition (for it is also a tradition) to the majority churches. First, with regard to the meaning of membership in the Christian community, there is the ethical import of the insistence that church membership must be voluntary. This means that we cannot do ethics for everyone. The obedience of faith does not make sense apart from the context of faith. The substantial guidance, the experiential and social resources of conversion and membership are presupposed for it to be possible to speak of one's behavior as expressive of faith and obedience. Cross-bearing in the hope of resurrection, enemy-love as reflection of God's love, forgiving as one has been forgiven, behavior change describable as expressing regeneration or sanctification, do not make sense in the context of unbelief.

Of course there is still a sense in which the Christian community can and must "do ethics for the world," i.e., cooperate in ethical discourse beyond the borders of faith, or in language not dependent on faith. But that is a different kind of discourse from the ethical deliberation of the believing community. Such discourse beyond the bounds of faith may differ in its conclusions about the propriety of certain kinds of action which would be excluded from integral Christian discipleship but would be less easily excluded from the wider society in which faith in the crucified and risen Lord is not affirmed. I can, for instance, expect pacifism of a fellow believer who is committed to the same Lord, as I cannot expect it of other fellow citizens in a value-pluralistic nation. To see what that difference means for ethics would call for extended exposition.[9] All I am saying here is that it makes a structural contribution to the ethical discussion to insist on distinguishing between the voluntary obedience of believers and other kinds of ethical discourse in which a personal confession of commitment to discipleship cannot be presupposed. The latter become necessary where the church has taken on the mission of doing ethics for everyone.

To say that the church, being constituted voluntarily, is a distinctive kind of society is a formal observation in two senses of the word. It is "formal" in that it talks about the structure of Christian ethical reasoning and in that it talks about the shape of the Christian community. This is what is capsuled in the alternative label used since Max Weber to describe this tradition, "the believers' church."

The other distinctive mark has to do with the substance of ethics and consists in the rejection of violence, most categorically (since the word "violence" has a dozen meanings today) of killing one's fellow human beings. This is no place to argue for its own sake the issue of violence and pacifism. I am simply agreeing with the historians for whom it has become a prototypical issue, so much so that the radical reformation churches are also sometimes called "historic peace churches."[10]

For our purposes it is not an unfair reduction to concentrate on these two prototypical issues of membership and violence. Yet they are not exclusive issues. Behind the issue of the meaning of baptism and membership in the community there lurks a long agenda of further differences: the meaning of the Eucharist, the form of moral discipline, the status of clerical ministries and the laity, the status of supracongregational offices and assemblies, etc. Behind the difference on the question of violence as well there is a longer series: truth telling and the swearing of oaths, property ownership and accumulation, the use of even nonviolent civil power for selfish purposes. It would thus be improper to describe minority churches as making a hobby of a single issue or two. The choice of those single issues on each level, which made of them later the marks of dissident minorities, was made when the majority church in the age of the Constantinian shift chose to forsake earlier precedents at those points while maintaining earlier views on other matters. The selectivity with regard to issues on which to lay corrective emphasis, by which the radical churches later came to be identified, is the response to an earlier selection by the Constantinian churches of issues on which to forsake the pre-Constantinian ethic.

The Handicap of the Minority Conversational Stance

Since the radical view only comes to be formulated in a debating context where convictions diverge about how renewal should proceed, the historian does not encounter this view standing alone or beginning from scratch or taking full responsibility for a total culture. For some, it may be a weakness that this view therefore cannot be set forth as if it were standing alone as easily as the other views. It tends to come into being as a reaction against inclusivist religion. Thus the most representative marks of this position are those which are provoked by its stance over against others. I do not know to what extent a Roman Catholic view needs the Eastern Orthodox alternative to make itself clear or vice versa, or the extent to which Presbyterianism needs Catholicism to explain itself. The distinctiveness of the "radical" view does include accounting for the "mainstream" alternative which it argues against. In the formative past events, this challenge addressed to mainstream alternatives was far-reaching and costly. These views came to be borne by separate ecclesiastical bodies only because people who held them were forced out of larger bodies.

This leaves open a serious question for a more ecumenical age. Our divided denominational situation is the product of a period when it was assumed that church organizations should be ethically unified. Ethical dissenters were expelled, or they withdrew. Many church leaders would no longer proceed that way, but it has not yet become clear what the alternative would be, how ethical diversity can be tolerated without schism yet also without debilitating pluralism or thoughtless majority dominance. If the specific witness which in the past has led these groups to be rejected and expelled is no longer to encounter that sanction from the custodians of mainstream authority, i.e., if dissent is no longer persecuted, what might be the nonseparatist form which those concerns would then take? Could the same ethical commitments be lived by a community that would not be rejected by other communities? How would a different way of dealing with that problem differ? Can a pacifist position be taken within a nonpacifist church without its representatives being either expelled or told they must accept not being heard? If they are told that the price of their remaining in a larger body which no longer expels them is their acceptance of not being heard, would that be ecumenical unity? If the larger body gives their view a free hearing, would this include rescinding the normativeness of the commitment to the just war tradition? If not, then the separatism is not only on the side of the minority.[11]

There was, of course, one time when the ethical orientation referred to here as the free-church view was dominant among Christians, or at least among those Christian teachers of whom we have record. This was the church of the first three centuries. Here there were divisions and divergences among Christians, but with regard to the morality of violence, the oath, wealth, and high imperial office the views in the ancient literature were largely those which were renewed by the Anabaptists and Quakers. This is an indication that it is possible for this ethical position to exist without being a reaction to some other, dominant form of Christianity.

In this pattern of standing over against other traditions, which I have characterized as historically largely inevitable, although unwarranted, one finds that some of the traditional keys which were of importance to interpret other systems are not much help. In the Lutheran context the interrelation of the levels or dimensions of law and gospel is very important to understand the location of ethics within the life of faith. That is of less help in our context, since the voluntary quality of the commitment of those in the community for whom we are doing ethical deliberation means that there is no moral guidance that is not of the gospel. But the relationship of morality to the person and work and teachings of Jesus also means that there is no gospel which does not have the form of Torah, i.e., of necessarily calling for and enabling specific commitment in the style of moral relations (which other Christian groups do not hold to in the same way).

A mainstream Catholic tradition, being concerned to give account of the way in which the values of non-Christian reason are gathered up in a "catholic" synthesis, will be concerned to give account of the relations of nature and supernature or nature and grace. I am still willing to be shown that this distinction is helpful at the point of providing moral guidance. It may well be illuminating as a principle of classification and description. The morality of discipleship would be classified by some as a morality against or above "nature." Others would claim it to be most natural. How we classify it is neither here nor there, as long as one is clear that discipleship is what God asks of those who confess Jesus as Lord.

A Detour Concerning Logic

Just as the radical stance cannot step out of past conversation and avoid relating to Catholic or Lutheran or Enlightenment alternatives, so also one must respond to the way in which academic practitioners of ethics sharpen our ability to identify specific styles of logic as correlated with or representative of specific religious traditions. Is Christian ethics deontological, practicing certain virtues and avoiding certain vices, doing good deeds and eschewing bad ones without claiming to calculate the consequences? Is it characterial, locating goodness or badness in a way of being whose effect on behavior is not to be boiled down only to deeds? Is it teleological, whereby deeds have no specific moral quality of their own, except as they contribute to moving the total social system toward good or bad ends? Or do Christians evaluate only the heart, so that whatever is done out of love is the right thing to do?

My response at this point must be twofold. As an ethicist, I am not convinced that these categories are helpful for anyone in any tradition. They almost necessarily suggest that it would be possible to do ethics with one of these dimensions at the cost of all the others. I doubt that this is true in logic or in real human moral experience anywhere. I would say that whatever might be my own ethical convictions, whether they were Catholic or Marxist or chauvinist. But in any case, even if that prejudice of mine on the level of systematic ethics were not acceptable, I must say as a historian that it is not possible to characterize the ethical specificity of the free churches as focused on law or motivation, on character or pragmatism. With regard to the discussions of violence there are those who do believe that the pacifist rejection of violence is legalistic. Yet we have not been shown how an alternative reasoning pattern would work which would explain the necessity of violence without the appeal to some kind of law. Now it may be that the law for the sake of which we need to kill people in the minds of some and the law against killing people according to the conviction of others are laws of different kinds or shapes or styles. But it will not do simply to assume that one is law and the other is not.

That would seem to be a fair sample of a more general observation about the limited value of efforts to reduce substantive moral debates (i.e., differences about what to do) to formal description (e.g., "you are a legalist and I am a situationist," or "I am utilitarian and you are character-oriented"). Serious moral debate only takes place when both available choices are being talked about in the same language, in the same universe of discourse, and by appeal to commensurate warrants. It would thus be fitting to say that each major moral tradition which can be described by a distinct ecclesiastical base has its own deontology, its own utilitarianism, its own characterology—not that one reasons in one idiom and the other in another idiom. Only exceptionally and only on selected topics could the approach which correlates denominations with logical styles be of any use.

For example, at first sight, as I said, many have attempted to argue that pacifism is deontological, whereas the readiness to use violence is utilitarian. To put the question this way however begs two basic questions. What is the cause for the sake of which we must use the violence which is pragmatically justified? That ultimate cause (national sovereignty, political liberties, the lives of the innocent) to which we will sacrifice the lives or the freedom of our adversaries is not itself justified pragmatically.

Nor is the utility calculation nearly so simple as it claims to be on the other side. By categorizing the pacifist as an absolutist, the nonpacifist tends to dispense himself from hard realism in his own case. How do we know that violence will be effective toward the ends which are posited? Has a long enough time frame been allowed? Has there been attention to the possibility that social changes imposed by superior forces are less stable, or that the people living under unfreedom are less productive than when social change is achieved without violence? Has really serious legal process or really serious social science analysis been invested in testing whether the violence one is ready to resort to is really the last resort, and whether there would be no nonviolent alternatives offering a comparable percentage of probability of achieving comparable results? It is generally the pacifists, who are accused of being rigidly deontological, who ask these pragmatic questions more carefully and write studies about "how to do it," and the nonpacifists, who claim to be pragmatic, who leap to the conclusion that "there is no other way."

It seems self-evident from the majority perspective that this kind of moral discernment must lead to a principled withdrawal from the exercise of certain social functions or from "the use of power." It is obvious that the systematic analysis of the advocates of the majority position would make this assumption, so that the choice must appear to be between involvement (which cannot be ultimately critical) and noninvolvement. Then the mainstream tradition chooses involvement. The radical reformation perspective, however, refuses to stand that choice on its head and withdraw, but rather challenges the prior logical analysis. By no means is the exercise of all kinds of economic power contingent upon what Jesus calls the service of mammon. The proclamation of jubilee, the feeding of the poor, the release of prisoners, even the healing of the sick, the economic sharing of the Jerusalem community and the collections of funds in Europe which Paul called *koinonia* and carried back to Jerusalem were all forms of the exercise of economic power. Similarly the exercise of civil power need not be boiled down by definition to the wielding of the sword. A sectarian ethic can, when it has a chance, govern an American colony (William Penn) or can exercise major institution-building pressure and creativity (Gandhi, King, Dolci). Thus to argue that for believers to derive their ethic from Jesus demands that they withdraw from society is petitionary, an argument which follows neither from empirical experience nor from the content of the gospel message, but from the hermeneutic aprioris of the majority traditions.

THE FORMS OF ETHICAL DISCOURSE

What are the axioms of radical reformation ethics? Which of these matters the most will depend on the perspective of the interlocutor. The primary substantial criterion of Christian ethical decisions for the radical reformers is the humanity of Jesus of Nazareth. What he did is the primordial definition of the human obedience which God desires. There are issues concerning which his example gives us no guidance and for which other kinds of wisdom will be indispensable, but at those points where his example is relevant it is also revelatory and is not to be set aside in favor of other criteria.

Jesus was not only a model actor, but he was also a foundational teacher. He thereby incorporated into the body of guidance of which his disciples dispose an accumulation of wisdom which not only is predominantly Jewish in idiom and origin, but also no less Jewish at the points where he differed from some other Jewish traditions. That body of moral wisdom includes notions about nature and human nature, God and God's law, which can of course be classified in several types. General rules such as the love commandment, specific rules such as the prohibition of the oath or adultery, and parabolic examples combine to provide a rich repertory of tools for illuminating moral decision. This excludes any single-issue system, whereby one holds out the promise that once one key theme is struck (law and gospel, or nature and grace, or love and justice, or providence, or creation, or vocation) the rest of ethics will unfold simply, almost deductively.

There would be no memory of Jesus if it had not been for the early communities' recording and interpreting his words in the ongoing process of defining the meaning of obedience in the first-century Mediterranean world. We have in the New Testament canon the ground floor of a few decades' experience. Stretching from then to the present we possess an additional nearly infinite accumulation of applications and interpretation. The extent to which various strata of these traditions can be fruitful for our guidance is a question too complex to unfold here. The radical reformation was with Protestantism in general in claiming that the canonical witness remains the baseline for judging subsequent evolution. Yet it would be a misinterpretation to be led at this point into a simple repetition of the naive sixteenth-century debate about Scripture versus the church.[12]

The knowledge of the meaning for today of participation in the work of Christ is mediated ecclesiastically. The bridge between the words of Jesus or of the apostolic writings and obedience in the present is not a strictly conceptual operation, which could be carried out by a single scholar at his desk, needing only an adequate dictionary and an adequate description of the available action options. The promise of the presence of Christ to actualize a definition of his will in a given future circumstance (i.e., future to Jesus or to the apostolic writers) was given not to professional exegetes but to the community which would be gathered in his name (Matt. 18:19) with the specific purpose of "binding and loosing" (Matt. 18:18). Classical Protestantism tended to deny the place of this conversational process in favor of its insistence on the perspicuity and objectivity of the words of Scripture. Catholicism before that had provoked that extreme Protestant answer by making of this hermeneutical mandate a blank check which the holders of ecclesiastical office could use with relative independence. The free-church alternative to both recognizes the inadequacies of the text of Scripture standing alone uninterpreted, and appropriates the promise of the guidance of the Spirit throughout the ages, but locates the fulfillment of that promise in the assembly of those who gather around Scripture in the face of a given real moral challenge. Any description of the substance of ethical decision-making criteria is incomplete if this aspect of its communitarian and contemporary form is omitted.

A popular slogan which has become operative in the contemporary search to recapture the validity of the radical reformation tradition is the notion of the "hermeneutic community." Finding its expression in 1 Corinthians 14:25ff., the same passage in which Luther and Zwingli both initially rooted their argument in favor of congregationalism (which they later abandoned in practice),[13] the Anabaptists and the later Puritans affirmed that the way God leads is that the Spirit gathers believers around Scripture. The Spirit, the gathering, and the Scripture are indispensable elements of the process. A technical exegete alone in his office could not replace the actual conversational process in empirical communities where the working of the Spirit is discerned in the fact that believers are brought to unity around this Scripture.[14] This "hermeneutic" process of conversation will often not be done with much explicit self-awareness in terms of the styles of ethical discourse or metaethical self-criticism. It is thus not possible, as it is in some of the other traditions, to distill out of the body of ethical teachings a few very broad axioms from which the total system is derived. One could as an ethicist try to formulate such a distillate, but it would be the observer's own concoction and would not be recognized as representative of what really happens when two or three gather and find Christ speaking in their midst.

This gathering process is in one sense a situational ethic. It does not seek advance wisdom on problems not being faced. It takes off immediately from a problem or an offense. In addition to 1 Corinthians 14, the primary textual reference of this approach is Matthew 18:15ff., dealing also with the mandate to act in God's name in the unity of the body, where the immediate occasion is a particular offense.

NEITHER WAX NOSE NOR EMPTY CIPHER

Since the Christ around whom we gather is confessed the same yesterday and today and forever, and since the ground floor of the canonical witness is a body of relatively clear texts, this flexibility to begin in a given situation will never amount to an impressionistic or intuitionistic improvisation. No one speaking in the Spirit can deny the Lordship of Christ (1 Cor. 12:3). If Christ is who the texts say he is, no one gathering around him can affirm a mandate to kill or to oppress. Thus there will be considerable principled solidity (or what the ethicist would describe thus) in the body of ethical decisions which will develop out of the life of community, but we do not understand that solidity best when talking about the status of general principles, so that we would need to detail formalistically how they are known, how clear they are, what exceptions they might admit. It resides rather in the status of the story of Jesus as paradigm.

A minority ethic must also be a missionary ethic. The sixteenth century did not make as clear as our century is doing it the implied differences among the several reformations with regard to the meaning of Christian evangelization. In the sixteenth century, established Protestantism generally disavowed the concept of world missionary outreach for a number of explicit reasons. It is not unfair to suggest an implicit reason as well, namely that the numerical fusion of church and society made it simply unthinkable that the Christian faith could be propagated in another form than the extension of the political and cultural sovereignty of Christendom. Later, when Protestant nations also had their empires, Protestant renewal movements did have a terrain for mission. But in the sixteenth century the only Protestants to create or retain or renew a notion of missionary sending were the Anabaptists.[15] In the seventeenth century it was only the Friends who sent emissaries to parts of Europe where their sovereign had no sway. It is only with the collapse of empire that it becomes clear that the problematic of mission goes much deeper than a simple discussion of whether the commandment of Matthew 28:20 is still a valid commandment (the form in which the overseas missionary imperative was debated among Protestants around 1800), but rather that it has to do with whether the meaning of Jesus of Nazareth is of sufficient importance for knowing the nature and will of God that it is worth bothering the rest of the world with that identity and its Jewish antecedents, when people can be religious without that.[16]

It is no surprise, from the radical reformation perspective, that those communions which for centuries have linked Christianity with the power and prestige structures of the Western society with which they hoped the church would be numerically coterminous, and whose fathers had no compunctions at all about linking missionary expansion with colonial expansion, now feel as well that missions in the name of Jesus are an embarrassment when colonialism is disavowed and seek rather to accredit as "anonymous Christians" or as "valid religions" the faiths of peoples for whom the names of Abraham and Jesus are not determinative.

In conclusion I turn to the specific questions raised when my topic was assigned.[17] First, how is it possible for Christians using the same sources to come to disparate conclusions? It is unavoidable that the conclusions should be disparate if the axioms with which people relate to Jesus and the Scriptures as well as to the ethical agenda itself are different. If, since Constantine, one tradition has assumed that it is the duty of Christians to be the chosen organs of God to guide history in the right direction, if it has been decided on a priori grounds that the teachings of Jesus with regard to Mammon and Mars were not meant to be obeyed, or that we have in "nature" or "common sense" or "culture" or somewhere else a body of ethical rules which outrank the teachings and example of Jesus, then obviously the conclusions will be different. It is not the case that we "all use the same sources of revelation" when for some the openly avowed value of certain traditions in the name of which they move beyond the common authorities is such as to set aside the normativeness of the earliest common sources.

In the first chapter of my *Politics of Jesus*[18] I surveyed some standard shapes of argument whereby mainstream Christians with a good conscience have set aside the normativeness of Jesus. To the cases identified there, which have to do especially with whether Jesus was a political figure, I would need in the present context to add a number of others having to do with the revelatory status of nature, of common sense, of the lessons of history, of generalizations arising out of the observation of social process, of readings about what people can understand or will take seriously, and many other kinds of guides, which are operative consciously or unconsciously in some ethical traditions and which the radical reformation tradition in all meekness seeks explicitly to place in a subordinate position. It does not say that those other kinds of wisdom are to be smashed or cursed. Jesus and the apostles themselves use them in subordinate ways. The question is how to keep them subordinate to the centrality of the guidance of Jesus.

Second, how can or does ethics contribute to or hinder the cause of Christian unity? First of all, let us look at the hindrance. Roughly the same thing needs to be said about the two distinctive marks being represented here. The notion that membership in the Christian community should be a matter of adult decision has been a subject of division among Christians since the sixteenth century, one with which the organized ecumenical efforts of our century have had great difficulty in dealing. In the various study approaches of the World Council of Churches, this issue has never been dealt with head-on. A few prominent Baptist, Disciple, and Mennonite theologians have participated in the WCC activities and have never formally been placed in a position where to go along with the majority of pedobaptist churches they needed to deny their faith, but neither has the issue been a subject of direct encounter in a responsible debate comparable to the attention given to most other questions of faith and order. Thus the WCC carries on into the present undigested the deepest division of the sixteenth-century reformation.[19]

The same needs to be said with regard to the problem of Christian participation in war and the violence of the state. The issue was identified in the 1937 conference of the Life and Work movement, one of the parent bodies of the WCC, as an issue seriously needing attention. It was identified in similar terms at Amsterdam in 1948 and at Evanston in 1954, and again but somewhat less clearly at New Delhi in 1961. Each time it was said in Assembly documents that this matter needs to be studied as a major issue concerning which the division between Christian traditions has not been overcome. Yet never has a thorough study process taken place under WCC sponsorship directly on the subject.[20]

What is said here about the WCC, as one place to take a reading, could be said just as clearly about other levels or other agencies of concern for Christian dialogue or unity. These two issues represent the most recalcitrant themes for debate between traditions. As long as we are divided about them, they represent the most fundamental structural barriers to genuine mutual recognition.

Yet it is just as possible to pick up the other side of the invitation. "Can Christian ethics contribute to the cause of Christian unity?" If we were to think of Christian unity not as a consensus already present, needing only to be explicated, nor as a compromise between deeply different settled positions needing to be hassled and haggled through to a barely tolerable halfway statement, but as being led forward beyond where we were before into the discovery of a position which will not say which of us were right in the past but will renew our unity because it deepens the definition of our mission, then it could be claimed that this ethical agenda bears special promise for rediscovery of a new sense of united mission which still lies ahead of us.

First of all, on the level of the general structure of Christian ethical deliberation, all Christian thought has been renewed by the last few generations of biblical studies, reaching past the traditions to the text and reading it afresh with sharpened instruments of grammatical, historical, and literary interpretation, so that it is more clear than before how the whole canon centers upon the ministry of the human being Jesus – how the meaning of Christian ethics is determined by ecclesiology and eschatology rather than simply being derived deductively from uniquely "moral" postulates. While we could not unite our old structures of systematic ethics, we may still encounter ahead of us a new perception of the call of Jesus to community and hope.

With regard to ethics in the sense of the structuring of the Christian community, all Christian bodies are in one way or another leaving behind the heritage of the Constantinian age and moving into a world in which adherence to the believing community will have to be an adult decision. In numerous traditionally pedobaptist traditions, the question of the appropriateness of infant baptism is being raised, not out of respect for Baptists, Pentecostals, Disciples, and Mennonites, but from a renewed honesty about the place of the church in the world. In other contexts, the same result derives from renewed seriousness about the meaning of the sacrament of baptism, by way of renewed concern for catechesis, confirmation, or continuing education for ministry.

An analogous hope can be projected for the specimen issue of violence, as its pertinence has been clarified through our encounters with racism, exploitation, revolution, and modern war. Whether it takes the path of a new seriousness about letting the doctrine of the just war have a critical negative impact upon the conditioned willingness of Christians to accept some violence in the civil order, or whether it takes the more radical path of vocational or personal integral pacifism, there is widespread agreement—once again joining Roman Catholic thinkers with participants in the WCC—that militarism and nationalism conceived in a military tone constitute the fundamental challenge to the unity of the church and of humankind which must be condemned and transcended in our age. A common commitment to bring to bear on the menace of war and tyranny the full critical capacity of the total Christian community would be a path to Christian unity in mission, which would probably be more promising than a resumption of the older patterns of negotiating from the fixed, correct positions of established confessions. Then the contemporary ethical consensus might be the needed "end run" past the lines set up to defend already obsolete alternative ecclesiologies.

6. Anabaptism and History

Long ago Roland Bainton, now the dean of American historians of the Reformation, identified "primitivism" as a trait common to the whole Reformation, yet most consistently carried out by the Anabaptists:

> Erasmus was fond of rebuking the superstition and intolerance of his own day by the example of the early church. From him, probably Luther, and Melanchthon in a measure, and more especially Zwingli, learned this device for combatting the church of Rome. But they were speedily to recoil, having been made aware by the Anabaptists of the too radical implications of a complete restoration of primitive Christianity, for the New Testament provides no warrant for infant baptism or the union of church and state.[1]

From here Franklin H. Littell picked up the theme and systematized it, as not simply a trait but a definition of Anabaptism, in his *Anabaptist View of the Church*,[2] from whence it became a commonplace in Reformation historiography.[3]

The most apparently emphatic dissent from this interpretation is that of Hans Hillerbrand,[4] who does not deny the presence of the restitution theme in Anabaptism, but contests its usefulness as a definition on numerous grounds. The *terms* "restitution" and "restoration" meant quite different things in sixteenth-century usage. They were used more freely by Spiritualizers than by Anabaptists. The theme of renewing original Christianity was common to all reform tendencies.[5]

This proposal to set the concept aside was hardly conclusive,[6] but it suffices to indicate that the systematic reformation/restitution distinction needs further definition if it is to be usable to describe not merely an argument but also an ecumenical stance. This present survey, too brief to review the literature, seeks to suggest the lines of an interpretation which would make the label "restitution" objectively

123

usable as a label which friends and critics alike could use to identify a real sixteenth-century difference.

RESTITUTION IN SEARCH OF DEFINITION

Some recent discussion has failed to clarify because, disregarding sound practice in the history of ideas, it mistook a word for a concept. The word *restitutio* (like its relatives *restauratio, renovatio, regeneratio, reparatio*) had all kinds of meanings.[7] Most of them did not center on the particular attitude toward the history of the church of which Bainton and Littell are speaking. But that does not mean that the term is useless for the historian. It only means that the historian's usage must be defined structurally, functionally, as descriptive not of a verbal occurrence but of a thought pattern.

That pattern sees in history three movements. There was once a normative state of the church. There was then a "Fall," leaving a degenerate state, so intrinsically deteriorated as not to be reparable without discontinuity. Then there is the radical renewal. This pattern, thus broadly stated, is common to most historically oriented religions. To sift out its varieties we must look closer.

For many, the "Golden Age" (a term Littell uses) was a mythical or an historical Eden, a "state of nature," an original "simplicity." The term "primitivism," which was current in the work of Arthur Lovejoy[8] when Bainton first used it, leads the reader's mind in this same direction. To avoid this misunderstanding[9] I prefer the more formal term "normative state."

More attractive in the sixteenth century was the restoration of the Davidic Kingdom. Christendom in its fallenness being a religious/political unity, it was natural to look for models of restoration in the shape of righteous kingship, validating in the present or the near future not the practices of the New Testament church but its expectations, interpreted as parallel to the prophecies of the book of Daniel and all the promises of a new David.

Those whose restitution hope was thus concretized then differed according to how they saw their own work relating to that fulfillment. Some saw themselves as its precursors; not yet the New, yet still, as its privileged heralds, a part of it. They are then not so much a return to the beginning, as the beginning of the End. This "John the Baptist" self-image was that of Melchior Hofmann, perhaps of Hans

Hut, and of Thomas Müntzer in 1524. Müntzer in his last frenzy, and more effectively Münster, represent the other alternative, where the "elect" are themselves already God's instruments[10] – although here, too, a far wider divine intervention, still future, was counted on. By no means would such a Davidic restoration be a return to the New Testament. It would be a new, culminating stage in salvation history. The weakness, suffering, and ethics of the early church and the corruption of medieval Christendom would both be left behind. In this respect the millenarian enthusiasts were joined by the Spiritualizers, for whom "restitution" meant a new age of mystical or rational illumination.[11]

In contrast with all of these approaches, the ecclesial Anabaptists[12] stood with majority Protestantism (and some Catholics) in ascribing to the Incarnation a normative significance such that we do not hope to go past Christ either backward (to David or Adam) or forward (to a new, unaccountable "Spirit" or kingdom). But then the question is *how* Christ (or Scripture) is normative for reformation. Again we must itemize alternatives.

The restitution claim does not begin with the present but with a judgment on the past; i.e., with the concept of the Fall. In normative Catholicism, one can speak of fallenness and degeneration. Yet what is fallen is not the Church as such, in her essence, as defined theologically and historically through apostolic succession. Even a morally unworthy man becomes *as bishop* a valid bearer of that essence. The Church properly understood is indefectible, and the locus of that indefectibility is in the apostolic succession.

The restitutionist alternative is clear. The fall is more serious than that. Its locus is precisely the point where indefectibility is claimed. The visible church *defined by succession* has apostasized. There can be no cure in continuity with what is, because the organ of continuity is itself in enemy hands and must not be granted control of the pace or shape of reformation.

This alternative is not intrinsically schismatic. The critic of the restitution alternative assumes that it is, because in some cases of restitutionism (in situations under someone else's political control) a new ecclesiastical body sprang up. But this is not inevitable. Every view of reformation has produced new churches. Restitution does not have to or hope to. The restitutionist calls on other organs than the bishops (a council, a prophet, a gathered *Stadtgemeinde,* the "grass roots") to reform the whole church.[13] Since unity was itself one of the characteristics of the New Testament church, restitutionism cannot be schismatic in principle, but only when forces beyond its control make valid unity in renewal unattainable.[14] Hillerbrand's formulation is thus inexact when he generalizes that "the Anabaptists did not share the agony of the early reformers" with regard to schism.[15] A less pre-judged statement would have been that they did not recognize the (already divided) state-church structures as adequate organs of that unity whose breach is schism.[16]

The majority form of official[17] reformation, as Bainton said, be-gins with restitution argument but soon finds itself defending the prod-ucts of post-Constantinian history: the church/state liaison, just war, repression of dissent. The claim to renewed recourse to biblical au-thority for change, including the concept of the Fall of the church, could not be abandoned by the official reformers, but now it had to be redefined. Not the form of the Church but the faith or the message of the apostles is the norm. The adjustments made by later churches in other areas may be accepted as long as the message or the doctrine is maintained. Or: the standard is not the early church but the totality of Scripture, all on the same level of authority, so that for issues re-lated to society Joshua, David, or Josiah are more useful models than Jesus or Paul. Thus the interpretation of the criteria of restitution is more complex and must be reserved to qualified teachers. In order for the corpus christianum to be united around their teaching, they must be authorized and supported by prince or council. Thus they have a solid base to attack certain specifically Catholic abuses; but none to call into question the corpus christianum arrangement itself, since its structures are being used to implement the cure. Far from condemning the fusion of church and world in corpus christianum, it is to be welcomed, as a step forward under Providence, beyond the apostolic age.[18] It cannot be condemned since it is the only place the prophet can stand to denounce the bishops.

From this comparison it arises that, if we wish the label "restitu-tionism" to be usable for technical discrimination between radical and official reformation visions, it must a) include an alternative to the social shape of the fallen Christendom it rejects, not only to doctrinal formulations or churchly practices. It must further b) identify *within* Scripture its baseline, especially with regard to the relationship of the Testaments; and it must c) locate the authority to read Scripture some-where (the prophet, the congregation, everyman) outside the estab-lishment. With these refinements the concept of restitution becomes objective, manageable for the historian. It describes Francis, Waldo, Chelčický, the ecclesial Anabaptists, radical Puritans and others of the same mold since, and not the official churches they opposed.

Restitution and the Reading of History

There are a limited number of possible ways to take history seriously. One may do so by arguing against its importance; this is the stance of the Spiritualizer. One may reject the past globally in the name of a present or future takeover: the apocalyptic. One may accept its results, subject to continuing critique and reformation within the frame it has produced; so the official churches. In any of these cases one is free to study the data of the past or not; the meaning of truth and obedience goes on from today. The past must however be taken seriously in a very different way if one claims to critique the course of history using as criterion a point within history, namely the Incarnation, or the canon. Thus the critics of "restitution" are farthest from the facts when they describe it as "historyless" (Sidney Mead) or "apolitical" (Walter Köhler, Georg Wünsch). An ahistorical bias is incompatible with restitutionism; historiography is theologically necessary. By standing in judgment on particular fruits of historical development such as the state/church linkage, episcopacy, and pedobaptism, restitutionism accepts the challenge to be critical of history and thereby to take it more seriously than do those for whom some other criterion than the New Testament determines the faithfulness of the church. A classical Tridentine Catholic affirmation of the teaching authority of the hierarchy, or a classical Hegelian affirmation of the relevatory power of the Spirit of Western culture is "serious about history" in the sense of accepting the results of the particular evolution of certain institutions in European experience. It however need not and perhaps even cannot deal with history *critically,* since it has totally affirmed its own path as its norm. Dialogue is by definition questionable. On the other hand, a view which criticizes what has come into being in the course of history, on the grounds of criteria which themselves are also drawn from within the course of history, is thereby obliged to be concerned with historical data in a way different from those traditions which claim each in its own way to be the "mainstream."

One simple example of this is the thinking about the origins of

infant baptism which went on in the very first months of the Anabaptist movement. A Catholic or an Oecolampad could affirm infant
baptism as having been practiced always everywhere by everyone,
meeting the test of catholicity. That freed them from facing any dis-
parities between their time and apostolic practices, or from asking
how things had come to be. The Anabaptists on the other hand, rejecting present practice, had to explain how this practice had arisen,
if it was not in the New Testament. This they did, by attempting to
reconstruct the origins of the practice of pedobaptism.[19] Since their
reconstruction was done within the limits of the tools of the time,
there is no need for us now to evaluate their explanations as historiography. What is important relative to the present question is the fact
that such a reconstruction had to be done as a part of the integrity
of their own critical vision. This would not have been the case if their
stance had been ahistorical.

But radical reformation is not history-oriented only in the sense
of needing to study how things went wrong. It is also historicist in
that it affirms the character of man as a being who within the temporal order makes decisions which themselves determine history. To
speak of the present or the immediate future as an age of restitution
by the Spirit is to take the uniqueness of every moment, and the importance of every decision, more seriously than when one sees the
career of the church as an unbroken gradual climb and one's present
institutional and doctrinal stance as obviously the best possibility for
the present.[20] The radical reformers read their Bible because they
took their own time seriously as one more *kairos* of choice between
fall and renewal. A picture of past and present as made up of crucial
particular choices, on each of which the future depends, is far more
earnest than one in which an indefectible church and a pious government have things so in hand that only natural catastrophe and the
exotic infidel are to be feared.

Thirdly, the radicals were history-minded in that the norm whereby
they judged the present age was not a timeless garden of Eden or primitive simplicity, not a speculative utopia, but the very particular story
of the New Testament. Jesus, the prophets before him, and the apostles
after him, as a base for evaluating what has been done since in their
name, are to be found fully within the researchable, debatable particularity which according to the New Testament witness is the meaning of Incarnation. (There is another, high-church concept of Incar-

nation, which sees it as an apotheosis or divine approval of humanity as a whole; the effect of this kind of "Incarnation" on the capacity to critique history is of course the opposite).[21] The Anabaptists did not reject the present for its failure to be Eden, or the New Jerusalem (as some spiritualists and some revolutionaries did). Their indictment was rather that one particular set of decisions, accepted by the churches at large in the fourth century, symbolized by Constantine, had been wrong when measured by the New Testament. It was not wrong because it was later than the New Testament, but because wrong fourth-century options were chosen rather than right fourth-century options.[22]

Anabaptist historiography sees the pre-Constantinian fathers in a strikingly favorable light. If apostasy (as distinguished from finitude or peccability), though real, is inexcusable, it must also have been evitable. Faithfulness must also be possible. We should then expect to find faithfulness in history as well. Locating the Fall in the age of Constantine means granting the benefit of the doubt to over two centuries of fallible, divided, confused church life, during which nonetheless the vision of the major teachers was structurally sound. It is not claimed that history always goes wrong or always needs to be reversed. A particular fall necessitates a particular restitution. These earlier centuries are part of the Anabaptist historical claim, in that they document how the New Testament vision was understood by those closest to the origin of the texts,[23] as well as attesting to the modesty and feasibility of the restitutionists' demands. This respect for the early centuries continues to this day to be edifying in Anabaptist circles.[24]

Further, restitutionism is historically serious in that among the various trends of polemic it sought to determine which was the root, which abuse caused the others. It agrees with official Protestantism that the papacy is apostate in the authority claims it makes for itself, but doubts that that error has its roots there. It agrees in rejecting justification through good deeds, and in denying that the mass is the kind of sacrifice which negates the sufficiency or the finality of the Cross, and in claiming that if Catholicism teaches those things then the gospel is imperiled, but again it doubts that doctrinal deviation is self-generating, seeking rather a deeper (and earlier) explanation in a shift in church/world relations from which other degenerations naturally followed.[25]

How then can interpreters from within the official churches transform the restitution call into a pretended undiscriminating insistence on the timeless imitation of first-century details? The shift in categories is only possible because they themselves, being part of the power structure of their own age and indisposed to subject it to the judgment of Christ, assume that their positions, where they differ from the New Testament, were imposed by the course of events; either literally imposed (not decisions at all), or correct and wise adaptations to new circumstances. Only when one assumes that the choices leading to where we are now were right, can one equate the criticism of those choices with the rejection of history as such. Thus the course of history becomes its own justification. It can be judged only by immanent criteria; thus the contingency of the present is denied. Only a reference point in the past can be equally accessible to all and a judgment on all. Only the normativeness of some past afford us critical leverage on the present.

In medieval Europe it was at least credible that the present was the best of all possibilities. One could see the world as unified, under one church and one Caesar, moving necessarily forward under Providence. One did not have to notice that the Syrians or the Russians were of another mind. But since the Renaissance, Reformation, and Enlightenment it is increasingly visible that for any one – be it a Hegel or a Spengler, a Marx or a Pannenberg – to claim that history has or will have a definable meaning is in fact to have chosen a particular provincial vantage point, whereby every power structure forms its own constituency and meaning system. In contrast, the claims of Christ, by virtue precisely of their historical objectivity and distance, enable a genuine catholicity. Pointedly said: only the mental structure of restitutionism can be at once Christian and serious about history.

Carefully to test the adequacy of this view as a theologically coherent self-understanding, we would need to move beyond the reading of one crisis in history, where it is quite at home, to other levels of generality:

1) does it facilitate the reading of other crises as well?
2) does it enable an alternative overview of church history?
3) does it reach helpfully beyond historiography to contemporary issues of the mission, structure, and unity of the church?

In this article only one specimen response can be suggested for each of the first two questions; the third would take us too far.[26]

Restitutionism on the Frontier

The nineteenth-century American "Churches of Christ" or "Disciples" movement,[27] whose most widely noted spokesman was Alexander Campbell, faced a situation as different from sixteenth-century Zurich as one could ask. In place of ancient Catholic culture, the context is the still largely unsettled Midwest. In place of enforced religious conformity, the challenge is chaotic and competitive diversity. The state/church link, central to the debate in the 1520s, could not be an issue. Yet in this different milieu the "Disciples" found their way to a mission of strikingly similar shape: the generalizing of ministry and the relativizing of "clergy"; pacifism, which many of the Disciples held to during the Civil War with more vigor than some Mennonites, including obtaining conscientious objector status from the Confederate government;[28] congregationalism in polity, with intercongregational agencies respected but relativized; believers' baptism.

Because sectarian division was their special concern, the Disciples sometimes stated their restitution vision in an apparently minimal way: "nothing that was not as old as the New Testament should be made an article of faith, a rule of practice, or a term of communion among Christians."[29] Yet the claim to have found in a newly clarified biblicism a way around denominationalism demanded special attention to issues of church polity, as one could claim to illuminate these from the perspective of a claimed "New Testament pattern."[30] At this point Campbell was nearer to the radical Calvinist than to Anabaptist forms of restitution. It was Calvin, not the Anabaptists, who claimed to find prescribed in the New Testament a specific pattern of "fourfold ministry," eldership and synod.[31] Similarly the Puritan "Cambridge Platform" of 1648 claimed: "The parts of Government are prescribed in the word, because the Lord Jesus Christ the King and Lawgiver of his Church, is no less faithful in the house of God than was Moses, who from the Lord delivered a form and pattern. . . . The partes of Church-Government are all of them exactly described in the word of God . . . & therefore to continue one and the same, unto the appearing of our Lord. . . . So that it is not left in the power of men . . . to add, or diminish, or alter any thing in the least measure therein."[32]

It can be argued that the later history of the Churches of Christ indicates that this narrowing of the restitution focus to formal polity issues, concerning which the New Testament is more pluralistic than on some other questions, may have contributed to discrediting the idea of restitution.

One reason reformation historians would do well to study Disciples' history comparatively[33] is that the post-establishment political context gives the restitution concern a new shape. Another is the adjustment to a different intellectual climate, post-pietist and post-Enlightenment. In the age of rationalism symbolized by Locke, with its new confidence in the ability of any honest reader to find the meaning of ancient texts simply by being careful with plain language and suspicious of intervening traditions, Campbell and his associates claimed a possibility of renewal, present as it had not been before, precisely on the basis of cultural development. This repeated in a new key something of the way in which the Renaissance, symbolized comparably by Erasmus, had trusted the possibility of getting "back to the sources."

Thus the fact that we are given in a particular age a new instrument for restitution is not a mere repetition or return to "go," but progress, Providence. The fact that in every age particular dimensions of apostasy are identified, denounced, and dismantled, is a way of discerning the real substance of salvation history. Thus Campbell's belonging in his century exemplifies the statement made before, that the doctrine of restitution does not deny but rather enables real historical progress under God. It does so by identifying in each age the criterion of progress, namely the capacity to identify the new forms of apostasy, so as to restore accordingly a redefined faithfulness.

A third reason for more attention to Disciples' restitutionism is that the most coherent modern refutation of the vision is that called forth by its American expressions. Whereas the European critics tend to presuppose the normativeness of their own inherited official alternative and to condemn by cliché without a hearing, the American critics argue in a context where the forms of restitution have been at least negatively successful (no state church, no enforcement of ancient forms, a lay voice in polity, voluntary membership). Some of the most pointed criticism comes from the movement's own children,[34] some from more general historians.[35]

Restitution As Succession

Can history, or church history, be read as a continuity under God? Is restitution a story of its own or merely a recurrent recalcitrant footnote to the main story? Professional historians, trained in the schools of the mainstream, lean toward the latter view. Baptists and Quakers in puritan England came out of Anglicanism under Calvinist influence; the Anabaptists were radicalized Erasmians and Zwinglians; Hus was an official churchman. Yet there persists another line of witness. Van Braaght[36] prefaces his sixteenth-century martyr accounts with an extensive compilation of reports of Christians from every century who obeyed the New Testament, who baptized on confession of faith, who rejected state control of belief, and who suffered at the hands of government.[37] This approach became more credible when it was repeated by the non-Anabaptist Gottfried Arnold[38] and later by Ludwig Keller.[39] It has been the dominant self-understanding of the Plymouth Brethren,[40] of the ("Dunkard") Brethren,[41] of the Churches of Christ,[42] of American Mennonites before this century,[43] and of Swiss Mennonites to this day.[44]

One obvious pitfall of this kind of counter-historiography[45] is the temptation to imagine genetic connections where there were none, thus shortchanging the study of proximate real causes.[46] There are cases, some of them demonstrated and others arguable, of causal lines from one restitution group to the next, but other beginnings were clearly new products of fresh criticism within official churches.

A second temptation is to assume that all suffering dissenters must have agreed at all other essential points. In fact, while many rejected infant baptism, not all did. While all rejected state control of the church, not all rejected war and the oath. While most had more affirmative attitudes toward work and marriage than did the official church, the Albigenses, influenced by Cathar Manicheism, may not have.

But behind these pitfalls is a deeper one, an unwitting misunderstanding of the deep originality of the restitution claim on the part of some of its apologetes,[47] who nearly fall into an inverted form of the majority view. If it is not public institutional succession which accredits the faithfulness of the mainstream church, then why should it be a clandestine institutional succession which accredits the faithful church? Should the alternative not be a continuing series of new beginnings, similar in shape and spirit, as the objective historicity of Jesus and the apostles, mediated through the objectivity of Scripture, encounters both the constants and the variables of every age to call forth "restitutions" at once original and true-to-type, at once unpredictable and recognizable?[48]

When John Robinson bade farewell to the Plymouth dissenters with his since famous phrase, "The Lord has yet more truth to break forth from his holy Word," his claim was not that in the face of high-church persecution there was also a clandestine connection with Waldo and Wyclif. He believed that the apostolicity of the Pilgrim cause was certified by its conformity with the apostolic documents;[49] reliably recognizable because even across the sea the same Spirit will lead again, reading the same documents in fresh yet similar ways. To trust this constancy despite the repetitiveness of men's infidelity is the most hopeful view of history, the one most free to read the facts as they stand in any century without either official apologetics or spiritualistic unconcern, the way most able to proclaim the continuing sovereignty of the Word Incarnate over all the words that seek to speak His echo.

7. The Constantinian Sources of Western Social Ethics

Christians in the first century were a minority in a hostile world. Their ethical views were attuned to that context. In the twentieth century, Christians – especially if by that noun we refer to people voluntarily committing themselves, at some cost, to living in the light of their confession of Christ – are also in a minority in a world committed to other loyalties, yet we do not reason as the early Christians did. This study shall seek to show summarily how some of the axioms of Western social thought are the product of the deep shift in the relation of church and world for which Constantine soon became the symbol.

Our concern is not with Constantine the man – how sincere his conversion was, what he believed, how he intended to use the church. Nor do we suggest that the year 311 represented an immediate reversal without preparation or unfolding. The great reversal certainly began earlier and took generations to work itself out. Nonetheless, the medieval legend which made of Constantine the symbol of an epochal shift was realistic: he stands for a new era in the history of Christianity.

This new era was to include far-reaching changes in Christian social ethics. For example, the pre-Constantinian Christians had been pacifists, rejecting the violence of army and empire not only because they had no share of power, but because they considered it morally wrong; the post-Constantinian Christians considered imperial violence to be not only morally tolerable but a positive good and a Christian duty.[1] But our attention must move deeper, to the levels of ecclesiology and eschatology.

THE NEW ECCLESIOLOGY

Obviously the composition of the church changed. Before, Christians had been a minority – some scholars estimate no more than ten percent of the empire's population – and intermittent persecution worked against making anyone's adherence cheap. It took at least a degree of conviction to belong. After Constantine the church was everybody. Being counted as "Christian" was the rule, not an exception. Paganism was soon declared illegal, and within another century the government was actively repressing heresies, i.e., ruling on what constitutes orthodox belief and punishing dissent. Henceforth, it would take exceptional conviction not to be counted as Christian.

What this means, of course, is that the meaning of the word "Christian" has changed. Its moral, emotional, and even intellectual meanings were changed by the reversal of the sociological and political pressures. This shift called forth a new doctrinal refinement, namely the doctrine of the invisibility of the true church. Whether defined from the godward side (the "elect") or the manward (those whose faith is sincere), the class of *true* Christians continues to be a minority. Though we are unable to determine just who they are, we can have some notion of the signs which suggest who are not of their number. The major architect of the concept of the *ecclesia invisibilis,* Augustine, thought that perhaps the true church would be five percent of the visible one.

The definitions of the faith could thus no longer take the assembly of believers as its base. As a result, therefore, the eyes of those looking for the church had to turn to the clergy, especially to the episcopacy, and henceforth "the church" meant the hierarchy more than the people.

The New Eschatology

The apostolic church confessed Jesus Christ as Lord; risen, ascended, sitting at the right hand of the Father, i.e., ruling (1 Cor. 15:25ff.) over the not yet subdued *kosmos.* The principalities and powers, though not manifestly confessing His Lordship, could not escape from His hidden control or from the promise of His ultimate victory. In ways that took account of their rebelliousness He denied them free rein, using even their self-glorifying designs within His purpose.[2] A later term for this same idea was "Providence." But with the age of Constantine, Providence no longer needed to be an object of faith, for God's governance of history had become empirically evident in the person of the Christian ruler of the world. The concept of millennium was soon pulled back from the future (whether distant or imminent) into the present. All that God can possibly have in store for a future victory is more of what has already been won.

We are in a position now to capsule in a phrase the reversal of ecclesiology and eschatology underlying the changes in ethics and in dogma. Before Constantine,[3] one knew as a fact of everyday experience that there was a believing Christian community but one had to "take it on faith" that God was governing history. After Constantine, one had to believe without seeing that there was a community of believers, within the larger nominally Christian mass, but one knew for a fact that God was in control of history.[4] Ethics had to change because one must aim one's behavior at strengthening the regime, and because the ruler himself must have very soon some approbation and perhaps some guidance as he does things the earlier church would have disapproved of. The conception of a distinctive life-style befitting Christian confession had to be sweepingly redefined. It could no longer be identified with baptism and church membership, since many who are "Christian" in that sense have not themselves chosen to follow Christ. Its definition will tend to be transmuted in the definition of inwardness. Its outward expression will tend to be assigned to a minority of special "religious" people. "Mission" in the sense of calling one's hearers to faith in Jesus Christ as Lord must also be redefined. Beyond the limits of empire it had become identical with the expansion of Rome's sway. Within Christendom, since outward allegiance to Christ is universal, compulsory, the concern of the preacher will be with "renewal," i.e., with adding inner authenticity to an outward profession which is already there, because obligatory.

Two further symbolic shifts spell out the implications of the Constantinian age at the borders of Christendom.[5] Once "Christendom" means Empire, non-empire is a new challenge. The era of Charlemagne demonstrates the option of annexation and fusion. Germanic values, legal traditions, social structures, and ruling families are "baptized" globally. This does not mean, at least not for most of them, conversion in any deep sense. It rather means that the *name* of Jesus is now intoned over a Germanic culture without changing its inner content, as it had been intoned over Graeco-Roman culture for half a millennium before.[6] "Syncretism" is probably not the best label for the resulting mixture, since there is not so much genuine fusion and reconception as there is an overlaying of two cultures.

The other symbolically powerful event is the Crusade. When the other "world" at the border is not open to interpenetration, the collision becomes a holy war. Mohammed will have to be met on his own terms. The outsider is not only no longer privileged, as he had been for Jesus and Paul, as the test of one's love (Matt. 5:43ff., Luke 6:32ff.) or as the proof of the new age's having come (Eph. 2). The outsider is not simply ignored, or disregarded as "barbarian" or heretical, as Christian Rome had largely done. Now the outsider has become the "infidel," the incarnation of anti-faith. To destroy him, or to give one's life in the attempt, has become a positively virtuous undertaking, quite without regard for the ordinary criteria of justifiable violence (the so-called just war theory). Our world has a divinely imparted duty to destroy or to rule over their world.

The New "Servant of the Lord"

Having these consciousness-changing events in mind, we now may proceed to identify their effects on our view of history, especially those assumptions that have become for us so axiomatic that it can hardly occur to us to question them. Certainly one is the view that *civil government* is the main bearer of historical movement. History is told as the history of dynasties, their conflicts and alliances. The ruler, not the average person or the weak person, is the model for ethical deliberations. A moral statement on the rightness of truth-telling or the wrongness of killing is tested first by whether a ruler can meet such standards.[7] "Social ethics" means not what everyone should think and do about social questions, but what people in power should be told to do with their power. The place of the church or of persons speaking for Christian morality (including academic theologians) is that of "chaplaincy," i.e., a part of the power structure itself.[8] The *content* of ethical guidance is not the teaching of Jesus but the duties of "station" or "office" or "vocation."[9]

There is no point here in arguing for or against this shift: suffice it to observe how deep is the change in bearings. From Genesis to Apocalypse, the meaning of history had been carried by the people of God as people, as community. Leadership *within* the people was dispersed (Moses, prophets, priests, judges). When kingship was introduced in order to be "like the other nations" it did not work long or well, and the king was not elevated above common humanity. Other rulers (Nebuchadnezzar, Cyrus, Caesar) were historically significant only as they have an incidental part in the history of the people of God. But the fact that with Constantine the civil sovereign becomes God's privileged agent is thus not merely a shift of accent but a change of direction.

A NEW UNIVERSALITY

After Constantine not only is the ruler the bearer of history; the nonsovereign ethical agent has changed as well. The "Christian" used to be a minority figure, with numerous resources not generally available to all people: personal commitment, regeneration, the guidance of the Holy Spirit, the consolation and encouragement of the brotherhood, training in a discipleship life-style. But now that Christianity is dominant, the bearer of history is Everyman—baptized but not necessarily thereby possessed of the resources of faith. Ethical discourse must now meet two more tests:

1. Can you ask such behavior of everyone? Are not servanthood and the love of enemy, or even contentment and monogamy, more than we have the right to expect of everyone? Is not the love ethic of the New Testament unrealistic, too heroic? The pressure builds rapidly for a duality in ethics. The "evangelical counsels" will be commended to the religious and the highly motivated. The "precepts," less demanding, will suffice for catechesis and the confessional. Two levels, two kinds of motivations and sanctions will be discerned, entailing different specific duties (contradictory ones, in fact, at points such as power, property, marriage, bloodshed, which were morally proper for the laity but not for the religious). Then the Reformation polemic against works righteousness and monasticism removed the upper, more demanding, level.

2. What would happen if everyone did it? If everyone gave their wealth away what would we do for capital? If everyone loved their enemies who would ward off the Communists? This argument could be met on other levels,[10] but here our only point is to observe that such reasoning would have been preposterous in the early church and remains ludicrous wherever committed Christians accept realistically their minority status. For more fitting than "What if everybody did it" would be its inverse, "What if nobody else acted like a Christian, but we did?"

A New Value for Effectiveness

A third dimension of the great reversal is the transformation of moral deliberation into utilitarianism. Minorities and the weak have numerous languages for moral discourse:

— conscience, intention, inspiration, and other similar "subjective" measures of right action;
— revelation, "nature," "wisdom," and other "received" standards;
— covenant, tradition, "style," reputation, training, and other "community-maintenance" criteria.

Each of these ways of moral reasoning has its logical and psychological strengths and limits. We cannot evaluate them here. Yet it is important that each can, in given circumstances, lead persons to act sacrificially, for the sake of others, or for the sake of a "cause" more important than the individual. Each can lift decision and action above immediate cost/benefit calculation. But once the evident course of history is held to be empirically discernible, and the prosperity of our regime is the measure of good, all morality boils down to efficacy. Right action is what works; what does not promise results can hardly be right.

Perhaps the most evident example of the dominion of this axiom is today's debate about revolution, liberation, and violence. Any ethic, any tactic, is, in the minds of many, self-evidently to be tested by its promised results.[11] To them, the rejection of violence is morally sustainable only if nonviolent techniques are available which are able to promise an equally rapid "revolution."[12] Again it would be petitionary to argue that the utilitarian world view is "wrong" or that an ethic of "principles" would be "right."[13] For the present our concern is only to report that the dominance of the engineering approach to ethics, reducing all values to the calculation of pressures promising to bring about imperative results, is itself a long-range echo of the Constantinian wedding of piety with power; it is an approach foreign to the biblical thought world and makes no sense in a missionary situation where believers are few and powerless.

A New Metaphysic

A fourth, more doctrinal implication of the Constantinian reversal must be named: it is the victory of metaphysical dualism. Historically the source of this view is predominantly Neoplatonism. But naming its source does not explain its success. Certainly one reason it took over was the usefulness of dualism to justify the new social arrangement and resolve the problems it raised. The church we see is not the believing community; the visible/invisible duality names, and thereby justifies, the tension. The dominant ethic is different from the New Testament in content (Lordship is glorified rather than servanthood) as in source (reason and the "orders of creation" are normative, rather than the particularity of Jesus' and the apostles' guidance). What could be easier than to reserve the ethics of love for the inward or for the personal, while the ethics of power are for the outward world of structures? Interiorization and individualization, like the developments of the special worlds of cult and meditation, were not purely philosophical invasions which took over because they were intellectually convincing. They did so also because they were functional. They explained and justified the growing distance from Jesus and his replacement by other authorities and another political vision than that of the Kingdom of God.

THE EVER NEW SHAPE OF ESTABLISHMENT

But is this not all ancient history? Have we not long since left the age of Constantine behind? Did not church and state again separate in most of the world? This counter-question has perhaps been in the reader's mind for some time and merits a closer look. Perhaps the strongest proof of the depth of the great reversal is the fact that it survives even as the situations which brought it forth no longer obtain.

Speaking schematically, we can observe one shift which took place as Renaissance, Reformation, and other more directly "political" changes brought about the modern sense of nationhood, replacing "Christendom" as the definition of cultural identity and historical meaning. It becomes more important now that one is French, or Spanish, or Dutch, or English, or Swiss, than that one is part of the unity of Christendom. What is the response of dominant Christian thought to this shift? The social arrangement remains, but on the national scale. One can now have wars, even holy wars, against other Christian nations. No longer can a bishop call a king to Canossa, for the bishop is the creature of the king. Despite some voices of regret or critique, most "Christians" adjusted with conviction to the new arrangement. For the Protestants this was easy, since the creation of a new national Protestant church in the sixteenth century was the work of the nation-state; but in other ways Catholicism can also take on a very national coloring. The basic Constantinian vision remains, only on a much smaller, provincial scale. Let us call this "neo-Constantinianism."[14]

Another shift comes with Enlightenment and Revolution. Religious liberty and disestablishment bring it about progressively that church and state *as institutions* become less linked. Each has greater autonomy over against the claims of the other. Yet even with this shift, the moral identification changes little, as the U.S. especially demonstrates. Once the separation of church and state is seen as theologically desirable, a society where this separation is achieved is not a pagan society but a nation structured according to the will of God. American patriotism remains highly religious.[15] For nearly two centuries, in fact, the language of American public discourse was not only religious, not only Christian, but specifically Protestant. Moral identification of church with nation remains despite institutional separation. In fact, forms of institutional interlocking develop which partly deny the theory of separation (chaplaincies, tax exemptions). Let us call this arrangement "neo-neo-Constantinian." The social arrangement has been changed deeply and formally, but remains informally powerful.

In our own century yet another step is taken. The government may actually oppose Christianity as value system and as institution. Perhaps this new phase began at the turn of the century in France, but the most striking cases are the "People's Democracies" of Eastern Europe. Yet even under this reversal of the stream, Christians remain patriotic. Their objection to the disadvantages or even persecution they suffer takes the form of claiming that their faith does not make them disloyal to the nation. In international and ecumenical contacts their national loyalty is professed, and the view of world affairs held in their homeland is shared, despite criticism in detail of their "disestablished" position. Or in some cases the churches are in fact not disestablished, but financed by a Marxist regime. This continuing moral identification despite mutual ideological disavowal might be called "neo-neo-neo-Constantinian." The social arrangement has been changed sweepingly. Civil authorities profess the intention that the church shall wither away, yet for the time being they support it from the resources of the socialist economy. Churchmen are outspokenly loyal not only to their people and their culture but even to their regime's current policies.[16]

There is yet one more possible step. One can identify God's cause and Christians' loyalty with a regime which is *future* rather than present: with a "revolution" or "liberation" which, being morally imperative, is sure to come. In our time the most vocal expressions of this are neo-Marxist, but it can occur as well in the name of some other future. "What God is doing in the world," or "hope," or "salvation" is spelled out as a better power system yet to come, with which Christians proleptically should identify. This then would need to be called "neo-neo-neo-neo-Constantinianism."

The friendly sovereign is not even there. The social arrangement is only a vision. Still the theologians' projections prefer models of partnership with power.

Each view along this progression is clear in rejecting the former one as having been wrong, and in blaming the blindness of earlier generations of churchmen for having accepted such identification with an unworthy political cause. This sense of rightness over against the others blinds each generation to the fact that the basic structural error, the identification of a civil authority as bearer of God's cause, has not been overcome but only transposed into a new key.[17]

It is not enough to say that the basic error has not been overcome; in a sense it has been heightened with each "neo" stage, with the sacrifice of a part of what had made the medieval synthesis, if not biblically correct, at least understandable and in a sense noble. There is first the sacrifice of catholicity. Constantine did not *really* rule the whole world. To link the church with Rome and Byzantium meant writing off the known neighbors to the north, east, and south, some Christian, to say nothing of the rest of the globe. Nonetheless we can understand those who felt that the part of the globe which God in Constantine was now controlling was the *oikumene,* as the Roman Empire called itself already in gospel times (Luke 2:1). But then the empire was reduced from the whole Mediterranean world to Charlemagne's Europe, and then to the nation. In our time of participation and regionalism even the nation is too large, and when we move on to the last level, the bearer of the hope of the future is only a segment of society, the proletariat, or more realistically, the "party" or morally elite minority, which despite its narrowness claims the duty to destroy God's enemies. That churchmen should see the poor or the proletariat or the party as the churches' allies in moving the world is mean-

ingful only when Marxist construals of history are appealing. Long
before, however, the same moves were made when it was the nobility,
or the bourgeoisie, who seemed to be the bearers of liberation.

Yet the progressive abandonment of catholicity is not the only loss
as the Constantinian stance resuscitates from stage to stage. At each
level the church's capacity to be critical decreases as well. The capacity to be critical of the regime has both institutional and cognitive
dimensions. Whatever else was wrong with the Middle Ages, these
dimensions were still present then. The hierarchy had a power base
and a self-definition which enabled independent judgment. An emperor or a prince could really be forced to listen to the bishop by ban
or interdict. The criteria of just war theory and other limits on the
prerogatives of princes (the rules of chivalry, the Peace of God, the
civil exemptions of clergy, the immunities of pilgrims) had real effect.

Most of this moral independence and critical capacity of the church
is swept away in the first shift. The Reformation does away with the
church's institutional autonomy, Renaissance skepticism destroys the
power of the interdict, and in the Reformation confessions the just
war theory becomes an affirmation where previously it had been a
question. Evidently, each further shift, as the church seeks to hang
on to a status slipping from her hold, decreases even further the capacity to be concretely critical. Least of all can one be concretely critical of a projected future.

A New Start

The intention of this text is descriptive only. What a coherent non-
or anti-Constantinian option would be, would demand a quite different study. For present purposes it must suffice to have sustained two
theses:

1) that the fourth-century shift continues to explain much if not most
   of the distance between biblical Christianity and ourselves, which
   is a distance not simply of time and organic development, but of
   disavowal and apostasy;
2) that many efforts to renew Christian thought regarding power and
   society remain the captives of the fallen system they mean to reject.

Still another study would be needed to unfold the specific missio-
logical perspectives of the disavowal of Constantine.[18] On the one hand

"mission" by definition should mean a forsaking of the Constantinian setting for a pilgrim status in someone else's world. The "forsaking" in mission has been as complex and as burdened with unpurged vestiges as the "overcoming" in Western experience. Suffice it to suggest that "to deconstantinize" or "to disestablish" might be a more concretely usable verb for the critical changes still needed than are the more current verbs "to contextualize" or "to indigenize," because the changes include:

—an element of repentance and judgment on the Western past;
—an awareness of the centrality of the power problem (whereas some discussion of "contextualizing" is often more narrowly semantic);
—a warning against a too easy conformity (to the indigenous scheme) to correct for the old ("foreign") one.

To conclude with a biblical vocabulary: if *kenosis* is the shape of God's own self-sending, then any strategy of Lordship, like that of the kings of this world, is not only a strategic mistake likely to backfire but a denial of gospel substance, a denial which has failed even where it succeeded. What the churches accepted in the Constantinian shift is what Jesus had rejected, seizing godlikeness, moving *in hoc signo* from Golgatha to the battlefield. If this diagnosis is correct, then the cure is not to update the fourth-century mistake by adding another "neo-" but to repent of the whole "where it's at" style and to begin again with *kenosis.*

WHAT IF THERE HAD BEEN A STRONGER FAITH?

As we look back over the "Constantinian reversal," with all that we now see that it meant, it is evident that there was one point in the standard descriptive analysis where a step in the argument is omitted. As we watched Christian thought adjusting to the presence of Caesar in the church, the reasoning went, "of course we cannot ask of Caesar that he live like a Christian (i.e., like what the earlier Christians had thought Jesus wanted their pattern of life to be)." That seemed self-evident at the time. But a critical observer, watching the logic of the argument without being in the situation, could very well ask, as did one editorial advisor, reading an earlier version of this text, why that should be. If it is the case that God is providentially in charge of history, even though that has not hitherto been visible, would not that divine sovereignty be able to bless the believing obedience of a Caesar who, taking the risk of faith like any other believer, from his position of relative power, would love his enemies and do justice? Does the argument need to grant that if a Caesar had done that, in the context of authentic faith as previously defined, the results would have been bad? What would have counted as bad results in that case?

This question prefigures debates that will stretch all the way to the present. From the time of Constantine to that of the sixteenth-century Swiss Brethren leader Michael Sattler, including the witness of fifteenth-century Czech Brethren leader Chelčický, people have assumed that what it takes to be a Caesar is firmly defined by "nature" as a life-style and a set of moral assumptions that is counter to the gospel. The choice then, as it was stated by Chelčický, and by Sattler, is that a Christian simply cannot do that. He can withdraw or be thrown out. It would however be logically possible to argue the other way around. One could say that Caesar would be just as free as anyone else to take risks in faith. In fact, in an authentically imperial society, where there is respect for monarchy, where there is not a theory calling for him to be rejected by a revolution, and where there has not been established a pattern of frequent assassination or usurpation, Caesar would be perfectly free (for a while) to bring to bear upon the exercise of his office the ordinary meaning of the Christian faith. It might happen that the result would be that his enemies would triumph over him, but that often happens to rulers anyway. It might happen that he would have to suffer, or not stay in office all his life, but that too often happens to rulers anyway, and it is something that Christians are supposed to be ready for. It might happen that he would be killed: but most Caesars are killed anyway. It might happen that some of his followers would have to suffer. But emperors and kings are accustomed to asking people to suffer for them. Especially if the view were still authentically alive, which the earlier Christians undeniably had held to and which the theologians in the age of Constantine were still repeating, that God blesses those who serve him, it might also have been possible that, together with all of the risks just described, most of which a ruler accepts anyway, there could have been in some times and in some places the possibility that good could be done, that creative social alternatives could be discovered, that problems could be solved, enemies loved and justice fostered. At least a systematic pessimism, denying that anything of that order could ever have been achieved even had Constantine taken on the substance of

Christian discipleship rather than only the name and baptism, would not only be equivalent to denying the rhetoric of Christian belief in Providence, but also the actual lessons of modern social experience, in which there has been at least some progress in the direction of greater humanity and justice. In the history of the development of Christian thought we shall have to wait for some very incomplete projections in the thought of Erasmus or of Menno Simons, and then later for some more ambitious visions in the context of Puritanism, before we can see what it would mean to try to put to the Christian sovereign that other challenge.

PART III

The Public Realm

8. The Christian Case for Democracy

The question to which this inquiry is devoted[1] is located on the level of ordinary discourse in the political arena. It is by no means a new question for political science, but it is not within the discipline of political science that lay or "ordinary" ethical questions get defined. Our situation is one in which the question we are least likely to ask is why it should be good that there should be rule "by the people." In every major election it becomes visible how in the rhetoric of both sides the appeal to "the people" is both unanswerable and on closer scrutiny undefinable.

The glorification of democracy as a new form of government categorically separate from the frailties of other forms is observable not only in the wars we fight in its name but also in our peacetime missionary stance. The morally careful criticisms of government by our own citizens in recent years have centered largely on the wrongness of "support" given to nondemocratic regimes around the world. This has extended nearly to the point of advocating interventionism against nondemocratic regimes overseas. Thus after the "Christian West" has lost the naive righteousness with which it thought it should export its religion around the world, we still seem to have a good conscience about exporting our politics. I do not make this observation with the thought that we should advocate an alternative overseas policy of supporting tyranny, but only as a reading on how self-evident it is to us that the value of democracy is irrevocably established and is of transcultural validity.

For over a half century now, since the downfall of the czar and the Kaiser, there are not many respectable royalists around in the North Atlantic world. Democracy as a slogan is so established that to ask about its credentials has become a nonquestion. Such debate as remains has moved to other levels.

1. One of the other levels is the discussion among historians about who may properly claim paternity for such a self-evidently valuable achievement. There is the claim of the Augustinians, for whom democracy is the necessary corollary of a pessimistic doctrine of sin: we need democracy because no ruler is trustworthy enough to be left alone with important decisions. There is the claim of the Enlightenment, which first affirmed the dignity of the individual citizen, who will know what to do once the facts are made known. There is the claim of the free churches, who modeled both dissent and dialogical decision-making.

2. Another level of debate is the discussion of the activitists about how to make democracy work better, realizing its full participatory potential.

3. Still another level of unfinished debate is that of the "realists," who under the umbrella of the rhetoric of democracy go on as before with the struggle among the elites who really govern. They do this with or without a conservative or a Marxist theory to the effect that the masses can only ever "govern themselves" through the instrumentality of the elite.

4. There is the ongoing debate about whether "democracy" can be exported, i.e., whether it can be the national policy of the North Atlantic peoples to favor more participatory and less tyrannical governments around the world, even seeking to bring pressure upon or to disavow antidemocratic regimes. This is a realm full of paradoxes; those most proud of our freedoms at home seem most ready to do business with authoritarian regimes abroad; we are more inclined to be critical of abuses in the Soviet sphere where they should not be surprising than among our client countries in the "free world."

I suggest that we might have a better handle on the problems of our time if we were to pick up the big question again. We might have a more realistic perspective on the struggle among the realistic elites, and a more prophetic understanding of the real contribution of the utopians (from the Libertarians on the one side to the Students for a Democratic Society on the other) if we were to keep the question open about whether and why (or when or where) democracy is really the best form of government. Then the derivative intellectual moves in ethics and the derivative tactical moves in politics could remain subject to the critique and the illumination which would flow from keeping the initial justification visible. We would be less crippled in speaking to situations where democracy is no real option.

Such disengagement of the assumptions might save us from repeating such anomalies as supporting a ring of dictators around the world in order to make it safe for democracy, or might lower the voltage of the standard circular debate about whether democracy can or should be exported.

The kind of review of the case of democracy which I suggest could be undertaken from numerous perspectives, traditional and revisionist, within the various disciplines involved. I here suggest only that we add, as one specifically ethical perspective, a theological accounting for the context in which Christians in particular ask whether and why democracy is the preferred form of government. The two pointers from which, I suggest, we might have something to learn are:

1) A New Testament realism about the nature of governmental power, as exemplified in the political choices of Jesus and the apostles;
2) a free-church realism about the ambivalence of "Christendom," as this doubt has been exemplified in debates within the Protestant Reformation from Peter of Chelčic to Roger Williams, rebounding in contemporary bicentennial discussion about "civil religion."[2]

It is not a simple matter, going back to our biblical roots to find a clear vision of how the world political order ought to be. We need to correct for our built-in habits of thought, to recognize that prescriptive visions for how things ought to be, in the world beyond the community of faith, did not come naturally to early Christians, or to early Israelites. Israelite nationalists did have a vision for the civil order of their own people. It was theocratic rather than democratic and in historical experience not viable after the first successes of the Maccabees and Zealots.

Obviously the Maccabees knew what they wanted to see happen to imperial pagan government, as did the Zealots. They wanted it to go away. The Maccabean vision included an affirmative design for government according to the will of God, but projected that hope only for the people of God, not for a better empire. There was a prescription for righteous kingship tying together the priest and the prophet in the unity of God's people, but not a vision for a better Rome. Joseph, Daniel, and Mordecai contributed creatively to making more livable the *existing* pagan imperial system. Frustration with or opposition to a system, or even the desire of the apocalyptic or the Zealot that it should go away, did not yet constitute an alternative affirmative description of what would be the best form of government.

Perhaps an exception to my generalization would be the vision of Micah 4 and Isaiah 2, with all the nations coming to Jerusalem to learn the law and then going home to live in peace. This is in one sense a vision for an alternative way of having God run the world. Yet it is formally marked by not fitting in the frame I am talking about. The event which will attract the nations who come to Jerusalem is not successful empire building, nor effective prophetic critique, nor progressive involvement in political vocations, but the End-time intervention of Yahweh, who will elevate the hill of Zion above all the surrounding mountains and attract the nations to come uncoerced to learn the law. One might speak of this as an alternative vision of a world empire, but it is just as much a vision of the end of world empire.

It obviously did not occur to the early Christians to ask whether empire was or was not the best form of government. Nor is the call for democracy self-evident in most of the rest of the world. The tribesmen or slum dwellers today do not ask the question. Nor do Soviet Baptists or Christians in China. To ask, "What is the best form of government?" is itself a Constantinian question.[3] It is representative of an already "established" social posture. It assumes that the paradigmatic person, the model ethical agent, is in a position of such power (and of such leisure—but that would be a further question) that it falls to him to evaluate alternative worlds and to prefer the one in which he himself (for the model ethical agent assumes himself to be a part of "the people") shares the rule. This paradigmatic ethical agent is assumed to be free, adult, healthy, male (as even our generic pronouns testify), an owner of property, and able to earn.

The Constantinian moral paradigm makes a number of interlocking assumptions about the nature of ethical discourse, each of them self-evident within the system and each of them questionable from a biblical or radical reformation perspective. It is easiest to demonstrate the bearing of these questions by looking at specific applications like the ethics of violence and war, or (in the sixteenth century) like truth-telling and the oath. But as the axioms behind moral logic they reach clear across the board:

1. There is the axiom of generalizability in terms of the social whole as agent. By virtue of the numerical dominance of Christians in

society, when you ask what is right for Christians to do, you are asking what the whole society should do.

2. There is the assumption of generalizability through putting myself in the place of the ruler. The meaning of an ethical statement is tested by asking how the society would go if Caesar (or Carter or Reagan) were to administer his society accordingly, not only in his face-to-face relationships but through the legislative and coercive powers of his office.

3. There is the further generalizability of putting myself in the place of "Everyman." I test a moral statement about myself by whether I can wish that it would be a law for all.

Once the question is identified, it is most evident that none of these assumptions about convincing moral discourse would have made sense to the earliest Christians. They do not really make sense today to a dissident Baptist Christian in the Soviet Union, or to Christians in extreme minority situations anywhere else in the world.

Once these assumptions are made, and especially once they are made so sweepingly and so self-evidently as not to be critically conscious, they open the door for a whole new view of the ethics of power. From this point on, there is obvious reason to declare irrelevant many of the biblical models. Therefore one must replace them with something else.

Once these assumptions have been made, then there is no difficulty in elaborating within them why we now see democracy as the best form of government. Each of the above parties claiming paternity (Augustinian, Enlightenment, free churches) can give their reasons, and probably all are right.[4]

Gospel Realism

The simplest expression of a non-Christendom alternative stance that I can offer in this paper will be the conscious anachronism and oversimplification of reaching back to the New Testament to state an alternative. I offer this example not as a proof text nor as prescription, but as a provocative paradigm.

We may see the alternative social analysis simply stated in a text which Luke places most dramatically (Mark and Matthew have its near equivalent earlier in the story) within the conversations in the

upper room, just after the "institution of the Eucharist" and between
two predictions by Jesus of how his disciples were going to fail him.

"The rulers of the nations lord it over them." Jesus does not suggest
that this phenomenon of "lording it" or exercising dominion is one
which will go away or for which he has an immediate alternative. He
is not an anarchist either in tactics or in theory. He admits the fact
of dominion among the nations.

But Jesus does not glorify or ratify this fact. He does not affirm
that it is a work of Providence or divine institution. He does not affirm the divine right of rulers, as a majority of Christians since Constantine have done, including the transfer of such moral ratification
to democratic regimes since 1776. Jesus neither says that dominion
is good nor that it is bad. There is in his words no ethical evaluation of "dominion" as a good or bad system *for the nations.* He is,
one might say anachronistically, a positivist. He just says that it is
that way.

"Those who exercise authority let themselves be called benefactors." Again
the text is a description and not a moral judgment. Jesus does not
say that the rulers of the nations are benefactors. He reports that they
make that moral claim. "They let themselves be called" is the specific
thrust of the middle voice. It is the case that even the pettiest Carib-
bean dictator, like the most powerful in Peking or Moscow, makes
claims to be benefactor. But Jesus is not a cynic. he does not say that
the claims are false. He does not, like a modern Marxist, brush them
aside as ideological window dressing.

*"But it shall not be so among you; you shall be servants because I
am a servant."* After having descrbied realistically both the fact of rule
and the fact of value claims being made for that rule, Jesus locates
himself and his disciples in a different ethical game. They are not
to take over that game of "rulers-making-a-case-for-their-benevolence"
nor are they to attempt to interfere with it. They are called simply
to do something else. The meaning of that "something else" is the
alternative answer to the question of government which is represented
by the servant Messiah.

In the immediate context of the narrative of the passion, Jesus
was explaining to his disciples why they should see through and reject the Zealot option which, the text makes very clear, was still their
picture of his coming Kingdom. The pericope began with their argument about their places in the coming government: "Liberation-
fighters-making-a-case-for-their-beneficence" was their picture of Jesus

and of themselves. He set it aside in favor of the cross-and-servanthood alternative.

By the time Luke wrote his Gospel, and placed this story in the midst of the passion narrative, the Zealot ethic was no longer a possibility. We must read Luke as telling us that this text takes on a wider relevance. Now it is a capsule of a general view of government as such. This view is wide enough to include both the relative acceptance of the "powers that be" expressed in Romans 13 and the realistic denunciation of those same powers when their claim to be benefactors is unveiled as idolatry in Revelation 13.

This statement in Luke deals separately with three levels which we have been taught to merge. One level is the fact of dominion. It is simply there, independent of and prior to any process of evaluation. Secondly there is the level of moral rhetoric used by the bearers of power to legitimize themselves. This legitimation language comes after the fact of dominion. And then there is the third reality, the ethic of Jesus and his followers, who take their signals from somewhere else.

Since Constantine we have fused those three levels: the facticity of dominion, the language of legitimation, and the differentness of the disciples. Thereby we have confused rather than clarified the proper diversity of language. This mixes the descriptive and the prescriptive, interweaving the language which justifies coercion with that which guides voluntary discipleship. Since Constantine, when talking about government, we have assumed (as Jesus could not have) that we are talking about government of Christians and by Christians. We have thus lost the distance which Jesus maintained between his realism about power and his messianic liberty in servanthood. We have not distinguished between an ethic which can claim the authority of incarnation for the content of messianic servanthood and that other discourse which talks with the rulers about their claim to be benefactors.

Although in other respects the age of Enlightenment meant the beginning of modernity, in this realm it did not. Bearing fruit (differently) in the American and French Revolutions, Enlightenment thought claimed to reverse the sequence, deriving the fact of dominion from a process of legitimation. Naturally that had to be done, not in favor of the regnant regime, but in favor of and by means of a revolution. Before that was worked out in a secularized form by the *philosophes* in the name of the dignity of "the people" as bearer of reason, it had been done by the *monarchomaques* of second-generation Calvinism (Huguenot, Dutch, Scottish, Roundhead) in the name of the Protestant people as bearers of divine justice. Since our revelation succeeded, what we have now must be "government by the people" (as Eusebius had said, "God gave Constantine the victory, so this must be the millennium"). Thus the three-way fusion initiated by the empire's success *in hoc signo* is replicated in an uncritical, undefined fusion with "democracy."

The benefits to be gained for Christian moral thought from disentangling these three levels again would be multiple.

Instead of dreaming about either past or future situations in which Christians did or would constitute the powerful majority in society, we could accept as normal the diaspora situation in which Christians find themselves in most of the world today and in which voluntarily committed Christians will increasingly be conscious of standing also in the "post-Christian" North Atlantic world. We should be more relaxed and less compulsive about running the world if we made our peace with our minority situation, seeing this neither as a dirty trick of destiny nor as some great new progress but simply as the unmasking of the myth of Christendom, which wasn't true even when it was believed.

Having accepted our minority place within society we shall be freer than before to make fruitful use of the self-justification language of the rulers, whoever they be, as the instrument of our critical and constructive communication with them. If the ruler claims to be my benefactor, and he always does, then that claim provides me as his subject with the language I can use to call him to be more humane in his ways of governing me and my neighbors. The language of his moral claims is not the language of my discipleship, nor are the standards of his decency usually to be identified with those of my servanthood. Yet I am quite free to use his language to reach him. This is potentially as possible for the benefactor claims of a Soviet premier as for those of an elected American president.

When I have the good fortune to find myself in a situation where part of the rulers' language of justification is the claim to have the consent of the governed, then I can use the machinery of democracy and am glad to do so. But I do not therefore believe that I am governing myself or that "we" as "the people" are governing ourselves. We are still governed by an elite, most of whose decisions are not submitted to the people for approval. Of all the forms of oligarchy, democracy is the least oppressive, since it provides the strongest language of justification and therefore of critique which the subjects may use to mitigate its oppressiveness. But it does not make of democracy, and especially it does not make of most regimes which today claim to be democracies, a fundamentally new kind of sociological structure.

The word of Jesus also makes a difference between the facticity of the "lording it" and the justification claimed for it by the rulers themselves. This is the point at which democracies are as much in need of demythologizing as are all the other oligarchies. The consent of the governed, the built-in controls of constitutionality, checks and balances, and the bill of rights do not constitute the fact of government; they only mitigate it. This is not the case because our government is capitalistic, so that a change in property regimes would make it go away. Nor is it the case because our government has already undergone creeping socialism, so that a return to libertarian anarchy would set us straight. It remains the nature of the civil order itself that its coercive control is prior to any justifications or qualifications thereof.

This biblical realism about the priority of the facticity of the sword[5] over any theories about legitimacy does not mean setting aside the imagery of the "social contract," the "state of nature," or any other kind of myth which may be found useful as fulcrum for constructive criticism. But the state of nature and social contract language lead us seriously astray when they give the impression or support the argument that if Christians don't take over the government we shall fall into anarchy. We are more likely to fall into international anarchy (i.e., war) or into domestic war when people do take over the government with too strong a sense of divine calling to set things right, with the national order as instrument.

It would go beyond our depth in the space available to attempt to unfold, as a complete theory of the church within the civil order, the implications of the separation of the three levels: the brute existence of dominion, the language of beneficence whereby the rulers justify themselves and whereby they can thereby be called to greater decency, and the distinctive ethic of the Messiah who chose to serve. Suffice it to say it would throw new light on many of our conversations, dominated as they are by the transfer from royalty to democracy of the claim to be the one righteous social order which glorifies God by its very existence and thus will also be used for God's global purposes.

THE POSSIBILITIES OF ANALOGY

Does it follow from the rejection of "lordship" (a) that there should be "in the Kingdom" (whether that should mean "the age to come" or the free church) nothing at all like lordship? Does it follow from the challenges addressed to the logic of generalizability (b) that "in the Kingdom" there would be no such reasoning of that type? (c) What language can one then use within the context of faith? Might there not be formally equivalent usages, i.e., ways to "generalize" which the view advocated here would affirm? Is there not a right use of "leadership" language, and a right use of "generalizability," i.e., of illuminating one more choice by analogy to others?

I do not intend to argue that in the ethic of the Kingdom or of the church there would not be leadership or value claims or ways of testing ethical statements: I object only to the way in which in the Constantinian tradition these ways of reasoning were used to set Jesus aside. That does not banish the language of authority, justification in terms of beneficence, and generalizability, as if these ways of reasoning could be completely set aside. To assume that that was intended is a part of the denominational stereotype, which it is good to surface in order to set it aside.

The answer can be given in any one of three semantic frames. Let us call the first "marketplace semantics"; it tries to use terms in their ordinary usage. In our case the market rules for language have been established by the likes of Troeltsch, Weber, and the brothers Niebuhr. Then "leadership" or "power" does mean lordship, and the disciple of Jesus accepts being shut out of the power game when that happens, though the disciple does not withdraw on his or her own. That does not keep the disciple from dealing with the same theme in other terms, both in dialogue with the civil society, where it is called "subordination" in the New Testament case, and in the internal organization of the believing community, where it is called "ministry."

The logic which tests a value statement by its applicability to others, which I called "generalizability," in its three forms (society as agent, the ruler as prototypical agent, everyone as agent) excludes faith and unbelief as significant variables and is thereby unusable.

But we could, in a formal way, establish a roster of parallels showing how the same themes recur in three frameworks:

Having the grid before us may make the prose more understandable:

	The Nations in their own terms: market-place semantics	The faith community speaking to the nations	The faith community speaking internally
Kingship as beneficence	The tyrants let themselves be called "benefactors"	Appeal to the tyrant's language to make him less a tyrant	Servant leadership in the way of the cross
Generalizability A: Society as a whole as agent	Fill all the slots so society can run	Stewardship investing skills where most significant	Every member has a (distinct) charisma
Generalizability B: Caesar as agent	How would this work out if you were Caesar?	If you were the victim?	If you were the brother/sister for whom Christ died?
Generalizability C: Everyone as agent	You can't ask moral heroism of every man	You can ask civility of almost everyone	You do ask love of everyone

Thus the ethic of the Kingdom and the ethic for speaking to the kings of the nations will use parallel sets of terms, will answer parallel questions, but in each circumstance they will have a different meaning.

For example, there will be one kind of beneficence language used by the leaders of the Christian community to explain their pattern of leadership and the decisions they make, but this beneficence language will not promise to the community the kind of gratification of pride and greed which is often a part of the promises made to his electorate by the pagan "benefactor." Leaders in the Kingdom will promise not bread and circuses but a mixture of the blessings of voluntary community and the cost of the cross (Mark 8:35ff., 10:29ff.).

Similarly there will be in the ethics of the Kingdom some rough analogy or counterpart to the generalizability logic used in favor of the need for a Constantinian ethics. Here too, however, the way in which the reasoning works will be modulated to take account of the fact that there are not one but two different bases of community. The *kind* of generalizability which concentrates on needing to fill all of the slots in society will be profoundly changed by the recognition that this is not a possibility with regard to Christians governing the wider society. It will be replaced by the stewardship of scarce resources, allocating the available Christian leadership discriminatingly in the places where it is most strategically significant. Within the Christian community, of course, there will be a commitment to fill every position, but this will be illuminated by a doctrine of the particularity and the dignity of charisma, such that the ordinary generalization patterns will hardly be applicable.

The second kind of generalizability, which asks us to put ourselves in the place of the ruler and to decide all together how we would decide if we were in his place, and thus to vote for what we want him to do as our surrogate, would also be modified by the ethic of charisma, recognizing that each agent of "ethics in the Kingdom" is in a different place and that those different places do call for different functions. Yet none of these functions has moral autonomy over against the structure of the servanthood of Jesus. This stance will also cast light on the vocational decisions of persons committed to Kingdom ethics as they decide how to be active in the wider society: their preference will not be for dominion roles but for servant roles. I am fully aware of the limited helpfulness of this verbal distinction, but that does not mean that it is false.

Within the "sons of the Kingdom" framework of the language of generalization, the alternative to "What would you do if you were in the position of Henry Kissinger?" is not that I would have a more ambitious or a more believing or a more sacrificial recipe, or a more modest one, to guide a secretary of state or a president. I would be interested in that too. But my first duty would be to insist that the paradigmatic person by whose situation my ethic must be tested would not be the oppressor but the oppressed, not the most powerful or even the most righteous powerful person, not my representative or my ruler, but the one with whom Christ in his servanthood is first of all identified. The search for an ethic for the person in positions of relative or great power should not proceed by taking the Caesar model and modifying it by adding certain kinds of Christian modesty and morality. It rather should take the model of the subject and servant and modify that to take account of the empirical availability of ways to be socially effective with integrity.

The third kind of generalizability, the assumption of value homogeneity, the axiom *I am Everyman,* must be denied *when* it operates to determine the way in which the sons and daughters of the Kingdom participate in the world of the nations. They can act responsibly and honestly only if they recognize that there is *not* one common value system. Their witness to the bearers of power will always be modulated by awareness of that distance. Within the community of the children of the Kingdom on the other hand, I must call for a greater value homogeneity than most North American Christian ethicists or churchpersons are interested in. It is in fact striking to observe, concerning the reorientation of priorities since Constantine, that most of the mainstream theologians with whom I converse want me to accept *greater* value homogeneity as a part of the American *civil* covenant but at the same time want *less* value homogeneity in the Christian community.

Looking back over this set of parallels, it is obvious that at each of the three identified levels the criterion of generalizability needs to work twice rather than once. On one level it is affirmed, but in a mediated way, as one of the tools which the children of the Kingdom will use to talk to the kings of the nations. At the other point it has a more solid function within the Kingdom vocabulary itself.

We can certainly call all of this "politics" or "government." Yet by the nature of the case we must now have subscripts to identify the respective semantic frames. One is the beneficence and generalization language which the kings of nations themselves use to justify themselves. The second is the beneficence and generalizability logic which the children of the Kingdom use to maintain their own community. A third is the bridge between the two, which the children of the Kingdom use to communicate with a wider world which they at the same time share responsibility for and cannot control.

Still another way to handle the semantic package would be to use what some could call a "Barthian" logic and to say that it is the usage of governmental language within the people of God which is the norm. The governmental logic used within the wider culture is then only a pale reflection, analogy, dilution, perversion of "true politics." Only the politics of Jesus is politics according to the will of God. The politics of the kings and the nations are distorted, fallen, counterfeits of the same. The norms of the kings are dealt with most responsibly when their claim to autonomy and clarity is denied by the church's courageous persistence in using Kingdom language first of all within the context of faith, never really granting the propriety of the expropriation of Kingdom language by the nations. In a context of catechism, of preaching, or of liturgy, this is the best of the three ways of reasoning. This is what I was doing in calling my book *The Politics of Jesus*,[6] or what Jacques Ellul means when he uses the phrase "The Politics of God."[7] It is misunderstood however in ecumenical and apologetic contexts. Therefore I would not attempt to impose it in a conversation with the children of Troeltsch and Niebuhr, for whom the pagan definitions are semantically prior.

Thus it would seem possible to say all of the same things under any one of three different semantic arrangements: just as in algebra it does not matter whether the variables are called a, b, and c, or x, y, and z. It is sufficient to be aware of the relativity of our linguistic rulings to be able to translate from one frame to the other. The right column above could stand as "covenant" semantics. Usually the left column stands alone as "realism." The formally more discriminating analysis would identify the parallelism, with subscripts, so as to compare analogous functions in the three columns. That can be done. I prefer, for reasons of catechism, and proclamation, and because I do not really believe in the ultimate epistemological sovereignty of the marketplace, to make the case for the "covenant" arrangement. Nonetheless I accept the language of the marketplace, in the forum where the rules have been set by the establishment reformers and their recent heirs Weber, Troeltsch, and the Niebuhrs.

The challenge which goes beyond the semantic is to define the difference between the two systems of ethical substance (the two columns on the right) rather than to choose at which level of terms to operate. What I reject (not in a total rejection but by questioning its unlimited application) is such an understanding of beneficence and generalizability that from it is drawn a new set of ethical norms, contradictory in their substance to the servanthood of Christ and which it is claimed arise self-evidently out of the nature of things. If generalizability and beneficence are *not* used with that kind of natural revelatory claim, then I am free on the "formal semantic" level to compare item by item or even on the "covenant" level to pre-empt the language of someone else's ethics for my own system. This I do when I show that my argument for democracy and against tyranny is independent of the cultural developments of Reformation and Enlightenment, whereas other views are dependent upon some particular Western cultural experience to make them convincing.

Now we can see the pertinence of my warning against misinterpretation due to denominational stereotypes. By claiming that we might still learn from the separation of three levels in the language of the New Testament with regard to the function of the sword, I am not advocating systematic abstention from modern society, or even from "government," as the "Christ against culture" caricature of H. Richard Niebuhr or the "sect" concept of Troeltsch would have it. The interlocking of society is far more than civil government. What we call "government" today is by no means only the sword. I am rather pointing to a great variety of styles of involvement, of which "the sword" should not be the dominant paradigm. What we saw above in the New Testament description of the power of the sword, which recurs in classical political theory, was for one school the "definition of the state." When modern social orders assign to "government" the administration of many other kinds of services, it is by no means necessary to apply to them all the same church/world dualism which the New Testament applied to servanthood and the sword. When modern societies institutionalize opposition and the separation of powers, it is not evident that all "involvement" in public office need be swordlike.

The assumption that commitment to a minority ethic, derived from a minority faith, must issue logically in withdrawal from significant involvement in the social process, including the refusal of office holding or adversary roles, is itself an outworking of the establishment axioms which I am challenging. It assumes (with the first definition of generalizability above) that the relevance of an ethical stance depends on the readiness of its constituency to fill all the posts in society. It assumes (with the second definition of generalizability above) that the paradigm of the exercise of social responsibility is not the civil servant or the opposition legislator, the minority agitator or the political prisoner, but the sovereign. It assumes (with the third definition of generalizability above) that for us to collaborate in making the social system work there must be value homogeneity. These assumptions made sense for Constantine, for Charlemagne, for Calvin, for Cotton Mather, but they are antidemocratic assumptions, and we need not let them define the limits of the pertinence of a minority ethic. It is possible that in a totalitarian culture every possible segment of society is poisoned by the overarching coercive claims of the rulers, but that is the extreme abuse, not ideally normative nor empirically typical. Thus my concern to debunk the claim of nationalist democracy to be as such a whole new style of government does not set aside the relative claim of all welfare states (whether democratic or not) to provide usable structures of mutual service.

In summary: if we claim for democracy the status of a social institution *sui generis,* we shall inflate ourselves and destroy our neighbors through the demonic demands of the claims we make for our system and we shall pollute our Christian faith by making of it a civil religion. If on the other hand we protect ourselves from the Constantinianism of that view of democracy, we may find the realistic liberty to foster and celebrate relative democratization as one of the prophetic ministries of a servant people in a world we do not control.

In Favor of Holy Experiments

The negative case for democracy is the one that needed to be made first, for it is the most basic. It applies to the moral claims of any government anywhere. It has concrete textual rootage in the New Testament, not merely superficially in a proof text, but in a crucial christological context. It deals with the reality of government as it is.

It has been important first to clarify that particular call for democracy which is relevant to the more pessimistic view of our situation, to the more Niebuhrian view of the nature of institutions, and to the minority social setting in which Christians have lived in most of the world except for the West between Constantine and modernity. This does not exclude or in any way contradict the more hopeful case for democracy which properly arises in those places where their numbers, or their virtues, or their friends, or their good luck should give to Christians a chance for positive model building. In such favored contexts, there is another "Christian case for democracy" which must also be affirmed. It is the one which once almost succeeded, namely in the age of Milton and Cromwell. This is the vision of the Christian cultic commonwealth as a model for the civil commonwealth. In Christian community, where the Word of God is proclaimed, all should be free to speak and all should listen critically (1 Cor. 14). If that is the way divine truth is to be articulated in the words of our world, then those who have learned those skills of listening critically and speaking prophetically should be able as well to apply them to debates about human justice. The point is not that the Bible is to speak to every question of human justice; that would be the wrong half of the Puritan vision. It is that the people of God should know how to process other issues, once they have learned how dialogically and respectfully to process sacred truths. There is widely recognized evidence for a historic link between the Christian congregation (as the prototype) and the town meeting, between the Christian hermeneutic of dialogue in the Holy Spirit and free speech and parliament, or even between the Quaker vision of "that of God in every man" and nonviolent conflict resolution. It may work very creatively, but it can do so only if it goes all the way, to found its optimism on the logic of servanthood rather than mixing coercive beneficence with claimed theological modesty.

The Cromwellian adventure was sure to fail. It fused two claims: a moral mandate founded on the consensus of the people of God under the Word, and the concrete sanction of successfully lording it over one's neighbors. The incompatibility of the two modes became clear when the Levellers proposed not only to dismantle ancient privileges through Parliament but to replace the military chain of command with internal democracy in the New Model Army. Cromwell had to go back to taking power as Lord Protector.

The contradiction between consensus and rule was more credible at first in the newly founded Commonwealth of Massachusetts, since it had the privilege of beginning without strong adversaries to the left (like the Levellers) or to the right (like the Cavaliers). Yet as Massachusetts matured, it became more visible in its treatment of Friends, Baptists, and Indians that it again had to deny to others the freedom of faith which the founders had sought for themselves. Thus the several strands of the Puritan experiment confirmed that the only way to apply, as a paradigm for government, the open conversation of the church under the Word, is first to assure to any and all churches their own freedom by denying to any and all churches any civil privilege.[8]

We keep using the word "democracy" as a code word for a better civil arrangement. Yet what is most at stake is not for the *demos* to be able to *rule* but rather for other entities, first of all faith communities, and then by implication other voluntary associations and household structures, to pursue their own ends without any more central management, by the *demos* or anyone else, than the peace of the total community demands. So the irreducible bulwark of social freedom is the dignity of dissent; the ability of the outsider, the other, the critic to speak and be heard. This is not majority rule; it is minority leverage. When it goes to seed it can cause anarchy. But without it democracy becomes demagoguery or mindless majoritarian conformity. The crucial need is not to believe that "we, the people" are ruling ourselves. It is to commit ourselves to defending *their* right to be heard. We will not do that out of the goodness of our hearts. We will only be pushed to do that if *their* dignity is theologically founded along the trajectory from 1 Corinthians 14 to Fox's "that of God in every man."[9]

This is the element of truth in the by now widespread thesis of A. D. Lindsay. The origin of democracy in Puritan and Quaker meetings was not the product of a high view of human wisdom, nor were these people original at the point of their low view of human power. What was new was that peculiar commitment to the dignity of the adversary or the interlocutor which alone makes dialogue an obligation, and which can be rooted only in some transcendent claim.[10] So democracy, when thus defined, does not simply mean that most people get to talk or that everybody gets counted. It means a theologically mandatory vesting of the right of dissent.

This positive correlation between the free church under friendly skies and the viability of a generally dialogical democracy needs repetition, for it is too easily forgotten under the cheaper Enlightenment rhetoric of autonomous human dignity. Yet it hardly needs to be proven once again, or to be advocated. What we need is some way to be ready to revert back to unfriendly skies, without thinking that our only grounds for denouncing tyranny and counting on dialogue would have to be a too sanguine hope for the skies always to be sunny.

In sum: we can contribute to democratization either by using the tyrants' legitimation language against them, or by the ripple effect from faith community forms.

Neither of these approaches is the Enlightenment affirmation that "the people" can have the same voice as God, that the majority is right, or that the structures of oppression can be used for good if taken over by the other side. Those views hold that there is some such thing out there as a *demos,* which is capable of ruling, and that if the *demos* were to rule we would be well governed. There is no such animal. The *demos* is a mental construct, a useful cipher to stand for the claim of an insightful minority to express some pertinent criticism of the injustice of the present ruling minority and some credible projects for the alleviation of that injustice.

Each of these ways of approach has the merit of beginning from within what the community of faith knows internally about her own calling, rather than becoming tributary to whatever secular consensus seems strong at the time. From this base, elements of the Enlightenment critique of authoritarianism can be recovered, accountably, because they can be authenticated as transpositions of original Christian testimony. Elements of the optimism of bourgeois or Marxist humanism can be recognized as fragmentary translations of messianic hope, yet without their Promethean autonomy claims.

THE SHAMELESS TYRANT

The paper's first thesis, namely that the language we can use to critique any oppressor is his own ideology of legitimation, left another helpful challenge unanswered. If we state the rules of the game so that the criteria which we use against the abuses of the kings of nations are simply the criteria which they themselves proclaim as their argument that their domination is good for us, we lay ourselves open to the counter move that a crudely tyrannical ruler would admit that he is doing us no good; therefore we would have no language with which to criticize him. This is, of course, a theoretical possibility. It is not a very threatening real possibility, because most rulers do claim beneficence. We may consider this as a vestige of created goodness or as providential. Since the givenness of domination is the starting point of the description which I suggest is most realistic, I am not logically able (or obligated) to reach beyond that givenness to answer each question. It is in effect a new form of the Rawlsian "original condition" logic. If we were free to set up the rules of social ethical discourse so that there would be a possibility of criticizing an oppressive regime, how could they be so defined that the oppressor could not get out from under our critique?

My response must be a conversation between two heuristic logics, not between two views of the state. If there is such a thing as a tyrant who makes no claim to beneficence, he would not enter the original covenant thinking either. He would opt to take his odd chance at winning in a game of dog-eat-dog, rather than soberly counting the odds and choosing a livable system in which he would probably be the underdog. Of course Rawls can say that that tyrant would not be very reasonable in preferring the infinitesimal chance of ruling to the much broader probability of being a subject, but why should he want to be reasonable and Rawlsian if he does not want to be a benefactor?

The entire thought pattern which we recognize in various "social contract" or "original position" phrasings is a logical outworking of Constantinian assumptions. It asks, "if we had the power to set up the situation so as to be as fair and as foolproof as possible, how would we set it up?"

It assumes that it is in our power to state the rules of the game. Some of the contract theories are relatively pessimistic in that they see the purpose of the contract to be reciprocal control over the threats which we represent to each other. Others would be more affirmatively focused on what we decide we need to do together to have a good world. The more refined approach of a theorist like Rawls makes the more abstract assumption that we can bypass the choice between optimism and pessimism by asking more carefully, "How will my chances be the best if I cannot foresee in what circumstance I will find myself in the hypothetical new society?" This is an effort to get every citizen in the position of the sovereign, or, more precisely, to imagine oneself as sovereign only in the one act of setting up a system in which the odds are that one would be a subject. To say it another way: one attempts to describe the nature of the hypothetical political system in such a way that every participant in the process can be told that they have responsibility for it. This is never really the case through the exercise of the vote, since (except in the most simple town meeting or village referendum) the franchise does not deal with all the questions but only with the choice of oligarchies. So instead of basing the claim that "you are governing yourself" on the strength or weakness of the electoral process, the philosopher bases it on the idea that "you can imagine yourself in the position of deciding what kind of social order to have." This is itself a sovereign position, even though only hypothetical.

I do not mean to challenge the maieutic fruitfulness of the contract imagery as a way to articulate social criticism or to provoke the capacity to imagine better systems. The capacity to imagine better systems is one way to critique the present. One must, however, not be led into the kind of tacit assumption which the question suggests, namely that of reasoning as if somehow the freedom to ask "how shall we set this thing up?" were a real freedom. That freedom belongs only to the kings of the nations, and to them only inauthentically. It might be a very fruitful enterprise to analyze the recent discussions around the construct of Rawls to see how they do constitute new editions of the old notion that I have the freedom to decide what kind of a world I want. We are led astray if we think that it would somehow be possible for careful contract formulation to make abuse impossible, or that the real relevance of the citizen's criticism of the authorities could somehow be so defined as not to be dependent upon the affirmation by the authorities that the subject's criticism is appropriate.

This question may push us to conclude that the pessimistic empiricism which I saw encapsulated epigrammatically in a word of Jesus is actually a more realistic and a more reliable handle for critical witness than is the increasing abstractness of the contract metaphor. It is more important to know with what kind of language we criticize the structures of oppression than to suggest that we have the capacity to provide an alternative which would not also be a structure of oppression. The least oppressive form of government is what our custom calls "rule by the people." That is a better statement of the case for democracy than are claims rooted in "nature" or "contract."

9. Civil Religion in America

If we were discussing the biography of some person, the meaning of some law, or the platform of some party, the objective definition of what we were talking about would be relatively similar for all of the perspectives from which we would look at it. "Civil religion," however, is no such thing. It is an analytical concept used by some people to describe something they like, by others to decry something they dislike, and by others to locate a phenomenon with value-free scientific objectivity. This variety within evaluative views does not prohibit their talking about the same thing, but it does put the definition under considerable strain. It has·been pointed out that the people who were supportive of the fusion of religious language with civic values in the time of the civil rights movement found themselves on the other side of the fence when Richard Nixon started having church in the White House. As is the case with most subjects, this one has already been classified by Martin Marty, who has identified two different scales of variation distinguishing what various major interpreters mean by the phrase, so that with typical creativity he could entitle his analysis "Two Kinds of Two Kinds of Civil Religion."[1]

One way to get past this built-in source of confusion would be to define a normative vocabulary. Yet that solution would be deceptive. The definition of the nature of the problem *should* probably be different from each perspective. I need, therefore, first of all to suggest in what sense it is important that we deal critically with *on* of the various phenomena which might appropriately be called "civil religion."

The label assigned to me—"radical Protestant"—also needs definition. I take it to denote the common thread of critical testimony addressed to "established religion" by the Czech Brethren in the fifteenth century, the Anabaptists in the sixteenth, Quakers and Baptists in the seventeenth, and their heirs in frontier America.[2] Not being represented by any hierarchy or scholastic elite, this stance can never be spoken for with full representative authority; and by virtue of its aggressiveness it may well happen, especially in post-frontier situations, that it falls unawares into its contrary, into a form of "informal establishment."

The defining characteristics of "civil religion" that serve to locate the critique with which I am concerned are the following:

1. The community which carries and is carried by a set of religious understandings and practices is a civil community: i.e., one in which membership for most of its participants is not voluntary, in which a function of coercively sanctioned organization claims jurisdiction over all the participants, normally within a territorial definition of physical frontiers and normally with a substantial degree of centralization of power.

2. The identity, the welfare and the interests of this specific community, including the way those interests are recognized, defined and implemented by the governmental powers, are thought of as appropriately a special concern not only of the citizens themselves but of the deity they invoke.

3. The civil community is so defined as by its very nature to have outsiders and enemies. These are usually defined territorially, usually ethnically, sometimes religiously. Some of the major expressions of the alliance of God with the community's interests come at the cost of those "on the other side" – interests such as colonization, pushing back the frontiers, expelling aliens, winning wars.

4. Other significant differentiae of moral or theological commitment, it is thought, should be set aside in order for the religious resources to have the desired supportive effect without being undercut by narrower "sectarian" definitions of loyalty and identity. Such specific "sectarian" matters of identity are therefore set aside. Protestant, Catholic, Jew, and ethical humanist forget their differences and pull together. Confessional idiosyncracies are demoted to the level of folklore.

It is this common-denominator homogenizing effect which first led to the suggestion by people like Will Herberg that what we have here is not a coalition of faiths but a new religion, significantly different from each of the particular traditions it claims to transcend and to fuse.

5. It further follows backhandly from the above, that although no one ecclesiastical office or religious community can have distinctive standing or any claim to the support of the state, the clergy as

a whole or the Protestant/Catholic/Jewish/humanist elite spokespeople as a class do carry a new version of the ancient status of "establishment." They have access, as a group, taking turns, to subsidized chaplaincy services in public institutions. They reciprocate by assuring the powers that be of divine blessings in general and by reminding them occasionally of divine imperatives. The leadership figures of the religious and civil institutions will generally recognize one another as peers and usually as friends, sharing in a complementary way the leadership of the wider society. This is represented in the symbolism of the Middle Ages by the legend according to which Pope Sylvester and the Emperor Constantine exchanged documents and greetings ratifying one another's sovereignty. We might call this the affirmative side of the reciprocal recognition. The negative side was equally present in medieval memory in the legend of Archbishop Ambrose of Milan, who held so much moral authority and political wisdom that he was able affectively to discipline Emperor Theodosius for having committed a political massacre. In our age the positive form is probably best represented by the presence of religious figures pronouncing invocations at political events (It has occurred to practically no one until recently to attend to the fact that many in the audience do not recognize these clergymen as spokesmen for their faith). The negative form may be seen in the authority seized sometimes by clergy people (which loses its credibility if seized too often) to speak judgmentally of major moral offenses within the political order.

By transforming the separation of church and state from the original notion of the Anabaptists, Friends, and Baptists, which had been rooted in the incommensurability of two orders, into the pragmatic fair-play notion of the Bill of Rights—namely, that no sect should have an unfair advantage and that the matter of establishment should be left to the several states—room was created for a new and more powerful version of the fusion of civil and religious covenants. Thereby the religious ratification of civil purposes became all the more undisciplined, since the civil authorities could demand the allegiance of all the clergy in general but were accountable to none in particular. There is no longer a more-than-local manifestation of the people of God as unity. No denomination is that. No set of denominations with common views is that. No patriarch or synod can talk back to the president or the Congress. Thereby the President becomes an updated Constantine, all the more so because we have no updated Sylvester to grant him his dignity and no updated Ambrose to upbraid him.

There would be a number of additional objections to address to this pious mainstream tradition from the perspective of "radical Protestantism." I have selected and shall pursue those (above) which seem to be the most directly operational for present purposes, without meaning to exclude the others. Among those others, especially the following, not pursued here, would be worthy of more attention.

6. Radical Protestants have always been concerned for the inwardly authentic quality of personal experience and commitment. From this perspective one judges the run-of-the-mill piety which is satisfied with conformity to easily attained patterns of expression. This critical perspective on hypocrisy and superficiality presupposes a more authentic alternative, which is very difficult to define. Once it is clearly defined, that new, more authentic form becomes inauthentic in its turn; yet that kind of preoccupation always belongs as part of the radical Protestant vision. The "civil religion" is judged for being feasible; its demands are too attainable.

7. One would need to spell out, behind this potential for critique, the assumptions that it makes about the authority of Jesus Christ in relation to other authorities, the authority of Scripture in relation to other patterns of insight, or what is traditionally called the problem of "revelation and reason." Here I intentionally have set aside that more systematic way of stating the problem, because of the amount of digression that would be needed to deal with it adequately. Nonetheless, it must be said that for the critical thrust described here to "work," there must be a knowable, definable Word—be it Jesus, the Bible, or the prophetic event—clearly set apart from common sense in its ordinary meanings. A "civil religion" on the other hand is commonsensical; it can have no imperious Lord.

If there were space for conversation with the earlier corpus of analytic writings on "civil religions," it would probably be important to look more analytically at the interaction of all the above seven traits, to ask whether one of them is more basic than the others. Is one fundamental and the others derived from it? Are they all equally objectionable and for the same reasons? Are some of the objections more important from the "civil" side and others from the "religious"? For the purposes of the present critique I shall rather posit the assumption that we are dealing, not with basically distinguishable traits which could be evaluated separately, but with multiple aspects of one global phenomenon.

The "Ideal" Alternative Approach

I intentionally look at "religion" here as a multidimensional social phenomenon rather than as one central "religious idea." The obvious and most traditionally attractive alternative would be to pay attention only to one such idea or a set thereof. In the Declaration of Independence as a founding document, it is said that all men are equal by creation and that this gives to them inalienable rights of life, liberty, and the pursuit of happiness. The idea of a Creator is a religious idea, although it appears here in a somewhat watered-down form. The idea that all people are bearers of rights is important for social criticism and construction. The very notion that a particular government should claim to be the incarnation of a philosophical principle is radical in unprecedented ways. The use made of this foundational affirmation by later saints like Lincoln and King has given this pair of phrases a special status. Is that "idea" itself our "civil religion"? My choice not to use that kind of propositional focus for this analysis may need explanation.

1. That statement did not, for the people who made it two centuries ago, identify a genuinely transcendent fulcrum of judgment from which to criticize their own culture. The "all men" in question did not include women or blacks or original Americans. It reinforced, more than it criticized, the qualities of civil self-righteousness and defensiveness which I have identified above as part of our problem. By attaching the appeal to the Creator to such a self-serving affirmation of rights, they also devalued the genuine transcendence which biblical religion insists on being judged by.
2. The pop intellectualism which claims to derive institutions from a few key ideas is wrong as a social science; it cannot be the right way to use religious ideas.
3. Although the language of "rights" can explain an insurrection it cannot create or govern a community. It cannot explain the realistic anthropology of federalism, checks and balances, and bills of rights, which had to move far beyond 1776 to create a viable government.

4. Far more important than the genesis of an idea is the sociology of its carriers, i.e., who the people are who will use such ideas as leverage for change rather than as window dressing for privilege, where those people will get their gumption and their social support. This is a question of community, not of the history of ideas.

It is true that more critically and creatively inclined people, including the two prominent prophetic Americans just named, were able to use this phrasing as an instrument for a more fundamental criticism and reconstruction. But that they were able to do so must be explained by reference to something other than what this phrase initially meant from the pen of Jefferson or in the politics of the colonies breaking with the Crown; it is that wider and more critical reference which I am seeking to interpret. What made it possible for them to make a prophetic rather than a defensive use of the creed of 1776? It was not that creed alone.

Establishment and Its Analogs

By setting aside this particularly intellectualistic interpretation of the "American religion," we have also prepared ourselves to move beyond the general description of our thesis to its historical location. Certainly a great originality of the great American system is disestablishment. The exercise of religion is constitutionally defended against infringement by governmental authority and the establishment of religion is removed from the purview of the federal government. Does that not amount to a resolution of our problem, in contrast to the various patterns of church-state linkage and subservience of the institutional church which had dominated the European scene since the fourth century? We can better locate our present problem by observing how it is that this apparent step forward was on a more fundamental level a step sideways: i.e., an avoidance of the problem on its deeper level by means of a reformulation on the surface.

Here we have reached the root of that specific critique of national or public religiosity which accentuates its continuity with that ancient temptation, whose victory radical Christians since the Middle Ages have been calling the "Constantinian fall of the church." What was wrong, in the fourth century, in that profound redefinition of the meaning of Christianity for which the first baptized emperor was to become the symbol, was not so much wrong for the empire as it was for the church. Church membership henceforth no longer meant belonging to a voluntary community of disadvantaged, if not always actively persecuted, believers but became compulsory. The Christian hope beyond history was relocated, to be juxtaposed with the prosperity of the imperial throne. From this redefinition of hope and of community followed all the other redefinitions of hierarchy, cult, and morality which later gave rise to the call for reformation.[3]

As the medieval synthesis ripened through the Crusades and the Renaissance, some called for reformation because the doctrines had gone wrong. Ideas were abroad which were counter to Scripture, or to the Fathers. True enough, but why had the doctrines changed?

Others called for reformation because the forms of church management and ritual had been deformed. These critics rejected the papacy, or pompous and formal worship, or the medieval understanding of the Eucharist. True enough, but why had that gone wrong?

Still others called for change because the church's moral vision had been lost; bishop tolerated or even implicated themselves in the avarice of simony and the violence of the Crusades. True again; but why had they arisen? The answer of the Waldensians in the twelfth century, of the Czech Brethren in the fifteenth, of the Anabaptists in the sixteenth, of the Baptists and Friends in the seventeenth, was that "establishment" was the error behind it all. So my assignment is to explicate the perspective from which what is wrong with American "civil religion," as the newest metamorphosis of the old dragon of religious establishment, is wrong not only as a bad way to be civil but, even more, or primordially, as a bad way to be religious.

Thus my assignment unfolds of its own accord. Concerning each of the already identified traits of the phenomenon, I need to demonstrate, in ways that others of any persuasion should be able to understand, that it is civilly bad, and in ways that make sense biblically that it is religiously bad. But before proceeding with that exposition, I must ward off one persistent misinterpretation, which claims that the only way for the religious critic to be consistent is for him to admit irrelevance to the political realm.

CRITIQUE IS NOT RETREAT

It is a common move, for those who consider themselves to be moderate or responsible in the custodianship of any majority tradition, to grant room for criticism but to do so by the patronizing maneuver of relegating it to the fringes. The "saint" and the "prophet" will find ready recognition from them, but at the price of the concession that their critical vocation is heroic, unique, and not to be taken as normative for others, nor as a judgment upon the unavoidable responsibilities that others must take upon themselves. Not only is the individual "vocational" withdrawal into irrelevancy granted a backhanded recognition; the "moderates" will recognize, as well, collective withdrawal by monasteries and Mennonites, friends of nature and Rechabites, whose collective rejection of some element of some dominant culture is recognized as having a kind of moral merit, with the proviso that it is worthy of respect only in correlation to the degree of consistency with which the withdrawal is carried through. What will not be recognized by these midstream persons who are willing to grant the moral integrity of "vocational withdrawal" is the possibility that they might be challenged on moral grounds not from the fringes but from within the system which their centrism is claiming to administer. It is therefore of fundamental importance that the "radical Protestant" view of which I am to speak is neither individual vocational purism nor communitarian countercultural withdrawal, but a challenge to the established system upon its own turf.

I said before that the error represented by the establishment is primordially a theological offense. It comes first, in the order of logic, to say that it is wrong for the church to be established. It is, however, no less wrong for a wholesome civil order that it should establish a religion. Therefore the denunciation of establishment occurs as much for the sake of the health of the civil community as in the defense of the fidelity of the religious community. Such denunciation is a service to society, not a retreat into purity.

The most pernicious effect of the Constantinian concubinage is not that it permits provincialism and community self-centeredness to go on. They would go on anyway. The worst is not even that God is made responsible for the mixture, though that is blasphemy. God is used to that. The worst damage is done by the system when it dictates the terms in which the critics can respond to it, casting their criticism as a mirror image of what they reject, rather than seeing that they refuse the standard formulation of the issue. This happens whenever free churchmen let themselves be told they must be anticultural or apolitical. The alternative to Christian nationalism is not religious treason, but more constructive—because more critical—reconception of the values a national community should stand for.

The alternative to idolatrous patriotism is not *un*patriotic. The alternative to the fusion of Christ and culture is not a Christ rejecting culture, but a more radically Christ-oriented transformation of the genuine values hidden amidst the mishmash called "culture." The alternative to the neo-Constantinian fusion of church and national power is not withdrawal to the ghetto, the desert, or the *bruderhof,* but the discovery of the next frontier where a more honest dialogue between the community of faith and her neighbors can build a more open pattern of civility. The alternative to buying into the power game as it is being played is not opting out, but inventing a new game. I would therefore have been falling into a trap if I had sought to formulate a simple negation by saying (assuming that we had solved the earlier problem of a common definition) that whereas some others consider civil religion good, and others call it ambivalent, I know it is simply wrong. Such a simple negation would be tributary to the wrong way of putting things which it sought to reject. What I must condemn is not that the phenomena of nation and power should be seen as important, or be a theme of religious concern and theological interpretation, but the particular ways in which that concern is shaped and in which that interpretation proceeds.

The issue is thus not one that can be clarified by a mere ruling as to how we should use words. Sidney Mead has preferred to use the phrase "The Theology of the Republic."[4] That means for him a perspective more critical than the religious patriotism of others, but that is because of Mead's own wise civility, not because the words are better. The question is not one of phrases, nor of agenda, but of direction. Is Christian participation in the costs and responsibilities of citizenship, insofar as those are accessible, a matter of claiming God's support for our purposes, especially the defensive and self-centered ones, or of pleading our support for God's causes? Neither a reassuring slogan like "responsibility" nor an alien one like "distance" can help us much. What we need is to look at cases.

I just said that the alternative to buying into the power game according to its old rules is to begin a new game. That alternative is not a pipe dream; it has been at work in the past. Over against the blind-alley models of Puritan establishment in New England and Anglican establishment on the southern seaboard, it was the free churchmen Roger Williams and William Penn who—no less practical for being guided more by their churchman's experience of the faith community than by England's experience of royal authority—were first not only to envisage but also to create a commonwealth with religious freedom, where the original Americans were recognized in the dignity of their languages and tribal culture. As Franklin Littell said decades ago in his insightful dash through the American religious experience, *From State Church to Pluralism,*[5] when Christianity in America sees itself as the youngest of the Christian nations of Europe, it renews the racist-nationalist sins of the old country with the vigor of youth. When on the other hand we see growing here the oldest of the younger churches, then the leverage offered in North America for cultural creativity is unparalleled.

The line goes on through the underbrush at America's growing edges. There were William Lloyd Garrison and Alexander Campbell holding together abolitionism and nonviolence. There were William Jennings Bryan and Norman Thomas and Harold Stassen, perennial near winners, seeing their victors soon defeated and some of their causes winning. There was Judge James E. Horton, who in 1933 sacrificed a judicial career in the attempt to give a fair trial to a black man. There was Martin Luther King, Jr., utterly Baptist when almost despite himself he became the most important churchly instrument of cultural change in our century. Most of them Baptist, most of them pacifist, most of them who would rather be right than president; they were the heralds of the agents of creative cultural change on a national scale precisely because they did not conceive of national power as their goal, but kept their eyes on the higher loyalty of Kingdom citizenship.

Thus the stereotypical notion, that a Christian commitment governed by such more critical and more promising visions drawn from the experience and the witness of the Christian community can properly be categorized as "apolitical" or "unrealistic" (as was done in the heritage of Ernst Troeltsch by the brothers Niebuhr) misreads the facts. A more demanding and more promising vision is not unrealistic just because it calls for risky faith. It would be unrealistic if it sought to impose desired behavior on others in the absence of conviction to support it (as in the national detour with the Prohibition of beverage alcohol). It would also be wrong if "faith" in due process and in the wholesomeness of tolerating dissent were identified with Christian commitment. But those are establishment mistakes. The figures just named made neither of those mistakes. But neither did they—and here is the discrimination misunderstood by the Niebuhrian analysis—conclude that because faith cannot be imposed, they should retreat to a world (or even to a church) where there would be only believers, or that because humane decency is less than the gospel it should be written off.

Is Religion Necessarily a Good Thing?

One strand of critical perspective which demands attention, although at first it seems to bring only confusion, is the increasingly open doubt which has been growing in different directions for the last century about whether the best way to talk about Christian faith is to put it within the wider category of "religion" at all. The strongest thrusts in this direction, after having been strongly stated earlier in our century, have been displaced by some more recent fads and trends, but not because they were soberly refuted.

There are profound reasons for doubting the adequacy of the term "religion," if and insofar as by that term is meant something which has about it sufficient clarity of definition that it will seriously help define all the categories of things that it means to cover. Without assuming that all of them merit our simply affirmative acceptance, I owe it to the dialogue to allude here to the half-dozen ways in which it has been seriously advocated that Christianity is best not understood as "a religion" or as "one of the religions."

There is a significant difference, although we need not pursue it at length here, between the two phrases just used. To suggest that Christianity is "one of the religions" is to posit a larger class, all of the elements of which are somehow similar in their basic structure or function, with the commonality of their belonging to that genus being more fundamental for definition purposes than their difference, and being already known to us.

On the other hand one may talk about the Christian faith as "a religion" without paying attention to all of the others. Then one gives to that term a meaning which is assumed to be understandable in itself as a part of Western culture since the time when in the fourth and fifth centuries Christianity replaced the kinds of "religion" that had been operative in the Roman world. What is being said about it when it is called a religion is not a comparison to any living analogs, but rather a description of the place in Western culture that it has taken over and from which the other ("false") religions have long been successfully preempted. It says that Caesar cult or sun worship have been displaced but not that Buddhism and animism are of the same genus.

Since the others are held to be "false" and ours is "true," established Christianity may be (as far as Western thought in the Middle Ages is concerned) the only one of its kind. Therefore when we say Christianity is a religion we need not ask about the others. Hendrik Kraemer, in his *The Christian Message in a Non-Christian World*,[6] worked out most carefully the implications of the line of questioning already being directed against this view by Europe's "theology of crisis" in the 1920s and by the "theology of the word" in the 1930s. If God is really God and not a projection of our best intentions, if we are really sinners and our ability to know, or at least to know divine truth, is negatively conditioned by the warping of our own wills against the truth of God, if the message of the gospel is that God has acted in ways we could not fully predict, could not do ourselves and cannot even adequately reflect upon in our own wisdom, then any response to this kind of message from God must on rigorously logical grounds be radically distinguished from those kinds of human behavior which in all societies express the efforts people make to come to terms with the complexity of life, to manipulate unseen powers, to find God by much searching, or in any other way to replace the simple acceptance of pardon by pure grace with some kind of human performance. Then to become a "religion" is the abiding temptation of Christianity rather than its essence. This critique of Kraemer's sees its polemic precursors in the argument of Augustine against Pelagius, or of Martin Luther against medieval Catholic works religion, or of the "theology of crisis" against liberal humanism. Christians may do religious things but in so doing they are no different from pagans. What is specific to biblical realism, says Kraemer, is the absolute subordination of the things Christians do and the ideas they cultivate to the prior action of a God whom they could never reach on their own and whom in fact they do not even have any criteria for accrediting. Human efforts to reach the divine, including human efforts to operate apophatic or ascetic disciplines so as to get out of the way and facilitate the divine's reaching us, are all the kind of self-salvation effort which Christian faith condemns as pride. Not only does it work at the wrong task; it exaggerates and escalates the basic problem, namely the epistemological presumption of our claim that we shall know truth when we see it if we only work a little harder at finding it.

This is not to say that Christians do not also do the kinds of things that "religions" lead people to do: they pray, they theorize about the transcendent, they meet physic needs . . . but that is not what makes Christian faith Christian. Those activities, when seen in themselves or in what they do for a person, are rather the temptation to faith than its nature.

This pattern of criticism by Kraemer and Karl Barth was a part of the breakthrough in the 1930s of recognition that old patterns of interpretation of Christianity as a "typical" human phenomenon were not working. By no means, however, was this critique the first of its kind. It seems rather that this critique made it possible that earlier ones, which had not been honestly faced or which had been observed but feared and not responded to, could also now be given attention. This meant reaching back all the way to Feuerbach, who was one of the first to draw the most thorough conclusions from the observation that a religion is a human activity, making God in our image or in the image of what we decide we need.

Barth also opened the door for some moderately respectful attention to the critique of Marx to the effect that "religion" has the defensive social function of weakening the critical perception which the poor might otherwise have developed of the injustices of their own existence and thereby defending the class interests of the people in power. It is no surprise that Barth was a socialist. He agreed with social conservatives that Christianity has in the past been a supportive factor in the defense of power relationships as they now stand.

Barth even made room for the cultural critique of a man like Nietzsche, for whom religion as a network of references to the transcendent cuts the nerve of a human dignity which ought to be affirmed in its own right.

Barth did not have to reach back even that far to make some room for the critique of Freud: religion is a special kind of illusion or compensation phenomenon which has the psychodynamic function of making sense of a world that becomes increasingly confusing as we grow up in it. Whether we focus on Freud's own further definition of the needs it meets as predominantly sexual, or go other directions with Adler or Jung or Erikson, in any case "religion" is explained "from below" as a human performance, and not the most mature kind at that.

It was probably a conscious prolongation of ideas initially encountered in Barth, but when Dietrich Bonhoeffer in prison elaborated his own critique of religion as the backdrop of a world view, he was saying something more. On the personal level, Bonhoeffer was critical of what he called "methodism." This meant no reference to the denomination. It was rather a designation of the way in which many think that to win someone for the Christian faith one must speak to him at the point of his weakness. One who makes this assumption is then predisposed to attend to the shadow side of human existence, since it is that which proves that "something more is needed." Such "methodism jumps on a man when he is down": it proves the need of God by proving we are no good without God. This is for Bonhoeffer the opposite of the gospel itself, which should be telling people, especially outsiders, about the love and goodness of God for its own sake, not trying to convince people of their misery or their guiltiness. Only if it is *not* seen as a response to weakness, only if its credibility does not depend on proving human weakness, is the gospel really the good news of the love of God as Creator, sustainer, Savior. Apologetic approaches that try first to make the point of human weakness and ignorance and lostness are hopeless, not because they do say something true, but because what they are interested in proving is not the good news.

The last phase of the reception and updating of the critique of religions was found in the early writings of Harvey Cox and in parallels and echoes near the same time as the publication of his *Secular City*.[7] For early Cox "religion" represents a normal, stable world view focusing upon the otherworldliness of basic reality. This preoccupation with the other world undercuts the importance of historic reality as fact and as mission, since it continues to claim that the higher reality is somewhere else than in history.

Behind all of these recent critiques of "religion," appealed to as a precedent by some of them, is the original Hebrew rejection of the religions of those days, condemning the great cosmic/imperial cults of Babylon and Assur, and in the same breath the local fertility deities of Canaan's hills. The first Christians reaffirmed that Jewish heritage and proclaimed it across the Mediterranean world, denying respect to the Hellenistic pantheon and obeisance to the divine Caesar. The theological name for misdirected religion is *idolatry*, "worshipping the creature instead of the Creator." The civil community, its values and its power structure, are as good a specimen as we can get of such a creature as should properly be respected, used, even honored, but not sacrificed to.

Yet another dimension of the "religious," one which the cultural anthropologist would make more of, is the unique status it gives to a few special persons: the shaman, the priest, the seer. Set apart by heredity, by initiation, by education, or by peculiar disciplines, that person renders to the society a service of linkage to the divine world which all the others gladly pay for. Over against this vocationally separated definition of the religious person, there stands the "laicizing" impact which Hebrew faith had upon the ancient near eastern religions, early Christianity upon Hellenistic and Roman religions, and radical Protestantism upon the sacerdotalism of medieval and magisterial Christianity. The cross-reference is evident to the fact that even a secularized and pluralistic culture still has a special slot for the "clergy."

The last form of this critique of religion centers on the agenda of the community. Priestly "religion" attends to the limits of manageable life; mortality and mystery, facing death and catastrophe. Or it celebrates rhythm; its ritual follows the yearly cycle of the crops or the life cycle of birth-puberty-marriage-parenting-death. For all this a separate ritual realm is helpful. Prophetic faith cares about ethics and politics, righteousness in history, poverty, power, justice, which it refuses to leave to the politicians by making the "religious" another plane.

What do all of these criticisms of "religion" lead us to? First of all, it should be repeated that I am reporting here the witness of Christian theologians, who "do theology" because of their concern with the authenticity of Christian faith. I am not talking about free thinkers, skeptics, enlightenment critics, or professional doubters, but about accountable professional theologians, who for reasons of integrity and evangelism are concerned to distinguish the Christian message itself from some of its broad equivalents and from its most evident counterfeits.

It is not true that any religion is better than none, so that, for example, all "religionists" should close ranks over against "secularism" or "irreligion." Nor that religion is alright, just so it does not get too involved in politics. It is rather the case that most religion is idolatrous and some of it is blasphemous. The first duty of churchmanship and of theology is then vigilance toward wrong religion. It is as a part of that vigilance that insufficiently critical attention to the intrinsic presumptuousness of civil powers and provincial communities must be denounced.

The several critics of wrong religiousness whom I have cited were not centering their attention expressly on the civil realm. They were working at other facets of the theological task. Yet each of their critiques applies with special aptness to the civil temptation and becomes most understandable when instantiated there. If their critiques are seen to be understandable, meaningful, verifiable, applicable to the real situation, then it is specifically at the line between "civil religion" and authentic belief that the particular kind of critique they call for would begin.[8]

The Alternative

The first thing wrong with "civil religion," on my list, was making the faith community involuntary. That is the one point where the American system preceded the rest of the world in pulling out of the medieval synthesis. It was possible for our governments to decontrol the churches, thanks to Roger Williams and William Penn, whose first concern was for the authenticity of free Christian allegiance. They determined as churchmen to decontrol the state. The first British Baptists and Friends did not want religious freedom as a better form of government; they wanted free, adult membership as the right way to be church. In that insight they went beyond the New England theocrats, who used the same language about the church but remained Zwinglian, or Calvinistic, about government. It can hardly be our theme here to review, as if it were news, the case against infant baptism – although it is news today in reformed Switzerland, in Lutheran Germany, and in Roman Catholic liturgical renewal circles. This is, however, the time to renew the warning that the fusion of evangelical language with political neo-conservatism – which right now claims to be gaining ground electorally with the avowed design of again putting the power of the civil sword behind the preservation of white Anglo-Saxon Protestant values – threatens to be one more tragic re-edition of that ancient mistake, all the more tragic when the media ministers leading the campaign are nominally Baptist.

We cannot ask of civil society that its membership be voluntary. But we must continue to object when the institutional separation to which all modern democracies have come by now is belied by a continuing psychological equivalent of establishment.

The second mark of the civil religion, on my list, was the invocation of the God of the Bible to bless this community in a way which redefines the very character of whom we understand that God to be. The way in which transcendence is defined determines the difference between the religion of the nation—into which established churches fall—on the one hand, and on the other Christianly accountable kinds of theological grappling with the meaning of the nation, which classically has been done by free churches. If the God-reference of civil religion is inward or upward, it provides no effective leverage for critique or transformation. The God-language of the Bible does not point inward to the renewed heart alone, nor upward to the "higher power," nor forward to the "hereafter," but backward to the salvation story, outward to the claims of the rest of the world, the enemies to love and the slaves to free, and forward to a city not of our own making. Of these, it is the historical reference from which we stand to learn the most. Only *it* will stand still to be counted. The irreducible historicity of Abraham and Moses, Jeremiah and Jesus, the demonstrable wrongness of Constantine and Charlemagne and the Crusades, the providential rightness of the renewals, spoken for by Peter Waldo and Peter of Chelcic, by Fox and Bunyan, Penn and Williams, of the call to obedience to a God whose sovereignty is not at the service of human dominion but who rather calls human power into servanthood; these are the memories that can best give substance to our hopes. The transcendence that counts is not a power from beyond that is now leashed to favor us, but the affirmation of values beyond our control to which we are committed, calling us to be ministers of peace and of justice above, beyond, and maybe even against our own interest. Ask not what God can do for America; ask what America owes humankind. This observation applies as well to the most valid of the less churchly civil theologies, like that of Lincoln.

The references thus far to God as transcendent, beyond our situation in time or in space, can become concretely effective within the civil community only if represented by a discrete empirical community, what we call the free church. All of the language of transcendence is but rhetoric unless there be a visible body of people who are able to escape conformity to the world while continuing to function in the midst of the world. It is their confessional commitment to living according to the transcendence we have been talking about which enables and in turn is enabled by their social visibility. The insistence upon the baptism of adult believers, which led some people to be called by their persecutors "anabaptist" in the sixteenth century or "baptists" in the seventeenth, was not the fruit of a psychologically preoccupied concern for the age at which it is possible for a person to have a valid religious experience. It was the sociological prerequisite for forming in the midst of the world a community of nonconformists whose culture and character cultivate an alternative construction of the community's history. That community is different from the surrounding community not because, like so many groups of immigrants in the American melting pot, they came from a different part of the old country, but because of the allegiance they confess to Jesus as Lord, over against other lords.

That God's transcendence is moral and not only metaphysical, that the differentness he demands is justice and not otherworldliness, is part of the reason no institution can claim his rubber stamp. The church can speak for God only under the proviso of forgiveness and subject to the contradiction of others. No government can speak for Him, no nation can count on His aid in its selfish pursuits or identify its adversaries as His enemies. Thereby we are driven on to our third point. The God of the gospel loves His enemies.

The beginning difference between the nationally defined vision of human dignity and the biblical one is the place of the outsider. The Abrahamic covenant begins with the promise that all the peoples of the earth are to be blessed. The early centuries of Hebrew experience seemed far from that goal, with the exclusion of the Egyptians and the Canaanites in particular and of the "enemy" in general from the scope of saving concern. Yet the story moves steadily toward the inclusion of all nations. The concern of the Mosaic laws for "the stranger in thy gates," Jeremiah's acceptance of the dispersion, Paul's mission to the Gentiles, and Jochanan ben Zakkai's acceptance of the fall of the second temple are only the most notable of the milestones along the way to the deterritorialization of the believing community. "They take part in everything as citizens, and put up with everything as foreigners. Every foreign land is their home, and every home a foreign land. . . ."

It seems clear that in the *ordinary* meaning of "civil religion," the American experience has always needed the polar outsider to precipitate a common self-awareness: the savage, the slave, the infidel, the "hun," the "Jap," the godless Communist. . . . It may be that our own ethnically mixed society demanded the foil of a racially polar bad guy nation to reflect upon ourselves a borrowed sense of natural unity.

The challenge is simple: if we accept that traditional territorial definition of the community under God, we deny the unity of the human race in creation, the cosmopolitan reality of the church in mission, and the eschatological vision of the world in redemption. The alternative is to accept the claim that this nation, any nation, every nation under God is called to multicultural reconcilation internally and to practical humanitarianism globally. Is it too much to ask of the United States that national interest be seriously qualified by commitments to the dignity of other nations and peoples, acknowledged in the form of real claims held by others upon our cultural and economic resources? If we are willing (as I fear we are) to leave it to the Swedes and the Canadians to project internationalism as a realistic policy, then let us at least not burden the God of Abraham with our provincialism.

I mention territorial provincialism first, in order that it be clear that the offense against the world vision of the God of Abraham and Jesus is first of all more than a matter of dollars or of lives. The first question is who the humanity is whom God loves. Yet the most dramatic expression of our provincialism is obviously not our general xenophobia or our disregard for other languages and cultures. It is not even our neocolonialism. It is that with a good conscience and with the resonance of congressional bipartisanship we continue (even in an age of national belt-tightening) to escalate our investment in the capacity to destroy, by the hundreds of thousands if need be, the citizens of nations we have let someone declare are our "enemies." At the same time that we make those peoples the hostage of our nuclear targeting, or of our discriminating acceptance of "moderately repressive" dictatorships, we state our convictions that the governments that rule over those people do not speak for them, are not morally legitimate; yet it is against their people that we prepare for war.

If the military expression of our nationalism is the most blatant, it may be that in peacetime its commercial expressions are more concretely destructive. The multinational corporation is in fact not even subject to the controls of one particular government. Yet in a broad cultural way it is the fitting expression of the patterns of not morally committed rational exploitation to which the "free enterprise system" commits its advocates, with the maximizing of profits finding a transnational terrain freed even from the antitrust regulations which the capitalistic nations enforce domestically. My concern here cannot be to analyze the good or the evil that these entities commit but only to recognize that, as a portion of our society sees in them a celebration of the special worth of our peculiar American economic system, we have raised provincialism to a global scale in the economic realm, as we had already done it in the realm of military technology.

It will not ward off this concern to say that in judging military patriotism I speak from the bias of a perspective which even since Constantine has been resoundingly voted down by majority Christianity. I am not now making a pacifist point. The war now being prepared for is condemned by the so-called "just war tradition" held by most Christian theologians since Ambrose. Obliteration bombing has been condemned by every pope since Benedict XV, by every major gathering of the World Council of Churches since 1937. It does not first become a sin when lives are taken. It begins to constitute idolatry when the particular interests of a given national regime are deemed worthy of our contemplating and threatening the destruction of another people for the sake of such interests. The idolatry crescendos when our best brains and dollars, minerals and energy resources are invested in tooling up for it, when the media and the schools are enlisted to rationalize it. If we did that all in the name of *avowed* self-interest, or of the virtue of the Aryan race or of the market economy, at least it would not be a blasphemy against the name of the God of Abraham.

As the free-church witness calls for decision from the individual, so it sets before the community not one way but two. With regard to territorialism as such, and again with regard to military nationalism, I have said we must look both ways. We might on the one hand assume that our context is pagan. Our rulers could admit, as political scientists of the style of Hans Morgenthau and Ernest Lefever do, that the basic interests of a nation should be selfish. That would have the virtue of honesty. But then it would become clear that the nation cannot call itself Christian, nor Protestant/Catholic/Jewish/humanist. The believing community should then set about, as it does today in Asia and Eastern Europe, living the life of faith in a culture it does not control. The other way, which would be a challenge and a choice, not a chaplaincy, would be to call the civil community to renounce short-range self-interest as a goal and global arm-twisting as a means of defending what we claim are the values of Western civilization.[9]

After the collapse of the slightly sanctimonious international optimism of the early Carter era, it may need to be underlined that a radical Christian judgment on American nationalism is not the same as naïveté. One of the differences is the relation to national pride.

There was a parallel between President Carter's earlier claim to "make the government as good as the people" and his dramatic insistence throughout the Iranian crisis that "we have no apologies" to submit to anybody. It is not from a posture of self-proclaimed innocence that the second biggest bully on the globe can teach moral lessons to smaller countries with more oppressive regimes but also more poverty.

The fourth mark of civil religion is its homogenizing disregard for the particularities of different traditions. The peculiar things some Jews do about food and about Saturday, the Lutheran thing about grace and the Baptist things about baptism, the special ideas some Evangelicals have about Jesus and some Catholics about his mother are all relegated to the status of dispensable folkloric appendages that we should not mind losing from view behind the pieties of the melting pot.

I note this mark with less emphasis, because others can concentrate their defenses there and because I cannot say that there are not some particularities which are worth submerging in a larger ecumenical stream. But on the other side of the relationship it must be noted that the ceremonial content of the civil pieties is most thin and sectarian and petty: the Memorial Day rereadings of the Gettysburg address which lose its note of repentance and tragedy, the various references of politicians to prayer, the nondenominational blessings invoked on flags and battleships, the trust in God which our money announces but our investment policies do not. The pieties of the melting pot do not, despite the hopes of Robert Bellah,[10] give a community enough to live from. The civil cult is a narrower, not a wider church.

The fifth mark of bad religion I named was the status of clergy as privileged: not as servants of particular, voluntarily constituted and accountable communities, but as a clerical caste within the society as a whole. Instead of "free exercise of religion" meaning the space for individuals to pray and for groups to be constituted, it has been transmuted into the right of clergymen in particular to divers discounts and tax advantages, or to the right of the bearer of a clerical collar to be treated differently by the police watching a protest march.

Radical Protestantism is not anticlerical in the sense of rejecting theological learning or doctrinal precision, but it does insist that the status of a "minister" is defined by an accountable relationship to the community he or she serves, and not "set apart" because of the "religious" quality of the language or rites involved in that ministry. Nor does radical Protestantism oppose the involvement of "the ministry" in public life, but it asks that what they say be honest and representative. Ever since Jeremiah's judgment on those who promised a too superficial "peace" (Jer. 6:14, 8:11, 23:16ff.), like before him Micaiah ben Imlah's condemnation of the prophets of well-being (1 Kgs. 22, 1 Chr. 18), the most authentic contribution the spokespersons of God can make to the wider society will most often not be the soothing reassurance in the face of mortality and crisis which a society expects of its priestly servants.

That more authentic troubling word is not one which the wider society will readily listen to, or pay for. Witness the rapidity with which Christian agencies are threatened with the loss of their tax-deductible status if their expressions of politically relevant moral preferences are too blunt.

Yet the issue focused here, namely the abiding respectability of clergy even in a secularized society, is only the tip of the anomaly. Despite the secularization of learning and despite the secularization in *substance* of the criteria of public decision-making about such matters as the dignity of human life, there remains a veneer of God-language over public discourse in the USA. Oaths in the name of the God of the Bible (which in its text tells us not to swear such oaths) are still part of the rituals of induction into high office. The less a political figure lets morality interfere with his decision-making, the more freely he will claim transcendent reference for his view of the nation's interests.

Once again the radical Protestant critique will be not a Rechabite return to the desert but the demand that if God-language be used, it be specified, and that if there is appeal to the God of Abraham and Jesus, there be submission to His revealed will regarding the liberation of the oppressed, the dignity of the outsider, and the unity of the race. Especially the correlation of God-language with provincial, national, or class self-interest will be consciously rejected and reversed.

I do not mean to say that negative prophecy is the only authentic public message. There may be times more desperate than our own in which only believers can hope, and where Christian dissent will consist in sharing that hope. Yet in the American experience currently the challenge is at the point of national self-confidence, gluttony, and pride.

My assignment here has thus far not seemed to call for direct dialogue with others who use the notions of "civil religion" or "Theology of the Republic" affirmatively, or who support the same position without using the words. The challenge they need to face is how that particular distillate of the national experience can be an instrument of genuine moral judgment as well as of consolation and encouragement. If one commends such a "religion" or "theology" a somehow "true," one must face all the hurdles any missionary faith must meet. Why should it be believed? How does it work to judge and to restore? Does the sociological fact that a coherent cohesive society *needs* a coherent value system, argued by Robert Bellah at the end of his *Broken Covenant*,[11] prove that such a system can actually be created or will be believed? Does Sidney Mead's own critical civility in wanting a "Theology of the Republic" to be self-critical[12] guarantee that the nation can affirm the crusading self-righteousness of the "Battle Hymn of the Republic" and still retain the tragic humility of Lincoln?

To take the advocates of civil religiosity more seriously would mean clarifying who their founders and church fathers are, and what their "canon" is, beyond a few phrases from 1776. My efforts to understand these colleagues are left unresolved because they do not sense the need to explain on what grounds, beyond taste and civility, they prefer the perspective of Lincoln and of King on the national identity to that of the Ku Klux Klan and our gunboat diplomats.

To take more seriously the theological exaltation of the Republic would also demand accountable reference to the ecumenical challenge. What is the relation of this vision of salvation and national calling to the rights and dignities of the rest of the world? To other religions? To other Christians? There may very well be good answers to these questions. What is significant in the debate of the last decade is that the advocates of the nationalist answer have betrayed no awareness of the need to spell out answers to such challenges before their claim to credibility can be granted.

Our subject is therefore by the nature of the case as ambivalent as when we began. If by "civil religion" should be meant the bare fact of our caring Christianly about public life, then the message would be the same as it is to an individual: a call to repentance, to the recognition of God's sovereignty, and to a commitment to live for the service of others. We would then have a positive Christian call to address to all public life. The "radical Protestant" version of that call would differ not in being unconcerned or impossible but in being more ready to run risks for the sake of a higher justice. But when what is usually meant is the religious undergirding of national interests at the expense of the wider righteousness, then the technical word for that offense, even if the name of Jesus be invoked over it, is idolatry. "Why do you call me 'Lord' and not do what I say?"

We call a nonviolent man "Lord" and in his name rekindle the arms race. We call a poor man "Lord" and with his name on our lips deepen the ditch between rich and poor. We call "Lord" a man who told us to love our enemies and we polarize the globe in the name of Christian values, approving of "moderate repression" as long as it is done by our friends.

The challenge of civil religion is not a fact, to which we could choose whether to say "yes" or "no"; it is an agenda. Is God, above all, our help? or are we God's servants?

Notes

1. The Hermeneutics of Peoplehood

1. This stance has been variously identified: "radical reformation" (George H. Williams), "free church" (Franklin H. Littell), "believers' church" (Max Weber and D. Durnbaugh), "sectarian" (E. Troeltsch), and "anabaptist" (the Reformation creeds). None of these designations satisfies. I shall use them interchangeably. The designations for the other alternative are no more satisfying: "established," "multitudinist," "magisterial," "state church." At the same time that I yield to the historical typology in order to locate a stance, I must object to the way such typologies tend to freeze the conversation. Even more do such typologies distort when they are spread over time, as when Mennonite emigration or Quaker humanism is taken as part of the original "typical" stance.

2. The reference here to a particular subtype of Protestant identity needs to be protected especially against one use made of that kind of typology in the past. One kind of "free-church" movement, especially in nineteenth-century America, has run the danger of being unhistorical in its claim that the reforming process can be completed, can have "restored" the "New Testament patterns" and stands no more in the need of reformation. Disciples Divinity House, sponsor of the Hoover lectures, represents that "Restoration Tradition." The danger of naiveté or self-righteousness about having restored "the New Testament church" does exist, but it represents a caricature. This characterization obscures for the critics and for some of the friends of this vision the difference between stating that the New Testament vision is normative and claiming to have fulfilled it. What the radical reformer criticizes in established reformation patterns is not the failure to be perfect but the specific apology, made on behalf of the "establishment" traditions, for being unfaithful, i.e., for aiming at some other point than the quality of obedience and community to which the New Testament writings were calling their readers.

3. The questions are still more serious if the specialist must be only male, if discharging this function is his livelihood, and if his authority to do so is independent of the local body of believers in which it is exercised.

4. Ronald M. Green, "Abraham, Isaac, and the Jewish Tradition: An Ethical Reappraisal," *Journal of Religious Ethics* 10/1 (Spring 1982), 1–21.

5. See my *The Original Revolution* (Scottdale, Pa.: Herald Press, 1972), pp. 93ff. A further difficulty is that Isaac was no infant, and participated know-

ingly. This is assumed by the Christian use of Isaac as a type of Christ, as well as by much Jewish interpretation (see Green).

6. For Kierkegaard's purposes it was unimportant to ask how Abraham knew God wanted that; for contemporary ethics it would be essential.

7. In the exposition which follows I propose to juxtapose simply some snatches from the New Testament and some brief references to the sixteenth century. This represents the simplification of the root paradigm, not a legalistic claim. Within the intra-Protestant debate, advocates of the less radical forms of reformation have regularly used the caricature of "legalism" to fend off a critique which is deeper than that. By looking in Acts and the Epistles for guidances to the process of discernment, I lift out specimens of continuing critique which were not given the same prominence in the sixteenth century or for that matter in any other reformation movement. Most of the Protestant talk about the priesthood of all believers did not develop structures to live up to the apostolic vision of every member's having a ministerial gift of her or his own. Authoritarian and pastorcentric leadership styles have developed just as well among groups which in other respects implemented freechurch concerns such as separation from the state or voluntary membership. This exposition therefore exemplifies in substance that which was said before in form: it applies the concern for continuing change, through appeal to the original tradition, to an agenda regarding which that change had not yet been realized. It thereby gives the lie to the "mainstream" caricature of the "free churches" that they think they "have it made."

8. One standard picture of "radical reformation" culture criticism is that it claims to recapture a pure first-century form and thereby escape historical contingency. In their more popular forms, the nineteenth-century followers of Campbell and Darby may have fallen into this trap; but certainly left-wing Protestantism as a whole did not. Its categories are more able to deal with *continuing* change and recurrent apostasy than are those of the official Reformation. See below, "Anabaptism and History," pp. 131ff.

9. Ulrich S. Leupold, ed., *Luther's Works*, vol. 53: *Liturgy and Hymns* (Philadelphia: Fortress, 1965), p. 64: "For I have not yet the people or persons for it, nor do I see many who want it."

10. Paul Ramsey, "Liturgy and Ethics," *Journal of Religious Ethics* 7/2 (Fall 1979): 139–171, and Donald Saliers, "Liturgy and Ethics: Some New Beginnings," ibid., pp. 173–189.

11. Sebastian Moore, *The Crucified Jesus Is No Stranger* (New York: Seabury Press, 1977).

12. Daniel Maguire, "Ratio Practica and the Intellectualistic Fallacy, *Journal of Religious Ethics* 10/1 (Spring 1982), 22ff.

13. "The Old Law showed forth the precepts of the natural law, and added certain precepts of its own. Accordingly, as to those precepts of the natural law contained in the Old Law, all were bound to observe the Old Law, not because they belonged to the Old Law, but because they belonged to the natural law. But as to those precepts which were added by the Old Law, they were not binding on any save the Jewish people alone." *Summa Theologica*, I/II, Question 98 Art. 5. The further elucidation of "law," in questions 90–108 adds a host of distinctions—between the precepts as common and as deter-

mined by positive law either human or divine, between duty according to reason and duty according to law, between precepts and commandments, between justice as being difficult for a person without virtue and its being easier for a person with virtue—but none of these has the purpose of enabling "ecumenical" discourse in the realm of the positive determinations of civil law (or moral law in the public arena) with persons rejecting Thomas's world view.

2. "But We Do See Jesus"

1. Gotthold Ephraim Lessing, *Lessing's Theological Writings,* trans. Henry Chadwick [A Library of Modern Religious Thought] (Stanford: Stanford University Press, 1957), pp. 53, 55.

2. Relativism is a mood more than a position. As the fairest viewers tend to agree (Arthur Dyck, *On Human Care: An Introduction to Ethics* [Nashville: Abingdon, 1977], pp. 144ff.; and Bernard Arthur Owen Williams, *Morality: An Introduction to Ethics* [Cambridge: At the University Press, pp. 20ff.]), it can weaken the claims of others but can never rationally sustain its own nor solidly falsify another's.

3. A most dignified and careful exposition of the claim that to be wider is to be truer is the distinctive usage made of the adjective "public" by David Tracy, "Defending the Public Character of Theology," in *Christian Century* 98 (1 April 1981), 350ff. What is most striking in his exposition is the circularity of his assumption that we share his definition of what it means to prove "publicly" the truth of what one argues, without any accounting for the selection of the particular value biases of the several "publics" one seeks to communicate to.

4. This would seem to be a fair though coarse characterization of what Paul Van Buren was seeking to do in his *Secular Meaning of the Gospel* (New York: Macmillan, 1963), pp. 158ff.

3. The Authority of Tradition

1. Without reaching back to the origins of this high scholastic debate in Bellarmine and Canisius, we find it very adequately summarized in a recent article by Kevin McNamara of Maynooth, on the thought of Patrick Murray, also of Maynooth, 1811–1882, in a symposium honoring the ecumenist and ecclesiologist Joseph Höfer: "Patrick Murray's Teaching on Tradition," in R. Bäumer and H. Dolch, eds., *Volk Gottes* (Freiburg: Herder, 1967), pp. 455f.

2. I say "units of information" rather than "propositions" because the way in which this knowledge was transmitted is not always held to have retained one particular fixed linguistic form.

3. Albert Outler, *The Christian Tradition and the Unity We Seek* (Oxford, 1975).

4. This paper was originally presented to a consultation at Notre Dame on "Remembering and Reforming: Toward a Constructive Christian Ethic."

5. William Visser 't Hooft, *No Other Name* (London: SCM and Philadelphia: Westminster, 1963).

6. This paper's concern for identifying unfaithfulness is not to be equated with discussion of what is "specifically" or "uniquely" or "distinctively" Christian or Judaeo-Christian. Distinctiveness is a semantically backhanded term. In using it one seeks to define oneself from the perspective of another, without having firm handles on who that "other" is. There is no point in denying that there is truth beyond the believing community; what is needed is a way to denounce the untruths held by those who profess to believe. There is no point in debating whether all moral concern will adopt and adapt language and information from beyond the bounds of church and Scripture; the need is for that adoption and adaptation to be discerning, not normless, chaotic, or self-defeating.

7. This way of remembering in reforming is a pattern for aggressive and optimistic forward movement in the life of the church. Not only is the church *reformata* and *semper reformanda*. She is also always in the process of further reformation. When the need for further reformation is affirmed, as in this standard slogan, yet without providing an instrument for it, the slogan *semper reformanda* becomes an acquiescence in imperfection rather than an affirmation of vulnerability to change. When the concrete subservience to political establishment belies the commitment to further reformation, then the *semper reformanda* becomes a defense ("nobody's perfect") instead of a power to renew. The standard interpretation of the position which others pejoratively call "sectarian" is, on the other hand, that it affirms the recoverable purity of the pristine pentecostal community. That would mean no forward movement but only a constant and always implicitly, almost immediately defeated effort to start over from scratch. That is not the vision that has been lived by any radical free-church community in history, nor is it the one I suggest. Each time a new perception of unfaithfulness is provoked by a new recourse to the canonical testimony, thereby calling forth from the ancient heritage "treasures old and new" (Matt. 13:4), the history of the community and even of the world has been moved not back but forward. It is not the free church but the establishment model that attempts to freeze history in the claim thereby to be taking responsibility for it.

8. My assignment has otherwise dealt with a purely formal question: normative past and debatable present, treason and fidelity. The theme would have been richer, but less manageable, if the debate had been specified materially as well. Might an ethic of martyrdom be more readily betrayed than one of stewardship? Might love of enemy be harder to hold to than love of spouse or of homeland? Might an ethic of vocation be more easily secularized than one of charisma? Then some elements of the Christian moral message might be more crucial, more in jeopardy of being jettisoned than others. In this respect, the just war sample is a good one.

9. There are at least the following quite distinct ways of using the language of "the just war":

a. The term was classically used to describe the holy wars of the age of Joshua and the Crusades, whose cause is transcendentally accredited by hierarch or prophet.

b. The same language is used to describe the moral autonomy of a ruler who is properly answerable to no one in his decisions about cause and means.

c. It may speak of the application of a set of rigorously logical formal criteria, whose objective clarity permits them to be applied by the citizen, the theologian, or the politician.

d. There is the transmutation of the logical and formal criteria into legal and procedural rules: conventions, tribunals, mediators.

e. There is justifiable insurrection, which claims that exceptionally the criterion of "legitimate authority" must yield to that of just cause.

f. There is the "nothing like success" argument, which claims that policies of mass retaliation and assured destruction, while contrary to the traditional rules of proportionality and discrimination, nevertheless are morally justified, because they deter effectively by making their application unthinkable.

g. There is what some now call "just war pacifism"; the application to particular contemporary cases of the classical criteria, in such a way as to condemn rather than approve of a war that is otherwise seriously likely, or is going on.

h. There is the "war is hell" view. The outbreak of war suspends most moral discourse. Everything we do is sin. Yet the judgments of military necessity must still be made responsibly. Hiroshima was still an atrocity.

These views differ in many concrete ways. Type c is structurally different from types a and b, although in the Middle Ages the distinction was not made clearly. Type f contradicts c in all its details, but agrees in its basically utilitarian logic. Type d is a development from type c. Type e is a development from c and/or from d. Type g is a serious revitalization of type c, beginning with its logic yet producing unprecedented conclusions. Type h is like f in that it differs deeply from c yet nonetheless claims to discriminate responsibly. Thus this *new* "tradition" does not have in its favor that it has done away with ambiguity.

4. THE KINGDOM AS SOCIAL ETHIC

1. The phrase "historic peace churches" seems to have become current first in the mid-1930s in the U.S.A., as Brethren, Friends, and Mennonites saw the need to band together in the light of the new threat of war.

2. A fuller presentation of this argument is presented in chapter 7, "The Constantinian Sources of Western Social Ethics."

3. The reference to Constantine in the following exposition has a code function. The first Roman emperor to tolerate, then to favor, and then to participate in the administration of the Christian churches is the symbol of a shift in relationships which had begun before he came on the scene and was not completed until nearly a century after his death. Although his thoughts and his deeds are eminently representative of the nature of the shift, it is not our present concern to discharge the task of the historian, to interpret the man by asking questions about his sincerity or his wisdom or his relative

causative importance. The symbolic value of Constantine as representative of that change was not an invention of his critics or of Christian radicals either in the twelfth century or more recently. It was rather the adulatory historians of the school of Eusebius of Caesarea who gave to his age and to his person that dramatic centrality. All that the radical historians did was to argue that the change was not all for the good, whereas "mainstream" theologians from Eusebius to Bullinger and Bucer saw him as initiator of the millennium.

4. The more methodologically self-aware ethical systems use phrases like "sphere sovereignty" and *"Eigengesetzlichkeit der Kulturgebiete."*

5. See in my *Original Revolution* (Scottdale, Pa.: Herald Press, 1972) the treatment of "the other lights" (pp. 134ff.). It is the merit of the age of Reinhold Niebuhr to have made this tension clear.

6. See chapter 6, "Anabaptism and History."

7. See the concept of teacher/*didascalos* as described above pp. 32ff.

8. The interlock of complementary ministries is detailed in chapter 1, "The Hermeneutics of Peoplehood."

9. H. Richard Niebuhr, *The Church Against the World* (Chicago: Willett, Clarke, 1935).

10. John C. Bennett, *Christian Ethics and Social Policy* (New York: Scribner, 1946).

11. Bennett's post-retirement work *The Radical Imperative* (Philadelphia: Westminster, 1975) deals with ideas, not with their social shape.

A powerful witness parallel to the works just cited was articulated two generations later by Julian N. Hartt, in his *A Christian Critique of American Culture* (New York: Harper & Row, 1967). The phrase "culture christianity," used to name what Hartt is critiquing, has a meaning similar to that in the Niebuhr volume thirty-three years before: Hartt's critical analysis is far more complex. His description of the church (especially pp. 292ff.) is likewise more complex in the way it characterizes the interaction between what the community of believers is called to be and what it is: not much more is said about concrete directions for the life of real communities which might incarnate ("inculturate") a critique like Hartt's.

12. Cf. Robert Tucker, "Revolutionary Faithfulness," is Martin E. Marty and Dean G. Peerman, eds., *New Theology* No. 6 (New York: Macmillan, 1969), p. 204, and Wolfgang Schäufele, *Das missionarische Bewusstsein und Wirken der Täufer* (Neukirchen, 1966).

13. Helder Camara's text by this name (Maryknoll, N.Y.: Orbis, 1981) is but one specimen of a genre.

14. See below in chapter 5, "Radical Reformation Ethics," my rejection of the duty/ends disjunction.

5. RADICAL REFORMATION ETHICS IN ECUMENICAL PERSPECTIVE

1. Presented orally at the Graymoor Ecumenical Institute, Garrison, N.Y., 27 May 1978, as part of a symposium on "Christian Ethics in Ecumenical Perspective."

2. See especially by Littell: *The Free Church* (Boston: Staff King Press,

1957); *The Origins of Sectarian Protestantism* (New York: Macmillan, 1964); "Church and Sect," *Ecumenical Review* 6/3 (April 1954), 262ff.; "The Historical Free Church Defined," *Brethren Life and Thought* 9/4 (Autumn 1964), 78ff.

3. Yet it is not necessarily the case that such marks of voluntary adult membership will be seen, by the very people who consider them important, to be representative of a different ecclesiology. A Baptist may argue simply that babies should not be baptized because they cannot have a "born-again experience," or a conservative Methodist may argue that a teenager needs an experience of commitment before being ready to function as a full member of the church, without their reasoning beyond these observations to their distinctive implications for our present subject. Even less would a Missouri Synod Lutheran or a Christian Reformed believer be inclined to recognize, as Littell does, that their "free" shape implies any noteworthy difference in ecclesiology or ethics from Luther or Calvin.

4. Among the shortcomings of the term, we may note these:

a. Such views, or such communities, can arise in other ways than *via* the radicalizing of a less radical reformation or the formation of a new "church."

b. The term "radical" is logically imprecise. Its meaning depends on some other thrust or process which it "goes beyond," without the direction or quality of that "beyond" being specified. Most "radicality" does not issue in free churches.

c. This usage tends to foster the use of the reformation experiences of the sixteenth and seventeenth centuries as dictating prototypes for confessional identity, as models rather than specimens. To give such foundational authority to one past incarnation of faithfulness is more acceptable to Roman and official Protestant traditions than to either the Orthodox or the free churches.

5. See John H. Yoder, "The Nature of the Unity We Seek: A Historic Free Church View," *Religion in Life*, Spring 1957, pp. 215ff.; and Yoder, "The Free Church Ecumenical Style," *Quaker Religious Thought*, Summer 1968, pp. 29ff.; "Could There Be a Baptist Bishop?" *Ecumenical Trends* (Graymoor) 9/7 (July/August 1980), 104ff.; "Einfachere Einheit für Knappere Zeiten" in Karlfried Fröhlich, ed., *Möglichkeiten und Grenzen der Ökumene Hete* (Tübingen: Mohr, 1982), pp. 107–111.

6. The name of the Emperor Constantine figures here and elsewhere in this collection, as it has since his own time, as a symbol of a far-reaching shift in institutional and value arrangements. Constantine himself did not bring them about, nor are we here interested in his personal biography.

7. That the normativeness of the New Testament was stated simply need not mean that its implementation was naive: see chapter 6, "Anabaptism and History."

8. Nobody in the sixteenth century would *directly* deny Jesus' moral authority. Not until the Jesuits of Pascal's *Provincial Letters* or Reinhold Niebuhr would moralists say straight out that they were doing something other than what Jesus meant. The question was rather for them whether Christian obedience meant applying Jesus' teachings straightforwardly in a social ethic or holding that he himself intended some other understanding. Often the best

test of how that was intended is the respective theologies' readings of the Sermon on the Mount; yet since Tolstoy that way of putting the issue is deceptive.

9. An early specimen of such "ethics adjusted to the world" is offered in my *Christian Witness to the State* (Newton, Kans.: Faith and Life Press, 3rd ed., 1977). See also pp. 000 below.

10. Other "restoration" churches with similar self-understandings and similar structures (Churches of Christ, Churches of God, Pentecostals) also originally were pacifist, although without working it out as firmly as the Brethren, Friends, and Mennonites.

11. The possibility of a "mainstream" communion which would no longer expel the advocates of a radical reformation ethic would not be the only way to break through the classical typology. It is also possible for the heirs of "radical" ecclesiology to become quasi-"established." Baptists and Disciples in the American South, while keeping some of the outward marks of "free" ecclesiology, have at other points evolved into new forms of "mainstream" mentality. This happens most easily on ethical matters.

12. Cf. the text on tradition above, p. 000.

13. For Zwingli's original congregationalism, see my *Täufertum und Reformation im Gespräch* (Zurich: EVZ-Verlag, 1968), pp. 110ff. For Luther, see his "That a Christian Assembly has the Right to Judge . . ." (May 1523), in *Works* vol. 31 (Philadelphia: Fortress, 1970), 303ff. Luther said of 1 Corinthians 14: "Let this passage be your sure foundation."

14. See my "The Hermeneutics of the Anabaptists," *Mennonite Quarterly Review* 41 (1967), 291ff.

15. Franklin H. Littell, *The Origins of Sectarian Protestantism*. See also John H. Yoder, "Reformation and Missions: A Literature Review," in the *Occasional Bulletin* of the Missionary Research Library, June 1971.

16. See my "The Disavowal of Constantine; An Alternative Perspective on Interfaith Dialogue," *Yearbook* of the Ecumenical Institute for Advanced Theological Studies, Tantur, Jerusalem, 1975/76, pp. 47ff.

17. The same preparatory questions were addressed to the four Graymoor panelists:

What are the criteria for Christian ethical decisions?

How is it possible for Christians using the same sources of revelation, and even of tradition, to come to disparate conclusions informing ethical decisions?

How does, or can, Christian ethics contribute to, or pose obstacles to, the cause of Christian Unity?

18. *Politics of Jesus* (Grand Rapids, Mich.: Eerdmans, 1972), pp. 15ff.

19. The most recent summary before this essay was drafted was *One Baptism, One Eucharist, and a Mutually Recognized Ministry* (Geneva: WCC, 1975), pp. 9–17. It reported no progress on the pedobaptism debate. It was more concerned to downgrade the value of a separate confirmation ritual, the more serious use of which would have been one step toward recognizing the anti-pedobaptist concern. Since then the new Faith and Order consensus document, *Baptism, Eucharist, and Ministry,* adopted in Lima in 1982, has been widely hailed for its irenic inclusiveness, but it again straddles the issue of pedobaptism. At the same time infant baptism is being challenged from within

the Reformed, Lutheran, and Roman Catholic communions, by their own pastors, on their own internal grounds.

20. See Donald Durnbaugh, *On Earth Peace* (Elgin, Ill.: Brethren Press, 1978).

6. ANABAPTISM AND HISTORY

1. Roland H. Bainton, "Changing Ideas and Ideals in the Sixteenth Century," *The Journal of Modern History* 8 (1936), 428.

2. Originally 1952, revised as *The Origins of Sectarian Protestantism* (New York: Macmillan, 1964). In the revision chapter 2 is "The Fall of the Church" and 3 "The Restitution." Littell has returned to the theme repeatedly but without major modification. His "The Anabaptist Doctrine of the Restitution of the True Church," *Mennonite Quarterly Review* 26 (1950), 33ff., deals with the substance of ecclesiology (baptism, discipline, community, etc.) rather than the idea of restitution as formal principle.

3. The index to George H. Williams's *The Radical Reformation* (Philadelphia, 1962), lists fourteen references to the theme, in addition to a partially intertwined further set dealing with universalism (for which the terms *restitutio* and *restoratio* were also used).

4. Hillerbrand, "Anabaptism and History" *Mennonite Quarterly Review* 45 (1971), 107ff. I say "apparently" because part of the debate is about verbal usage.

5. Since he is dealing with the Anabaptists in the article cited, Hillerbrand does not support in detail his statement that everyone used restitution language. He thus does not negate Bainton's nuanced statement that everyone used the language but that the Anabaptists carried out its logic more thoroughly, or that the official Reformers retreated from it as its implications became more clear. A careful study of which Reformers used restitution terminology, when, against whom, on which questions, could be rewarding. Pontien Polman, *L'Elément Historique dans la Controverse Religieuse du XVIe Siècle* (Gembloux, 1932) analyzes the Reformation debates thoroughly without using the term. Littell agrees that not only Anabaptists used the concept; he quotes a dramatic statement of it from Philipp of Hesse (*The Origins of Sectarian Protestantism*, p. 34). A Catholic example is the French specialist in anti-Lutheran polemic, Clichtove (1472–1543), whose biographer makes use of the contrast *restauratio/renovatio*; J. P. Massaut, *Josse Clichtove, l'Humanisme et la Réforme du Clergé* vol. 2 (Paris, 1968), 391ff.

6. Littell's "In response to Hans Hillerbrand," *Mennonite Quarterly Review* 45 (1971), 107ff., itemizes the points of controversy. Again some of them are semantic.

7. H. W. Meihuizen, "The Concept of Restitution in the Anabaptism of Northwestern Europe," *Mennonite Quarterly Review* 44 (1970), 141ff. (Originally *Het Begrip Restitutie in het noordwestelijke Doperdom*, Haarlem, 1966.) Some of the following survey is indebted to Meihuizen. The geographical difference between Meihuizen's and Littell's focus is significant.

8. Arthur O. Lovejoy and George Boas, eds., *Primitivism and Related*

Ideas in Antiquity (Baltimore, 1935), vol. 1 in a series: A Documentary History of Primitivism and Related Ideas. Lovejoy distinguishes many subtypes of primitivism, depending on the concept they have of "nature," of the historical process, etc. Gerhard H. Ladner, *The Idea of Reform* (Cambridge, 1959), proposes a comparable typology. Littell acknowledges early acquaintance with Lovejoy, especially in his *Landgraf Philipp und die Toleranz* (Bad Neuheim, 1957), where he is least critical of the equation of restitution with the Eden myth.

9. The idea of the restoration of pre- or proto-historical Adamic innocence arises on the very fringes of reformation radicalism, but is a phenomenon quite distinct from the one we are pursuing.

10. The only mainstream Anabaptist to use the term "restitution" in a title, Dirk Philips, uses it negatively, with this meaning. His tract *Van de geestelijcke restitutie* (n.d.) is an anti-Münsterite work. It argues that whatever promises and hopes of a restored Israel were left pending from the Old Testament were fulfilled in Christ, leaving no basis for a "third age" still to be expected, and that the fulfillment which Christ brought is in the church ("spiritual"), not national. From the perspective of the peaceable Anabaptists, Zwingli's use of the Old Testament's theocratic vision followed the same logic as Münster.

11. That the Spiritualizers and revolutionaries share the concept of a beginning "third age" is shown by Frank Wray, "The Anabaptist Doctrine of the Restitution of the Church," *Mennonite Quarterly Review* 28 (1955), 186ff. If our purpose were a full review of reformation typology, it would have to be argued that the "third age" is not technically restitution at all. What is wrong with the present is not that it has fallen away from Jesus or the New Testament but that it has not yet made the next step forward.

12. I suggest this more formal label for what Bullinger called the "general Anabaptists" and G. H. Williams the "evangelical Anabaptists," to refer to those who created ordered communities: the Swiss Brethren, the Hutterites, and the Dutch after Menno.

13. It is widely agreed that the Zurich radicals in 1522–23 began with the expectancy that the entire Zwinglian movement might "go all the way" with reformation. Fritz Blanke, *Brüder in Christo* (Zurich, 1955), pp. 10ff.; J. Yoder, *Die Gespräche zwischen Taüfern und Reformatoren in der Schweiz* (Karlsruhe: Mennonitische Geschichtsverein, 1962), pp. 29ff. Michael Sattler did not abandon this hope until he left Strasbourg early in 1527: J. H. Yoder, "Der Kristallisationspunkt des Täufertums," in *Mennonitische Geschichtsblätter* 1972, pp. 35ff. The objections of K. Deppermann to my interpretation (*Mennonitische Geschichtsblätter* 1973, pp. 24ff. and pp. 47ff.) do not strike the point being made here.

14. The earliest Anabaptist witnesses to their own beginnings were concerned to justify the exceptional breach of continuity represented by the baptisms of January, 1525: J. Yoder, *Täufertum und Reformation im Gespräch* (Zurich: EVZ Verlag, 1968), pp. 109ff. With that and one other exception, no known Anabaptist leader began baptizing without having first been baptized himself. Melchior Hofmann as the other exception demonstrates thereby a new discontinuity which Obbe and Dirk Philips later had to explain. This

concern for order is incompatible with Hillerbrand's picture of carefree separatism.

15. Hillerbrand (note 4 above), p. 111. Hillerbrand makes his point somewhat more defensible by using the undefined adjective "early." If he means before 1523 or before 1520, when Luther and Zwingli hoped to avoid or to repair the breach within Christendom, the comparison of course falls away, as there were no Anabaptists then. See my section "Der Wille zum Gespräch bei den Täufern," J. Yoder, *Die Gespräche zwischen Täufern und Reformatoren in der Schweiz* pp. 157ff.

16. In fact, the corpus christianum Protestant approach differs from all the others (Catholic, Anabaptist, and spiritualist alike) in that schism along geographic/political lines is the necessary effect of its implementation. "Restitutionism" is thus no more intrinsically divisive than "Protestantism" or Roman Catholicism. Each defines in its own terms the unity it seeks and the price (i.e., the kind of division) it will accept.

17. G. H. Williams's term "magisterial" says the same thing as is meant here by "official." The latter term is more translatable. To the double allusion to magistracy and magisterium it adds the dimension of parish office.

18. For Zwingli see Yoder, *Taüfertum . . .* , pp. 153ff. and notes.

19. Yoder, ibid., pp. 66ff.

20. "Restitution was not a strategy for irrelevant archaism, as though history could be reversed. It sought rather to restore in the present, by the power of the Spirit, the faithfulness of the first Christians. . . . The true church was to be made visible again. It had been driven into exile. . . . In some ages it may have disappeared completely. . . . But this was not the end of the church, for continuity lay with God rather than with men." Cornelius J. Dyck, "The Place of Tradition in Dutch Anabaptism," *Church History* 43, (1974), 34ff.

21. "The doctrine of the Incarnation, which says that redemption already exists in this world, has always tempted Christians to make their peace with whatever this world has been at a given time." Steven Schwarzchild, in D. Callahan, ed., *The Secular City Debate* (New York: Macmillan, 1966), p. 148.

22. Sixteenth-century historiography of course made of Constantine's "decision" to bless the churches and the churches' "decision" to accept the arrangement a point-event rather than a process of some length. Twentieth-century restitutionism needs to adjust at this point to an awareness of events as process, but that does not change the point at issue.

23. Sixteenth-century pictures of the early church probably assumed that every local congregation had the same Bible, which they all read and sought to understand in ways much like those of the 1520s. A more adequate picture of the varieties and the gradualness of canon-formation would only strengthen the case for this relative trust in the post-apostolic generation.

24. Eberhard Arnold, founder of the neo-Hutterian Society of Brothers, gathered in the 1920s a collection of patristic fragments to illustrate the life of *The Early Christians after the Death of the Apostles* (English version, Rifton, N.Y.: Plough Publishing House, 1970). Everett Ferguson's *Early Christians Speak* (Austin, Tex.: Sweet, 1971) does something similar for the Churches of Christ. Ferguson's selection is more attentive to forms and churchly practices, Arnold's more to mission and world view. Restitution does not produce

uniformity. Yet both testify to the contemporaneity of the earliest Christian experience as a source of perspective and creative alternatives in the face of the pressure of conformity to the present.

25. If twentieth-century restitutionism needs correction or refinement at this point, it would be to look for still earlier or deeper predispositions toward the Constantinian shift (anti-Judaism? Neoplatonism? creeping empire loyalism despite the commitment to pacifism?).

26. J. H. Yoder, "The Free Church Ecumenical Style," *Quaker Religious Thought* 10 (1968), 29ff., essays some suggestions in the third area.

27. W. E. Garrison and Alfred T. DeGroot, *The Disciples of Christ: A History* (St. Louis, 1948).

28. B. J. Humble, "The Influence of the Civil War," *Restoration Quarterly* 8 (1965), 233ff.

29. Alexander Campbell, *The Christian Baptist* vol. 2 (1825), p. 40: cited by Hughes, see below note 33.

30. The concern for "pattern" and "system" was the product of a specific kind of concern for unity in the face of squabbles over polity. One of Campbell's most popular works bore the revealing title: *The Christian System in Reference to the Union of Christians and a Restoration of Primitive Christianity, as plead in the Current Reformation* (4th ed., Cincinnati, 1863).

31. Henri d'Espine, *Les Anciens, Conducteurs de l'Eglise* (Neuchâtel, 1944), esp. pp. 33ff. Polman (note 5 above) pp. 69ff., shows that Calvin's concept of "return to antiquity" was distinctive in its concern with forms and polity, and in considering Augustine the prime witness to antiquity's norms.

32. W. Walker, *Creeds and Platforms* (1893, rpt. Boston, 1960), p. 203.

33. An initial contribution is Richard T. Hughes, "A Comparison of the Restitution Motifs of the Campbells (1809–1830) and the Anabaptists," *Mennonite Quarterly Review*, 45 (1971), 312ff.

34. Ralph Wilburn, ed., *The Reconstruction of Theology*, vol. 2 in the series *The Renewal of the Church*, ed. W. B. Blakemore, written by an unofficial panel of Disciples theologians (St. Louis, 1963). The articles in vol. 2 by Wilburn and by Ronald E. Osborn are especially critical.

35. Sidney Mead, *The Lively Experiment* (New York, 1963) can criticize with special vigor because Mead openly advocates an "American civil religion."

36. For the history of *The Martyrs' Mirror*, the foundational postbiblical document of Mennonite identity, see *Mennonite Encyclopedia* vol. 3, p. 527.

37. The standard designation for the faithful believers existing amidst apostate Christendom was the "rose among thorns," an allusion to Song of Solomon 2:2. Anabaptists were using the figure at least as early as the 1530s.

38. *Unpartheyische Kirchen- und Ketzergeschichte*, 1699–1700.

39. L. Keller, *Die Reformation und die älteren Reformparteien* (Leipzig, 1885).

40. E. H. Broadbent, *The Pilgrim Church* (London, 1930).

41. Donald F. Durnbaugh, "The Descent of Dissent: Some Interpretations of Brethren Origins," *Brethren Life and Thought* 19 (1974), 125ff. Durnbaugh also surveys the alternative historiographies in his "Theories of Free Church Origins," *Mennonite Quarterly Review* 42 (1968), 83ff.

42. James DeForest Murch, *The Free Church* (Louisville, 1966), pp. 36ff.

43. John F. Funk, *The Mennonite Church* (Elkhart, 1878), pp. 186f.

44. Samuel Geiser, *Die Taufgesinnten Gemeinden* (Karlsruhe, 1931; rev. 1971).

45. Robert Friedmann, "Old Evangelical Brotherhoods: Theory and Fact," *Mennonite Quarterly Review* 21 (1947), 202, reviews the debate as it applies to Anabaptism, less broadly than Durnbaugh (note 41 above).

46. One example is Broadbent's effort (pp. 85ff.) to connect the Waldenses genetically to the Bogomils of the Balkans.

47. The claim to underground institutional continuity is in fact a modernization. It is in Keller and Broadbent but not in Arnold or van Braaght. According to H. Bohmer's article on the Waldenses in the *Protestantische Realenzyklopaedie*, vol. 20, pp. 799f., the idea that the Waldenses go back to ancient underground Italian communities which never apostasized was the view of Beza. It was developed in full-fledged histories by the Reformed pastors Jean Paul Perrin (1619) and J. Leger (1669).

48. After having begun his report simply, "the Anabaptists denounced the past," Hillerbrand (note 4 above) corrects himself pp. 116ff. with a description of this kind of continuity claim.

49. The idea is as old as Tertullian: "the authority of the bishops does not derive from the physical succession, but from the fact that they hold the faith of the apostles. Their ability to show a direct line of succession from the apostles is not what makes them authoritative. . . . That is why even those churches which cannot show a line of succession from the apostles, if they hold to the faith of the church, can be accepted as apostolic on the basis of their kindred faith. . . ." Justo L. Gonzales, "Athens and Jerusalem Revisited: Reason and Authority in Tertullian," *Church History* 43 (1974), 24. See C. Dyck, note 20 above.

7. The Constantinian Sources of Western Social Ethics

1. It was this shift which G. F. Heering described as the "Fall of Christianity." The pre-Constantinian pacifism is best described by Jean-Michel Hornus in *It Is Not Lawful for Me to Fight* (Scottdale, Pa.: Herald Press, 1980). Cf. Roland Bainton, *Christian Attitudes to War and Peace* (Nashville: Abingdon, 1961), pp. 53–84.

2. This Pauline doctrine of the Lordship of Christ in relation to the "principalities and powers" has been summarized in chapter 8 of my *Politics of Jesus* (Grand Rapids, Mich.: Eerdmans, 1972). It represents a broad and growing scholarly consensus.

3. To understand the symbolic meaning attached for centuries by "radical Protestantism" to the name of Constantine, attention must be directed not to the man but to his veneration by later "established" historians and churchmen as the initiator of the age of the church's prosperity. This made him the symbol of the epoch of the great reversal; all that the dissenters did was to judge the change negatively instead of positively. The point was not that he was a man of blood, not that they doubted the spiritual authenticity of his conversion, or the propriety of his convening church councils and dic-

tating the wording of their creeds, but that he inaugurated the age of Christianity's being the official religion.

4. A thorough exposition of this critical view is offered by the Reformed theologian Leonard Verduin in his *Anatomy of a Hybrid* (Grand Rapids, Mich.: Eerdmans, 1976). Some parallel argument is offered in my "The Otherness of the Church," *Drew Gateway* 30 (Spring 1969), 151–160, and in the *Mennonite Quarterly Review* 35, October 1961, 286–296.

5. The word "Christendom," like the more recent correlate "non-Christian world," is itself a Constantinian creation.

6. The appropriateness of a term like "intone" points to another aspect of the shift: the development of "cult" as a godward activity distinct from the rest of life. Jesus is no longer a teacher to be heard, a Master to be followed: he is a metaphysical miracle needing to be recited.

7. During my 1976 visit to theological schools in South Africa, I observed that even some of the powerless agree that the paradigm of moral decision is the ruler. My presentation of New Testament ethics called forth from black South African students questions not about whether it was true to the New Testament nor about what South Africans could do (where both major racial groups, in different ways, consider themselves oppressed or threatened), but about whether John F. Kennedy could have attained the same results in the Cuban missile crisis by following the ethics of Jesus. Note the two unspoken assumptions:

a) that we see the world's most powerful people, rather than ourselves, as the meaningful actors in history and as the tests of the meaning of ethical statements; and

b) that the immediate issues of ends (i.e., to prevent the installation in Cuba of the kind of missiles which the U.S. had long had installed near the Soviet borders in Turkey) and of means (beginning with a blockade but stating threats all the way to nuclear war) are to be read as the U.S. government read them.

8. The "chaplain" originally meant literally a clergyman responsible for the prince's prayers. Modern application in the military, and more recently to chaplains to schools, hospitals, and factories, retains the administrative (and usually financial) dependence upon the ruler to the exclusion of any more properly ecclesiastical base within the people "served." In exceptional cases a chaplain may be critical or even "radical," but only within the limits of the elasticity of the ruler's tolerance.

9. The concept of "vocation" is one witness to the shift in meanings. In the New Testament, "calling" meant the status of belief as such; "charisma" meant intracongregational functions of teaching, shepherding, ministering, healing, etc. In the Middle Ages "vocation" meant religious separateness. With the Reformation it shifts again to "each serving in his place in the social structure," so that the prince, the banker, the tradesman, the soldier, are thought of as "called" to do just what each "station" involves. The language which in the New Testament meant newness, change, spirit-driven creativity, now means a divine rubber stamp for the present social order.

10. It is part of the larger issue of cause-confident utilitarianism (below). It further assumes that "everyone" does not include anyone on the other side.

Certainly if *everyone* loved their enemies, the Communists would be no threat either, for they too would love their enemies.

11. "Advocates of non-violence as a matter of principle need to ask themselves such questions as: may non-violent action emasculate effective resistance . . . ? . . . are you not in danger of giving the means . . . priority over the end sought . . . ?"

This specimen question from the excellent WCC document "Violence, Non-violence and the Struggle for Social Justice" (*Ecumenical Review* 25, October 1973) exemplifies the axiomatic place of ends-effectiveness reasoning in contemporary thought. In fairness it should be emphasized that the report in question is far less doctrinaire in this respect than many contemporary writings.

12. More thorough ethical debate would raise at this point other objections than the one we are here interested in. How clear is it that a given "revolution" will genuinely liberate? Must nonviolent techniques be ready-to-wear immediately whereas military techniques have had millennia to develop and millions of dollars and hundreds of thousands of lives to invest? Are the advocates of indispensable violence really ready to meet the test of efficacy? Do the "liberation martyr" images of Ché Guevara and Camilo Torres meet that test?

13. Another level of fitting critique, too technical to unfold here, is that self-proclaimed pragmatism is in fact self-deceiving in its polemic against "principles." The goals by which effectiveness is measured cannot themselves be defined by effectiveness. Somewhere down the consequential line there is a goal held to be valid for its own sake. My right, as a ruler or rebel, to impose upon you, as my subject or enemy, my choice of historical direction is in its logic also a principle prior to pragmatic reckoning.

14. This analysis is adapted from an earlier use in my *The Original Revolution* (Scottdale, Pa.: Herald Press, 1971), pp. 150ff.

15. Presbyterian historian John Smylie observes that the average American has assigned to nation rather than to church the functions of moral discipline, of defining personal identity, and of carrying God's action in history. See *The Christian Church and National Ethos,* (Washington: Church Peace Mission, 1963).

16. The most visible examples of this are the positions taken by East European churches' delegates in the ecumenical forum of the World Council of Churches or the Christian Peace Conference. It is not for us to evaluate, as some seek to do, the sincerity or the representativity of those statements. The same critics would not address the same objections to the equivalent spokesmen in the earlier phases.

Strong resistance phenomena like the central role of the Polish church in the 1980 movement, or of the black churches in the American civil rights struggle, represent the opposite pole from such accommodation as far as the particular regime is concerned, yet they too work within the fusion of the civil and cultic communities. They resist an oppressor from *outside* the national or ethnic society. Rather than seeing the churchmen bless the rulers, the churchmen become the closest available approximation to civil leadership when the machinery of the state is in the adversary's hands.

17. The above analysis was first formulated in the late 1960s to describe trends developing in the theologies "of revolution" or "of humanization." Since then some theologians "of liberation" do name the Constantinian synthesis as obsolete, or as a mistake. Yet without more precise analysis of what it was about Constantine that must be disavowed, the tools for critical reflection on the new forms of the same mistake are not developed.

As theologies "of liberation" evolve, they tend to outgrow the above description. Some come to struggle more deeply with the fact that "the revolution" will not come. Then they can retain their opposition to the present regime while becoming less uncritical in their advocacy of the next one. Some come to this through simple pastoral realism (H. Camara); others by renewed appropriation of the biblical visions of exile and apocalyptic (Rubem Alvez, Miguel Brun). For others the source is more thorough biblical theology (Comblin, Sobrino, Topel), for yet others the *praxis* of local community building (the *comunidades de base*). Here as well as in interpreting East European resistance there is ground for hope that the old conceptual molds may be broken.

18. J. Yoder, "The Disavowal of Constantine: An Alternative Perspective on Interfaith Dialogue," *Tantur Year Book* (Jerusalem) 1975/76, pp. 47–68.

8. The Christian Case for Democracy

1. The bulk of this material was presented by invitation to the Ethics section of the American Academy of Religion 29 October 1976 at St. Louis.

2. My reference to the "free-church" of "radical reformation" alternative, if not clarified, might open the door to misunderstanding as much as it helps clarify. From the creeds of the magisterial reformation through the systems of Weber and Troeltsch to the modern typology of H. Richard Niebuhr's *Christ and Culture*, free-church alternatives have regularly been interpreted through polarizations of the age of schism, or through the distortions of later history (persecution, clandestinity, emigration, ethnic isolation, ghetto counter-culture, sectarian defensiveness) of which Amish and Hutterian isolation of Pietist denial of concern are better samples than Roger Williams or William Penn. Rather than interpret the "radical reformation" or "free-church" alternative on its own terms, "mainstream" ethicists have used it as a foil to reinforce the case for the "ethic of responsibility." For the present let me refer to this distortion as "the denominational stereotype." What is being interpreted here is the adequacy, not of the ethos of the excluded minority, but of their testimony to the church as a whole, which as a whole may sometimes be a minority within society at large. An earlier treatment of a broader scope is my *Christian Witness to the State* (Newton, Kans.: Faith and Life, 1964).

3. Terminology is confusingly diverse here. Sometimes "post-Constantinian" means simply "after Constantine," i.e., in the epoch or the status of establishment. I originally used the term that way. But others take it to mean after the end of that arrangement. I shall therefore not use the expression; "Constantinian" shall be used here for the former sense, and "post-Christendom"

for the latter. For my doubts about whether "Constantinian" thought patterns can ever be left behind, see above chapter 7, note 3.

4. Nonetheless it is striking that in the situation of religious establishment Augustinian theology itself did not create Christian pressure toward democracy for 1000 years, whereas free-church dissent did so at least as early as Chelčický. But my concern here is not to argue that in direct causative effect the free churches are or the Enlightenment is more responsible for the growth of democracy than someone else. Claiming paternity may be a form of moral subservience. Perhaps "democracy" is not univocal or not always good. Our interest is rather to reach behind those "Christendom" assumptions to ask whether they are necessary, or what we would learn by no longer assuming them.

5. We are here discussing government as "sword," its legitimation and decision-making. Here the ruler's beneficence claim and his call for my consent is the difference that matters. But another difference also matters, perhaps more. Notions of the state as welfare agency, as coordinator of non-coercive services to a wide range of human needs: transportation, education, health, and so forth, may change its definition qualitatively. This may increase the room for "services" rendered within the civil structure with Christian integrity. But this possibility is not limited to democracies.

6. J. Yoder, *The Politics of Jesus* (Grand Rapids, Mich.: Eerdmans, 1972).

7. Jacques Ellul, *The Politics of God and the Politics of Man* (Grand Rapids, Mich.: Eerdmans, 1972).

8. Whereas the early Christians, the medieval sectarians, the Zurich Anabaptists and the early Quakers can be taken as a "pure type," John Calvin cannot. The movement from Zwingli to Roger Williams across British Puritanism is not a qualitative leap but rather a gradual evolution. Calvin's view of the civil order is neither very original nor very conducive to the development of democracy. It is conducive to the expansion of the governing elite and to the possibility that the lower-level civil authorities might occasionally replace a tyrant. But Calvin as a thinker *concerning the church,* and as a link in the ecclesiological development away from Zwingli, Erastus, and Bullinger toward Puritanism, does develop notions of substantial, albeit mediate, relevance for the development of democracy. These notions are not a theory of the state's mandate so much as a view of the church's autonomy and accountability. Calvin is one of the fathers of the movement toward a free-church vision of the work of the Holy Spirit in dialogue, of the freedom of individual conscience in dissent, of the incapacity of any civil authority to build the Kingdom of God, of the division of labor among leadership structures, etc. In these respects Calvin stands not with Zwingli and Bullinger but with the Anabaptists and later Baptists in understanding that to begin with a redefinition of the dignity, the dialogical character, and the autonomy of the visible church will yield significant leverage and some translatable models for participating positively in the civil order as well.

9. The phrase "answering that of God in everyone" was a frequent usage of George Fox. Howard Brinton's *Friends for 300 Years* (New York, Harper and Brothers, 1952), pp. 28ff. cites four such statements, culminating in a

call to "Friends in the ministry" to "come to walk cheerfully over the world, answering that of God in every one" (*Journal of George Fox, Eighth [and Bi-Centenary] Edition,* introduced and edited by Daniel Pickard [London: Edward Hicks, 1891] vol. 1, p. 316). The phrase presupposes a particular understanding of revelation. As Brinton paraphrases it: "it would be impossible to convince anyone of the Truth unless he already had the divine Seed of Truth within him." James Childress reviews and advances the debate about what Fox meant in his article "'Answering That of God in Every Man': An Interpretation of George Fox's Ethics," *Quaker Religious Thought* 15/3 (Spring 1974), 2–41.

10. Alexander Dunlop Lindsay, *The Churches and Democracy* (London: Epworth Press, 1934) and *The Essentials of Democracy* (Oxford: Clarendon Press, 2nd ed. 1935).

9. Civil Religion in America

1. Martin E. Marty, "Two Kinds of Two Kinds of Civil Religion," pp. 139–157 in Russell E. Richey and Donald G. Jones, eds., *American Civil Religion* (New York: Harper & Row, 1974). This text was first presented in a lecture series on "Civil Religion" sponsored by Wake Forest University and published here by permission of the publishers of the series volume.

2. For our purposes it is especially important to recognize that the witness I have been asked to articulate is not that of a specific denomination, but rather a perennial position taken, sometimes quite without coordination, in fact often without any knowledge of one another, by scores of renewal communities—including a dozen major, independently viable ones—across the centuries, and by renewal movements within established denominations as well. The "ecclesiological type" concept is worked out by Franklin H. Littell in his *The Free Church* (Boston: Starr King Press, 1957). The histories of some of the most representative examples are gathered by Donald Durnbaugh, *The Believers' Church* (New York: Macmillan, 1968). The use of the "type" concept for further analysis and illumination of history and contemporary churchmanship was begun by James Leo Garrett, ed., *The Concept of the Believers' Church* (Scottdale, Pa.: Herald Press, 1969). The adjective "radical" assigned to this stance by historians refers not to specific social issues but to the degree of thoroughness with which one attempts to implement the reformation.

3. See my interpretation of "Constantinianism" as a sociocultural reality independent of the fourth-century details in *The Original Revolution* (Scottdale, Pa.: Herald Press, 1971, pp. 150ff.) and in chapter 6 above, "The Constantinian Sources of Western Social Ethics."

4. Daniel F. Rice: "Sidney E. Mead and the Problem of 'Civil Religion'"; in *Journal of Church and State* 22 (1980), 53–74; and Richard T. Hughes: "Civil Religion, the Theology of the Republic, and the Free Church Tradition," ibid., pp. 75–87.

5. Littell, *From State Church to Pluralism* (Garden City, N.Y.: Doubleday, Anchor, 1962).

6. Kraemer, *The Christian Message in a Non-Christian World* (New York: International Missionary Council, 1947).

7. Cox, *Secular City* (New York: Macmillan, 1965), and Daniel Callahan, ed., *The Secular City Debate* (New York: Macmillan, 1966).

8. Not that this is the only such frontier. The religiosity of individual self-fulfillment without constitutive critical social awareness (represented by Dale Carnegie's churchly counterparts, especially as they become allied with sanctification of "the market" or "enterprise" as producers of prosperity) is a major temptation. The neo-oriental and neo-archaic cults will constitute perennial fringe phenomena, more attractive as the sense-making functions of mainstream religiosity fail to convince. But most of these other more bizarre "religious" sideshows do not—as the civil religion does—move people to kill one another.

9. The values that can be defended by means of global arm-twisting are not those of Western civilization but of the civilization of the Western: that artificial world in which the good guys always talk our language, shoot straighter, and turn out in the end to have been on the right side even when they had to break some rules along the way. It is the Western, together with its near neighbors in police and spy drama, which educationally celebrates the cultural values in which our society trusts. That is a world in which the fastest gun determines who was moral, and since it is fiction, it always does work out that way.

10. "The Birth of New American Myths," pp. 139ff. in Robert Bellah, *The Broken Covenant* (New York: Seabury, 1975).

11. See note 10.

12. See note 4.

Index